9/24/22.

MW01224185

Thanks for
great memories with
the (sic) Vikings.
You were one of the
best!.
Enjoy the stories
LeRoy.

leroy.johnson2001@gmail.com

Endorsements

Mike Babcock, NHL and Olympic Coach

"I recommend this book as an important chapter in Canadian International hockey history. It was a huge deal for young men to experience this high calibre international play at the Viking Cup. The European teams were jammed full of talent."

Jim Matheson, Edmonton Journal Sports

"LeRoy Johnson and his cohorts deserve a world of credit for turning a gem of an idea for an international junior hockey tournament over Christmas 40 years ago into a roaring, must-see, must-write-about success."

Chief Willie Littlechild, Canada Sports Hall of Fame (Jr Inspol Thunderbirds coach), former MP

"The Viking Cup brought unique opportunities to play exhibition games against teams from Europe. It brought international hockey to Maskwacis and other First Nations communities. The hockey was first class. You will like this book."

Roger Castle, former Professional and Viking Cup linesman, Edmonton

"When it comes to icons in sport, you don't want to overlook the Viking Cup."

One Printers Way
Altona, MB R0G0B0,
Canada

www.friesenpress.com

Foreword by John Short
Illustrations by Brian Stein

ISBN
978-1-5255-9644-5 (Hardcover)
978-1-5255-9643-8 (Paperback)
978-1-5255-9645-2 (eBook)

1. SPORTS & RECREATION, HOCKEY

Distributed to the trade by The Ingram Book Company

THE
VIKING
CUP

International Hockey

A Small College Town Scores Big Time

LEROY JOHNSON

"In researching this book, I have gone to great lengths to ensure credit has been given to individuals contributing quotes, memories, and images. However, despite exhaustive efforts, I was unable to contact the photographer of some images; I feel that omitting such images would render that section of the book incomplete. To the unnamed contributors to this book, I sincerely thank you. Also, many conversations come from recollections and are not always written to represent word for word transcripts. In such cases, they have been retold in a way that evokes the essence of what was said."

Table of Contents

FOREWORD

by John Short

When the offer to write this foreword was offered and gratefully accepted, I expected these few words to be vastly different than they turned out to be. The early plan was to write a warm paragraph or two about the value of sports and the contribution of events such as the Viking Cup to small communities around the world.

It didn't work out that way.

The story, from beginning to end, is much too large.

These words of contribution do not come close to describing the remarkable effort created by LeRoy Johnson, in either print or reality. I can find no way to express the effort and commitment required to create a book that is partly history, partly personal memoir, and partly—perhaps mostly—a tribute to the humans who did so much to build the Viking Cup from what might have been a trivial on-ice exercise into a tournament that attracted National Hockey League officials, international politicians, and rabid spectators to a small arena that was always just a little too cool between periods.

Here, you will read and sense the comfort of small, rural Camrose, Alberta, blended with the size and requirements of numerous nations, including Russia at a time when the world's political Cold War was an everyday reality. International politics, pure athletic competition, and large dollops of goodwill came together and created an event worth holding and a story worth telling.

You will learn that all sides benefited from the small-town habit of welcoming visitors to small private homes, although, at first, officials of visiting nations wanted no part in the idea. After the questions were answered, firm relations developed quickly. Several European hockey players drove automobiles for the first time thanks to their Camrose hosts. Many of the hosts and players from years ago still communicate regularly.

Because teams travelled by bus from one small town to another before starting a tournament, many visitors got a clear and welcome look at Alberta's wide-open spaces—which are still mentioned fondly and often in notes and letters.

NHL general managers quickly became part of the attendance at every tournament. Today, it is stated regularly that this tournament, which started as a simple exchange of good sportsmanship among team leaders in Canada and Europe, was the first top-notch opportunity for pro scouts to study European players up close and personal.

Big names? There are plenty. Big adventures? More of the same.

For many who watched the Viking Cup grow from obscurity, and for a group that played in it, the Viking Cup was a dream come true.

(John Short Tribute – page 44)

PREFACE
by Author

One more chapter in the Viking Cup still had to be written.

It was normal practice after each Viking Cup tournament, when all the guests had departed, to gather in groups over a cold beer or coffee and pizza to debrief – to wrap up, sum up, back slap a bit and share favorite stories. It was like the last chapter of the event, a celebration of accomplishments blended with a few dreams about the next one.

Consider this book to be the last chapter of a volume on the Viking Cup, with the thousands that participated over the years telling their stories or being touched by another story teller. The Viking Cup is a good story and it will be kept alive by being told and retold. Hopefully, that is what this book on the Viking Cup will accomplish.

I started this writing project four years ago by listening to the memories and reflections of many who were involved in the Viking Cup. To tell the story, I knew I had to listen to the story again, myself. I began by researching documents stored here and there —in libraries, newspaper articles, magazines, family scrap books, personal journals and other records that one might find if looking in a time capsule. They were helpful and certainly sharpened my own memories.

My greatest resources were the minds and hearts of the Viking Cup participants, including the players, coaches and volunteers who have so willingly shared their most vivid experiences. From Europe and North America, hundreds have been interviewed and you will find their memories and stories throughout this book. Overwhelmingly, people who were touched by the Viking Cup were happy and anxious to talk about it, and so was I. Those conversations were my greatest motivation to keep going. After all, what could be more enjoyable and therapeutic than reliving wonderful experiences with inspiring people?

The younger generation, however, had more questions than memories as the last Viking Cup occurred fifteen years ago. Questions asked were, "What was the Viking Cup?" or "Can you tell me about the Viking Cup?" It was then that I knew for sure that a book should be written, and many encouraged me to do it.

The book is intended to reflect and hopefully reignite the unique spirit of the Viking Cup itself. As you read, I hope you feel it. The scope is intentionally broad to paint the big picture of how far the Viking Cup reached out from our little hub in Camrose to many countries of the world and many levels of sport including the NHL. The big story emerged from smaller stories and the global story is gathered from many local places. The whole story focuses on the two decades, the eighties and nineties, when the trajectories of sport and government were uniquely intertwined and interest in international hockey grew from a new frontier. As Coordinator of the Viking Cup during this period, I have drawn heavily on my memories and records with a great deal of assistance from all in the Viking Cup family and other knowledgeable people. I regret that it is not possible to include all of the stories that I have heard. Rather I have chosen to include a sampling to illustrate and strengthen central themes and messages.

There are so many to thank for their support of this project and the written and spoken word fall short of expressing my true gratitude. Thanks to the hundreds of those inspiring people for so willingly sharing your memories, stories, photos and paintings. You are too numerous to mention here, but you are likely to find your name or thoughts or works of art somewhere in the following pages.

I want to especially thank Brian Stein for sharing his statistical records of all Viking Cups and Gary Zeman for his research on the early history of hockey in Camrose vis-à-vis the Hansen brothers. I also want to acknowledge the help of Audrey Ronning Topping, author and retired photojournalist (New York Times) and Marilyn and Julian Ronning Hansen of California for their assistance relative to the Hansen story and early Camrose and Camrose Lutheran College (Augustana) history. (Audrey's father, Dr. Chester Ronning, was principal of Camrose Lutheran College from 1927 to 1942.) Dr. Petr Mirejovsky of Augustana was especially helpful in writing and editing stories as were Alumni Dr. Lyle Hamm of the University of New Brunswick and Verlyn Olson of Camrose. Mike Johnston, now with the Portland Winter Hawks, was also a helpful resource, as was Chris Reynolds, formerly with the IIHF, and John Short, broadcaster and sports writer.

Thanks to those who critiqued manuscripts and shared better ways of writing, especially to my daughters, Lana and Beth. Thanks to the publishers for guidance. Most of all, thanks to all in my family, for your partnership in making this story possible right from the beginning, especially to my wife, Dianne who was an anchor and source of inspiration to all who knew her.

INTRODUCTION

The Lay of Land and Ice

A river does not just happen; it has a beginning and an end. Its story is written in rich earth, in ice, and in water-carved stone, and its story as the lifeblood of the land is filled with colour, music, and thunder.

— Andy Russell, *The Life of a River*

The vision of the Viking Cup originated on a wobbly train near Leningrad (St Petersburg) in Communist Russia, but the roar of the crowds echoed from the prairies of Canada—and beyond.

When the small college city of Camrose opened its doors to international hockey, the world came knocking—in search of gold. Gold medals, gold experiences, and golden careers in professional hockey. And they returned—again and again.

In Camrose the Stoney Creek flows through Mirror Lake, the central focus of the town's character and beauty. It flows in the summer to the larger Battle River, and eventually to the oceans of the world. But in the winter, it forms thick ice, attracting young skaters and hockey players. Like much of Alberta, Camrose is a hockey community, central to the hockey climate and interests of Western Canada.

Many of the first Europeans who settled in Camrose and throughout the surrounding area were of Scandinavian heritage. Most of them were Norwegians. Quite a few came to Western Canada after a few years spent in Minnesota, Wisconsin, Iowa, the Dakotas, or other parts of the American Upper Midwest. They were an enterprising, adventurous lot and they valued education—a lot. In 1910, they built a college, Camrose Lutheran College (CLC). In 1992, it became Augustana College and, since 2004, it's been the Augustana faculty of the University of Alberta.

It is hard to imagine a time when a Scandinavian college like Augustana would not have had a hockey program. At the college's founding, northern sports played an important role in the high school curriculum. However, the lay of the sport picture changed as Augustana began to follow a new stream in 1959, with the introduction of university programming. The direction was to change, but the water did not. Education of the whole person was still the theme, and sport maintained a high level of importance. In tune with its roots, the college's teams appropriately took on the name Vikings, and its international hockey exchange program was later dubbed the Viking Cup.

Nestled on a wedge of land between two streams and overlooking the Stoney Creek valley sits the beautiful Augustana campus, the heart of advanced learning in Camrose. Bridges over the Stoney Creek connect the campus to the city's arena, the community focus for all indoor ice sport and the home of the Augustana hockey team, host of the Viking Cup. From the start, college hockey was like a seam that knit the university and the community together, a key feature of the Viking Cup tournament, which began in 1980. This was a unique time for rural Western Canadians to experience international hockey in their home communities in an unprecedented way. Numerous centres hosted pre-tournament exhibition games, enlarging the circle of direct exposure to this exceptional experience and to the Viking Cup. Like the rivers of central Alberta's watershed, which flow from mountain glaciers permeate the prairie terrain on their way to the oceans of the world, the Viking Cup became a vessel of global connection for those it touched.

In Canada, the "Great Divide" in our nearby Rocky Mountains determines the direction of our river flow to the east or the west. At the advent of the Viking Cup, European nations also faced a "Great Divide," in the form of a wall separating the free flow of people, ideas, and competition. In the Communist East, government merged with sport in an attempt to demonstrate a superior political system, while in the west, professional hockey was challenged from its perch atop the global mountain of the sport. Like the floods of a spring thaw, hockey sprang a fresh course just prior to the Vikings' first hockey excursion to Europe in 1974–75. The famous '72 Canada-Soviet Summit Series opened the gates for a flood of interest in international hockey amid the storms of a Cold War.

A river, after all, does not just happen.

It responds to needs and opportunities to nourish the land and enliven communities. It balances the forces of nature, making new life possible. It drains our swamps and feeds our oceans. From our glaciers to our lowlands, it distributes our water when conditions of nature declare hunger and thirst and a need for change and help.

Neither did the Viking Cup just happen. It was a response to a hockey environment looking for change and a new direction, and it was a journey along the river across our political divide. And it was deliberate; rowing toward a better strategy for a small-town college and its community to navigate obstacles such as a financial squeeze and institution size. It was that extra boost needed for a small college to be competitive in the deep waters of competition as Augustana ventured into Alberta Colleges Athletic Conference (ACAC) hockey. Like the spring season, the time was right for new life in the college hockey program, and stellar teamwork gave its story new direction, flow, momentum, and life.

But the Viking Cup became much more than the building and strengthening of a hockey program. Central to the changing scene was a lively community supportive of the ideals of the Viking Cup and anxious to see its college and favourite sport thrive. And in their response, the people of the community found a treasure in themselves—rich hospitality, the capacity to succeed as a community, joy in celebration, and a love for a fresh brand of ice hockey. As the

Viking Cup became an exchange program involving the hockey nations, the world discovered a place, the town discovered itself, and students of Augustana discovered new labs of learning, at home and abroad.

This was an age of hybrid hockey, bringing the currents of the North American and European game together to produce a stronger flow and a more attractive product, especially when the fog of the Cold War lifted. The different streams coming from the major hockey countries of the world gave our river a unique character and life. The tournament's story traces the opportunity afforded to over 400 of its players drafted by the NHL, numerous Olympians, and numerous college and junior players who later played for teams in other countries. Through a thirty-year history, the Viking Cup exchange became an important happening in the hockey world. It helped to nurture a new and improved era for international hockey.

This is a sports story, but it is also much more.

It is a story of churning pools of politics and sport, of the mixing streams of culture and sport, of enjoyment and fun on the shores of social interaction and sport, of living family dynamics and sport, of education and sport, and of human values, spirit, and sport.

It is a story of a confluence of life and sport.

This is also a story about people in symphony. The music of many parts played to the sound of sharp blades on the ice and lively people—the committees, volunteers, teams, players, leaders, officials, host families, and fans all played their own creative and harmonizing part. Many leaders are honoured in this book as representing a whole cadre of willing workers.

The Viking Cup was for the spectator. It was highly skilled hockey with the breaking of new styles, a flair for the unusual, and a fountain of contrasting strategies. It was a celebration with colour, music, and thunder designed to fill the stadium with people and ignite a passion throughout the community. It was our (biennial) carnival, where sport and culture thrived. It was a new brand with a local label. And it was fun.

The Viking Cup embodied the marriage of proven ideas from many high-level tournaments worldwide with our own ideas; many streams made our river flow. The stories embody strategies to achieve excellence because it was believed that, in this environment, sport would have the strongest power to uplift the community of Camrose, the international sport community, and the community of participants at all levels.

Some will remember the Viking Cup from what was seen and known, like on the tip of the proverbial iceberg. Most will not have known what lay below the surface. These chapters augur deeper to reveal answers to questions of "why" and "how," and outside-the-box thinking at the time.

Ultimately, this book is about highlights of an historical journey. Along the way, it was enhanced by a collection of my own memoirs and those of the many participants who enthusiastically shared their favourite stories and reflections.

The tournament is now in the past, but the water still flows from the many streams that have made our game. The waters of the creek and veins of Camrose are still saturated with the memories and soul of the Viking Cup, and they still circulate in the hearts and minds of the many who have been touched on both sides of the ocean. And I am among them.

Winter on Mirror Lake, by Jim Brager (Viking Cup 2004)

CHAPTER 1

Forerunners . . . The Stars Line Up

Childhood experiences sometimes influence the course of our lives in unexpected ways. Early discoveries and experiences form a bedrock on which the rivers of our lives eventually flow. We live within and from our unique stories.

One of my early childhood memories is of a clear Alberta winter evening, riding on a horse-drawn sleigh into town with my parents. We lived on a farm four miles out and that winter the snowdrifts were far too deep for any car or even tractor to handle. Horse-drawn sleighs were king then. There were no snowmobiles—they came much later.

As I lay on my back on a bed of blankets, I gazed up, trying to make sense of the overwhelming swarms of stars that seemingly danced to the rhythm of the harness bells on each of our trusty horses. I could make out no order, only chaos. Seeing my puzzled face, my father challenged me to find the Big Dipper. He gave me a few clues. After some strain, I made a great discovery. Out of chaos, there suddenly appeared seven bold stars forming a cup and handle. I had seen this constellation for the first time. In my mind at that moment, it was the trophy of the skies.

The greater lesson to me, as I understood later, was that the seemingly unidentifiable parts could come together to form something meaningful and useful when viewed with an inquiring mind. Mathematicians say that the whole equals the sum of its parts. In chemistry, you can make the whole greater than the sum of its parts by adding energy. In sports, passion and spirit can catapult individuals and teams to higher levels and greater possibilities. I believe that my own "discovery" of the Big Dipper contained elements of all of these.

I spent the earliest years of my life on the farm. Later, my family moved into town (a village, really), which appeared to offer a great profusion of wonderful amenities. The one that was perhaps the most important to me then was the open-air skating rink. It was located close to where we lived. On many a winter night, I watched the older boys play hockey under a string of incandescent lights. Sometimes, when I got there early enough, I was allowed to help them fill the cracks in the ice or flood the rink with a hose and a forty-five-gallon barrel. Casey deRoon, a great community man and avid supporter of youth sports, worked tirelessly every year to make the ice in the late fall and to help maintain it throughout the cold winter. I used to think I was helping him, but maybe not. He was a hero, because he helped the kids.

I wanted to be a hockey player, too! But I had no hockey skates or stick.

So, I managed to get the village paper route to deliver the *Edmonton Journal* when it arrived on the bus early each evening.

Soon, I had collected enough money to buy a pair of good hockey skates and a stick. I had found some pucks in the snow banks surrounding the rink. Later, I bought the protective equipment.

I soon realized that if I rushed through my paper route, I would have more time with the hockey boys at the rink before the lights went out in the late evening.

Luckily, I had a Shetland pony. Sparky was his name, and we did the paper route together.

In the summer, he would carry my papers as I ran to each house with a quick delivery. He soon knew which houses to stop at and when to go to the next.

In the winter, I would hook him to a sleigh that my dad (Herman) had purchased for my *Edmonton Journals*. Now I could ride, standing tall and jumping off for quick drops. It went faster in the winter with the sleigh and Sparky didn't seem to mind the run, which kept him warm. Again, he learned where to stop and when to continue his rhythmic trot, always ignoring the many barking dogs we encountered along the way. We were a good team and he sure helped me to get more ice time to develop my hockey skills and interest. The day would end with a read of the sports news in the extra *Journal* I always ordered. I would often cut out special articles or photos to add to an expanding sports scrapbook, and when the World Series of baseball or the Stanley Cup playoffs were on, I was all ears, glued to the closest radio.

I have loved tournaments ever since I can remember. I love their excitement—the opportunity to identify the best teams, the star players, seeing many games in one place! I love the atmosphere, the excitement, the chance to make new friends—and to meet the old ones! When I was a kid, it didn't matter much to me whether the tournaments involved hockey, baseball, ping pong, or even crokinole. I loved them all. Invariably, I found them challenging. Sometimes, they challenged my abilities in unexpected ways. When I was a teenager getting to the annual baseball tournament in Lacombe and back from my home in New Norway forced me to bring my hitch-a-ride skills up to previously unseen levels!

And then there were the frequent trips with favorite hockey coach and teacher, Ken Alackson, to watch and learn from my favorite players on the Edmonton Flyers pro team, including Norm Ullman, Johnny Bucyk and Mr Goalie himself, Glenn Hall. The Flyers, being a farm team of the Detroit Red Wings, sent many stars into the six team NHL at the time. I followed their careers closely and called myself a Detroit Red Wing fan… until the Edmonton Oilers later entered the scene. I was impressed by the atmosphere and product of the professional game.

The organization and mechanics of running high-quality professional and international events have always intrigued me. My teachers and mentors encouraged me to get involved in a variety of activities—as an organizer, as a leader. The experience I gained in 4H and as a Boy Scout has been valuable, and the Scout motto, "Be prepared," has been like a guiding star in addressing details. In my teaching career, I specialized in administration, and the training I received and experience I gained as a school administrator helped me tremendously during my many years as coordinator of the Viking Cup.

A fresh exposure to international hockey in the 1970s provided an opportunity to fill a hockey void that existed in the Camrose community and Alberta Colleges Athletic Conference (ACAC) at that time. The Camrose Maroons, leaders in senior hockey for many years, had disbanded operations and there was no Junior A team in Camrose. The time was ripe for the Vikings hockey team to stake a niche, and we had accumulated some ideas about how it could happen from two European hockey tours of that decade.

But Camrose had its first exposure to international hockey much earlier, though few people remember or have heard about it. They were reminded, however, when Paul Newman's comedy movie *Slap Shot* came out in 1977, just as the Viking Cup was in its infancy. The movie was a comedy and farce that parodied the "punch-up" style of hockey made popular by the Philadelphia Flyers and other penalty-oriented teams at the time—the antithesis of the kind of hockey envisioned for the Viking Cup.

For me, the memory went back to my childhood, and the regular Sunday afternoon visits from my mother's (Anna Hovde Johnson) best childhood friend and neighbour, Clara Scotvold Lomnes. As I would listen to their chatter, the topic would often shift to sport, and sometimes hockey. Clara would talk of her famous cousins, the Hansen brothers. There were seven of them, all hockey stars who grew up on a large neighbouring farm just north of Camrose. Their mother was Marie Scotvold, who was married to John Hansen, and the whole family, of Norwegian descent, had immigrated to their Canadian homestead from South Dakota in 1909.

When the cows had been milked (by hand), the horses unharnessed, and the daily farm work done, the boys would put on their skates and play hockey on their homemade rink. Sometimes, they would journey across to the better Scotvold rink. Soon, they starred on the Camrose teams, playing skillful but very aggressive hockey. They were known to drop their gloves in defence of a brother in the tough games.

A relative of the family, Donnie Scotvold, tells me that when their parents thought the boys were fast asleep in their third storey bedrooms, they were actually sneaking out to play more hockey, having extended a rope from their top-storey window. Or could be they were just having fun time with their friends in Camrose. When they returned, they would climb the rope, one hand over the other, with their burly arms, and then place the rope under the bed. They, of course, were ready to report for work assignments in the barn early the next morning. No regrets, no comments, no complaints.

Stories of their toughness were many. Different accounts said they had the best competitive tempers you could find in hockey. "Oscar has the knack of playing his best game when the going is toughest." And so on. Camrose resident and descendant of the Hansen-Scotvold clan, Lester Millang, said, "They never backed down from anyone. They stuck together like syrup on the wall!"

The boys worked hard on their large farm, developing strength and speed far beyond the normal teenagers of the time. They were fearless and confident in all they did. And when it came to sports—all sports—their conditioning was top notch before they hit the ice (or track or diamond).

The Hansen brothers were all sent to Augsburg College in Minneapolis, a sister Lutheran college to Camrose Lutheran College, for their university education. The youngest, Oscar, had apparently attended Camrose Lutheran College. Likely, they went to Augsburg to play hockey, as well, and Augsburg did not anticipate such immense Canadian talent. The oldest brother, Julius, became captain and soon took on the name "Iron Man Hansen," justifiably so.

An Augsburg publication at the time describes the team:

> Although it was the first year they had played in a conference, the Augsburg team was already recognized as the collegiate power of the Midwest. The Auggies had gone undefeated in 1927, winning an unofficial state championship. The 1928 team was also unbeaten, and its reputation as a powerhouse spread. Fans nicknamed the squad the 'Hansons [sic] of Augsburg,' for five of the eight players were brothers: Louis, Joe, Julius, Emil, and Oscar Hanson [sic].

The Hansen brothers were anything but goons as they dominated the college league and earned a national spotlight. They were tough and full of raw skill—not exactly like the Hansons of *Slap Shot*, but their passion was not to be outdone.

Later, I learned that General Douglas MacArthur, chairman of the USA Olympic Committee, announced that Augsburg, because of its winning ways, would represent the US in hockey at the Olympics in Switzerland in 1928, but it would have to raise half the cost and the American Olympic federation would contribute the rest.

The Hansens were ready to donate.

One account indicated that "there was 10,000 bushels of grain stored in Camrose valued at $1,500." They could count on that!

The *Edmonton Journal* and *Camrose Canadian* newspapers featured the US Olympic team and, on January 19, 1928, reported:

> When the amateur hockey team representing the United States at the Olympics to be held in St. Moritz, Switzerland, sails from New York, five Camrose players will be with them to participate. These boys are well known, not only to hockey fans but also to the public generally. Their parents live just north of Camrose. Mr. and Mrs. John Hansen have every reason to be proud of their sons, Julius, Joe, Emil, Louis, and Oscar, who will lead the attack for the American team . . . they will sail from New York on January 25 and play their first game on February 11. The performance of these boys, who compose probably one of the most unique teams ever participating in the modern presentation of the Olympic games, will be followed with keen

interest not only by people to whom they are so well known in their own home territory, but also by the entire continent.

A headline from *The New York Times* read: "5 Hanson [sic] Brothers on US Olympic Six."

Unfortunately, the USA Olympic Committee changed its mind three days before departure, giving the reason that *"the Minneapolis team is not regarded as a representative team."*

But these "Canadians" had all been born in the US.

One account said the American Olympic Hockey Committee intended to ice the Hansens, but the Russians complained days before the event, claiming they were Canadian. Though General MacArthur had documented proof of their birthplace, the White House ordered the team off the ice completely as part of a political statement regarding the increasingly tense relationship with the Russians.

Other accounts indicate other reasons, such as "Eastern influences."

It is interesting to note that Canada, represented by the University of Toronto, won the 1928 Olympics by a combined score of 38-0 in three games. The University of Toronto varsity team has always been called the Varsity Blues and was coached up until then by Conn Smythe, who became the principal owner of the Toronto Maple Leafs. However, for the Olympics of 1928, Lester B. (Bowles) Pearson was appointed the Canadian coach. Lester Pearson received the Nobel Prize for Peace in 1957 and was prime minister of Canada from 1963 to 1968.

One thing is certain: Canada would not have had such an easy ride to victory in the 1928 Olympics had the US been represented. The US has won two Olympic golds in hockey—the 1960 games in Squaw Valley, California and the 1980 Miracle on Ice and in Lake Placid, New York. Each was considered an upset. They may have narrowly lost their best opportunity to win the Olympics much earlier, in 1928, when they withdrew their team. This was the only year in men's Olympic hockey history that the US did not participate.

Had Augsburg, with the five Hansens, been the American representative, the strong possibility existed for the University of Toronto, with a future prime minister as coach, to play off against a Camrose-dominated US team that would have been familiar with the Canadian style of game. That would have surely made the front pages of *The New York Times*, *Edmonton Journal,* and *Camrose Canadian!*

Following their college days at Augsburg, Emil, Emory, and Oscar all had professional hockey careers in the States. Emil was brought up to play games with the Detroit Red Wings in 1932, and Oscar played eight games with the Chicago Blackhawks in 1937–38. Emil and Emory returned to Camrose to manage the farm for a time and play with the Camrose Maroons. Emil also coached minor teams in Camrose. Joe Hansen became a teacher and school principal. Louis achieved his PhD in chemistry and became a distinguished American research scientist with several inventions to his credit. Dr. Louis Hansen invented a synthetic rubber film that would resist cracking and swelling at lower temperatures and wouldn't swell when used as a membrane to pump fuel into carburetors. This product was immediately put into use to help the Allies in WW II. Louis remembered his roots in Camrose: "We were always working with tractors and horses. Farm life really taught you to get up and go. We couldn't loaf, but we had fun."

Rod Scotvold, a former high school student of mine whose father, Harold, was a first cousin to the Hansen brothers, enthusiastically told me of his first duck hunting trip with Louis and Oscar in 1962, on the Scotvold family farm north of Camrose, near Round Hill, where I was teaching at the time.

> They drove up from Minnesota in a snazzy new Cadillac to go duck hunting on our slough. I was about twelve or thirteen years old and totally impressed. They had all the best in hunting gear—new shotguns (Louis's had a gold trigger, I recall), hip waders, loads of shells (they gave me a whole box). They had picked up a long-time friend from Camrose, Harry Cassidy, on the way out. We all waded out with our new hip waders and hid amongst the cattails and other weeds. When the first flock of unsuspecting duck flew over, Louis was ready, but didn't know the back force of his brand-new shotgun. He blasted one, two, three, each time driving himself back with his feet stuck in the mud until he was totally submerged with his dazzling new hip waders filled with the muddy water and new gun and hand reaching out for help. The others pulled him up to a vertical position to roaring laughter by all. Rod said 'it was absolutely hilarious. I guess he regained that old feeling of recklessly shooting pucks and scoring goals again.' They had so much fun and so did I.

Julius Hansen became a Lutheran minister. He was prone to dwell on the value of sports and the lessons to be learned by participating. He would say, "Ice hockey was good experience for the problems I was to face later in life. After all, life is quite a game, too, and hockey has helped many to play it square."

Julius married Hazel Ronning, a graduate of Camrose Lutheran College and sister to Dr. Chester Ronning, former president of Camrose Lutheran College and distinguished Canadian diplomat. Julius and Hazel's son, Julian Ronning Hansen, age eighty-five and living in California at this time of writing, recalls his father with respect and humour. The setting is a small town in northern Montana, but it could have just as well been any small town on the Canadian prairies.

The Hockey Rink

by Julian Ronning Hansen

The rink was built on a piece of flat ground behind the church and the parsonage. It had wooden boards to circle the ice, with electric lights for night skating powered from a large generator supplying electricity to the town of Hogeland,

Montana. The main street consisted of a gas station, grocery store, bar, automotive garage, and school, which had a basketball floor. Classes were held grades 1–12.

When the railroad left, the town gradually died. Today, the church is lovingly cared for and they have a small congregation pastored by the Lutheran Church, ministering to the farms and ranches. It remains the centre for weddings, funerals, and annual gatherings.

Alas, no rink.

The rink was supplied with water from a seventy-foot windmill, with water being pumped from the well through a pipe to a wooden barrel tank cut in half from an old, cast-off farmer's tank. When the tank filled with water it had to be dumped into the rink. Julius did this throughout the day and night with his unusual strength.

He could chin himself eighteen times with one arm. I remember the large bicep he had, something he acquired from earlier days at the homestead farm at Camrose where the boys had cleared the land of bush, using the horses that later plowed the fields. The rink was smoothed out using his car with a specially designed plow scraper.

His skills were honed as a graduate from Vermillion [sic] Agricultural College in Alberta, skills that helped local farmers with their mechanical and farming problems. One project I remember as a small boy of six or so years was an elevator to lift grain up into a metal grain bin. It was powered by a one lunger gas engine. This contraption eased the difficulty in accomplishing this job. Combines were also always in need of repairs and here again he was called upon.

The hockey players were from local farms. He somehow managed to train these farm kids. Although good goalies were hard to come by, they still managed to beat the Canadians across the border in Climax, Saskatchewan. Their uniforms came from the brothers returning to Canada after the professional season was over. I still have a goalie stick and regulation sticks up in my attic.

Many years later, my father retired and they were living in Oakland, California. My dad had passed away by this time, but Mother continued to attend Trinity Lutheran Church, where Dad had been a visitation pastor. At a service, the pastor started to mention the visitor from Canada.

Of course, Mother asked where he was from. "Climax, just across the border," he stated. She told him her late husband had been pastor at the Turner/Hogeland

Lutheran Church and he said, "You don't mean Julius Hansen? He came to Climax with his farmers to play the local team."

The Hansen reputation preceded them. The visiting pastor told Mother that the Canadians were afraid of Julius, as he was so tough on the ice and could not be handled or controlled. They beat Climax without a decent goalie.

I remember my father shooting wrist shots at cans placed on top of the fence. He could hit them, knocking them off the poles, one after the other.

In his retirement, we attended many hockey games in San Francisco to watch the Seals. Dad remembered that he had played hockey with one of the coaches' fathers. We were unable to validate this.

At any rate, in one game against Portland, there were two fans sitting next to my father shooting off their mouths about how lousy the Seals were. Dad asked them to quiet down, just like old times. The guy shoved Dad and we were in physical fight. Dad ended up on the floor between the seats and I stepped back when the gendarmes arrived. I got a chewing-out from my father for not flattening them.

With all the injuries sustained over the years—broken nose many times, and broken fingers—he somehow managed to protect his front teeth and beautiful smile.

Many years later, Oscar's son Jerry was a prominent race car driver and owner of Brainard Raceways in Minnesota. Through the racing business, he became a close friend of actor Paul Newman, who, in 1977, produced the film *Slap Shot*, a comedy about the Hanson brothers. The question arises over whether he had the Camrose Hansens in mind when he chose the name for the goonish players, the three "Hanson" brothers, in the movie about the Charleston Chiefs. "Hansen" had become a well-known name in Minnesota hockey history.

The hockey history blog, GreatHockeyLegends.com, includes the following account of the Hansen Canadian connection and their near-Olympic experience of 1928 and homage to *Slap Shot.*

One of the early great families in Minnesota hockey history is the Hansen brothers. No, not the similarly named Hanson brothers of *Slap Shot* movie fame, though they were the inspiration for Paul Newman's creating of those famous characters. . . The Hansen brothers were anything but goons, as they dominated the college league and were put into the national spotlight by their 1928 Olympic selection. The movie was a funny parody of their career, but in real life, the Hansen brothers were serious ice hockey players.

The Hansens from Camrose set a tone for the hockey that later surfaced and grew in the Viking Cup—seven bright young stars of the game with ideal team chemistry and loads of passion and spirit. The first hockey Vikings of Camrose. Their connection to Augsburg College was the first substantial journey into international hockey circles for the Camrose community, and Switzerland was almost the far point. Six decades later, the Augustana Vikings played games in Switzerland on a European tour and, in 2004 and 2006, the Swiss national U18 team played in the Viking Cup.

It was with this same Augsburg College of Minnesota that the (CLC) Augustana Vikings initiated their US hockey relationship for Viking Cup participation. During the 1976–77 season, the Vikings travelled to Minneapolis for exhibition games with Augsburg College and the St. Paul Vulcan junior team, both of which made reciprocal ventures to participate in the Viking Cup in later years. This, as it turned out, was to lay the groundwork for extensive American participation in the Viking Cup to follow.

.   .   .   .   .

To complete my high school education, I enrolled at Camrose Lutheran College, where the deciding attraction was the famous choir, which had been founded by Chester Ronning but was then under the direction of Professor Ed Marken. How disappointed I was to find out there was little emphasis on the sport of hockey. This was a football and basketball school at the time. By the second year we, the hockey-minded students, wasted no time in organizing a team, convincing the football coach, Rev. Karel Lunde, to serve as our manager. He had never skated before but we knew he had a spacious Buick to transport us to the games! Furthermore, he was just a great guy. A friend and I agreed to be the "playing-coaches." That was to be the beginning of a long tenure in college hockey for me, although there was a break as I completed my university education at the University of Alberta and the University of Montana.

I was hired as principal of the Camrose Lutheran College high school department in 1967. My colleague and friend, Dr. Garry Gibson, director of athletics, approached me to restart a hockey program, the intent being to prepare for ACAC competition. I would go on to work with the program for thirty years in different capacities, including coach, general manager, and Viking Cup exchange coordinator.

With a small enrolment of near 300 students, the first challenge was mathematical: to find enough players to form a team and meet a small budget. Luckily, the junior league that we entered (and helped to form) allowed us to use community (non-CLC) players to reach our numbers and hopefully be competitive. When we entered the ACAC in 1972, non-college players were no longer eligible to play on the team. One of those players, however, decided to enrol as a student at Augustana and soon became the captain of the team and an all-star defenseman in the ACAC. His name is Bill Andreassen, now a provincial judge in Camrose.

In our pursuit to establish college hockey in the Camrose community, I invited a group of businessmen to a meeting in 1970 to explore means of recruiting players and promoting the team. From that group, the hockey promotion committee, the first scholarship evolved and became the genesis for the community scholarship program, which continues to raise financial assistance for all Augustana students today.

The hockey promotion committee, under chair Mayor Rudy Swanson, dedicated itself to the development of college hockey in Camrose, and when the Vikings entered the ACAC, its members stood ready to support.

Surviving as a small college program in a "big" league meant the financial and competitive risks had to be offset by creative initiatives, the first of which was a return to the homeland, the real land of the Vikings. Soon the movement began and a relationship was built with the Swedish Ice Hockey Association. International hockey was new territory for college hockey in Canada, and the Vikings led the way in 1974. The first European tour was the spark that was needed to recruit a highly competitive team that won ten of twelve games in Scandinavia. Upon their return, the team won the Alberta Championship in front of lively, packed Camrose crowds, and then went on to win the Canadian College Championships in Nova Scotia.

Those were the days of the "Athletic Supporters," a student-led brass band that played at every game. "They would play the first seven bars of 'Smoke on the Water' by Deep Purple to get everyone pumped up. It became our theme song," says Russ Shandro, a rough, tough forward on the team. Dave Lefsrud, the lead trombone player with the brass band, joined team members thirty-five years later in Red Deer for their induction into the Alberta Hockey Hall of Fame as Alberta's first Canadian College Champions.

The 1974–75 season was a high point of Vikings hockey, and the stars were beginning to line up for a "Big Dipper" (Viking Cup) exchange program, that would shine in Camrose for the next thirty years.

Old Main, by Glenda Beaver (Viking Cup '96)

CHAPTER 2

Swing . . . Beyond the Game

As he began his illustrious hockey career, the great Gordie Howe was asked, "How long will you play in the NHL?"

His response? "One year . . . and then we will see what happens!" The humble Howe went on to have a career of twenty-six years in the NHL and six years in the World Hockey Association, a total of thirty-two years.

Like in Howe's career, the first year of the Viking Cup was like a tryout by a promising prospect. Predictably, it was a great success, followed by many more. The Viking Cup tournament had a history of twenty-six years, from 1980 to 2006, but the Viking Cup exchange, including trips to Europe that began in 1974, ran for a total of thirty-two years!

Like the long-held traditions of the Detroit Red Wings, for whom Howe played, the Viking Cup was built on unchanging objectives and standards. But each tournament introduced a freshness of ideas and teams. Howe played for his team and his fans. The Viking Cup evolved and was always an attraction for great teams and satisfied crowds.

Team

The CLC Vikings hockey promotion committee usually held its meetings in the college cafeteria. At one in March 1980, we ate our meal quickly as there was important business on the agenda. I gave a wrap-up report of the Vikings' trip to Sweden, Finland, and Russia, which had occurred three months earlier, and explained how it had led to a new opportunity. My report concluded with the words: "Gentlemen, the top Junior team for Sweden, the top Junior team from Finland, and the Canadian Junior Champion Prince Albert Raiders, have all accepted our invitation to come to Camrose for an international tournament over the Christmas break next season. I propose that we will call it the Viking Cup."

Including the home team, we had now already secured four excellent teams, and it was no problem to find two more to round out a six-team tournament. True to the track record of the promotion committee, all members were on board for another new challenge—this time Europe would come to Camrose!

The task at hand was to make the first Viking Cup an extraordinary success . . . and then we would see what happened. There could be no denying, though, that simmering under our enthusiasm were dreams of a tournament dynasty—maybe like the Spengler Cup of Europe.

The "first team" of the Viking Cup was its leadership team, chosen for the abilities of its members to fulfill unique roles, to be stars in their own positions but important links in the whole "Cup." As coordinator, my role was to assemble the pieces—the stars, so to speak—to coordinate their work and spirit, and to set high standards. The team members soon gained valuable experience, shining at tournament after tournament through high energy and passion that made each event better than the last. They were consistent winners—all stars like in the arrangement of the Big Dipper. It was determined that my title would be "coordinator," as it best described the type of leadership that would be necessary in our situation.

The framework was built in short order and the goals and mandates established to coincide with Camrose Lutheran College's philosophy and objectives. The coordinator, an employee of that college, represented its interests and worked as chair of the community steering committee.

The Viking Cup was an invitational tournament. Its sanctioning by the Canadian Amateur Hockey Association (later to become Hockey Canada) and the International Ice Hockey Federation (IIHF) basically meant that those organizations gave approval for the teams to participate. The arrangement handed the steering committee a great deal of flexibility in operating the tournament and arranging pre-tournament exhibition games as part of a package for visiting teams. The inclusive atmosphere served the Viking Cup very well.

The tournament became a laboratory, on and off the ice, for exercising and improving on leadership skills at all levels, and discovering new "stars" in new positions. There was always room for creative thought, as new features and teams were incorporated at each tournament to give a unique freshness to every Viking Cup.

Tom Gould, CLC Vikings alumnus (1974–76) and presently a Calgary lawyer, may have expressed it best in his articles in the *Viking Cup* magazine in 1996 and 1998, entitled "The Vikings: A History of Leadership and Innovation" and "The Genesis of a Hockey Tournament."

"Sure, the Vikings were warriors who sought to dominate and conquer," he wrote, "but they also had the fierce spirit and determination to dare to be leaders, to try new things, to be first. . . Since 1982, each successive tournament has resulted in streamlining and fine-tuning an already impressive and well-received concept."

Change is inevitable and the Viking Cup steering committee was always alert to innovative ways to achieve team competitiveness and maximize quality of experience for the participants. For example, when the opportunity arose for the Vikings to tour behind the Iron Curtain, we proceeded, as it enhanced the Cup's educational objectives. When we looked to include the Soviet National U18 team in Viking Cup '88, the format was adjusted to an eight-team tournament that included the Soviets and the U of A Golden Bears. This broadened the format and enhanced the spectator appeal. And following Viking Cup '94, we established a summer English language and conditioning program to accommodate the increasing number of European draft picks as they prepared for pro training camps.

As I reminisce on the great work of committee members in the Viking Cup, I am reminded of the amazing US rowing team from the state of Washington that won Olympic gold in Berlin in 1936 in front of leading Nazi officials. A story in *The Boys in the Boat* contains this quote from famous boat-builder George Yeoman Pocock: "When you get the rhythm in an eight, it's pure pleasure to be in it. It's not hard work when the rhythm comes—that 'swing,' as they call it. I've heard men shriek out with delight when that swing came in an eight; it's a thing they'll never forget as long as they live."

Our team of workers featured many multiples of eight and we had "swing"—the simple notion of everyone grabbing an oar and pulling together. There was little we could do singularly but a lot we could do collectively. The more success we encountered, the better we rowed. And the better we rowed, the more effective we were in steering the Viking Cup boat through new winds of challenge—and the gales of opportunity that always seemed to follow.

The best indication that we'd achieved that "swing" could be found in the continuity of workers and volunteers from year to year. As I recall, we were never short. Many will express their experiences of the Viking Cup's "swing" in the chapters of this book.

Theme

When Alberta's iconic premier, Peter Lougheed, first met his cabinet after the election of 1971, his first words were: "Ordinary just doesn't cut it." Premier Lougheed was never known to operate with the handle of a dull knife, and that tone had constituency appeal. He also recognized and rewarded the extraordinary. His government went on to serve Alberta for fifteen years, and his party remained in power for over four decades.

In 1975, following the Vikings' first trip to Europe and a Canadian College Championship, Premier Lougheed presented Coach Joe Voytechek and Manager LeRoy Johnson with the Alberta Achievement Award. It was an auspicious beginning to the Viking Cup's international exchange program and an omen of things to come.

Alberta Achievement Award
(Premier Lougheed, Joe Voytechek, LeRoy Johnson)

Like the halls of government at the time, the bar was set high for the Viking Cup, with an overriding theme of "excellence attracts excellence."

The Viking Cup was not an ordinary hockey tournament. It was different. It was modelled to fill stadium seats.

There was little other choice.

In the beginning, there were no major sponsors, no government grants to lean on, no track record. And the dream was only that of a team and an athletic department—not even the college itself. Our only choice was to rely on a business model that would realize a financial gain for the Augustana hockey program. We reasoned; sponsorships would evolve, media would promote a good product, and central administration would be less nervous about the venture if it was an early success. Our hope was to build a quality product on the ice and in the community, wrapped in our theme.

Like the Norwegian founders of our college, we were pioneering a new investment that could pay great dividends in the future—but it needed a strong beginning. Success would beget believers and believers would support success.

Philosophy

The Viking Cup represented an opportunity for elite junior, college, and university hockey teams to compete under the finest of hockey ideals. The superior competition was characterized by a clean, aggressive style where the fundamentals of skating, passing, shooting, and checking were stressed at the highest level. Alberta's most qualified referees were assigned to the games and controlled the action in accordance with the tournament objectives.

The Viking Cup promoted goodwill and friendship among young hockey players, coaches, managers, and fans. Its participants represented different countries, backgrounds, and training and playing strategies. The Viking Cup was a learning experience in sport and cultural exchange. Through participant interaction, it was hoped that hockey skills would improve, friendships develop, and understanding and goodwill be enhanced to make our world just a little bit better.

Mandates

Mandates were clearly enunciated for each committee in a manual the coordinator prepared. To foster smooth teamwork and avoid duplication, the manual was cross-referenced and coded so that each committee member was aware of all the expectations and happenings (by date) of all other committee members as well as their own. Each committee chair prepared a formal written report at the conclusion of each tournament with recommendations for future events. Details always mattered.

In keeping with a fierce agenda of advanced preparation, a pre-tournament information and appreciation night was held involving all volunteers and workers. We hit the ground running.

Hockey Canada (CAHA) president Murray Costello later commented: "An event of this magnitude is simply not possible without the considerable organizational expertise of a highly efficient Augustana University College Organizing Committee and its numerous volunteers, and we commend each of them for their dedicated contribution."

Business Model

The operation of the Viking Cup was an anomaly to institutional governance's centralized decision-making and bureaucratic structure. Its administrators followed a business approach familiar to the many businessmen chairing committees. Augustana owned the event, but the authority to run it was handed to myself as athletics director/international relations director. I would work with a community steering committee in an effort to put together a tournament that reflected a positive image for the college and suffered no tournament deficit. In essence, the coordinator was the CEO for the Viking Cup, responsible for ensuring that decision-making occurred in a timely and efficient fashion. Initially, the Viking Cup coordinator was directly responsible to the college president, circumventing the usual bureaucratic processes within institutions. I maintained the position even when I later assumed other administrative and teaching positions.

In that role, I approved all tournament transactions; business plans, including budgets, were approved by the president. Revenues were generated from gate receipts and sponsorships from the business community, corporations, and interested local families and individuals. Advance ticket sales and a small service charge to hosts of pre-tournament exhibition games helped to stabilize cash flow.

Sponsorships

The number of major sponsors corresponded with the number of teams in each tournament—usually six or eight—and each sponsor was assigned a team. A major sponsorship typically included company logos on all sweaters and helmets, advertising in all Viking Cup publications, and large, colourful, custom-made banners that were prominently displayed in arena decorations. Upon the arrival of each team, volunteers would be seen collecting both sets of sweaters to be delivered to seamstresses for overnight crest application before games the next day. A package of game and banquet tickets was included for sponsors' employees and their customers. Major sponsors were given first option for sponsorship of the same country team the following year. For example, Joe Branco of Branco Concrete in Wetaskiwin always wanted the American team after establishing great relations the first year. Ross Agri Supplies, through ESSO, surprised us one year with a significant bonus for their major sponsorship package of an early Russian team. The Rod and Sheilagh Ross family also served as billets for the Russians.

The complete list of sponsors was exhaustive each year, and always, of course, included the families who billeted the players.

Over the years, the tournament successfully met its own budgets and, until the later years, maintained a modest surplus that eventually formed the Viking Cup Endowment fund. Today, this endowment supports the Augustana hockey program through scholarships and direct program assistance.

Leadership

The original committee chairs were made up the first Viking Cup steering committee included: LeRoy Johnson, chair and administrator, participating teams/European tours, finance, including sponsorships; Verlyn Olson, billeting and hosting (later, Terry Ofrim and Cindy Trautman became chairs); Lorne Broen, ticket sales; Ken Drever and Jim Brager, publicity; Mayor Rudy Swanson, public relations and advertising; Len Frankson and LeRoy Johnson, protocol; Bill Andreassen and Earl Berry, rules, officials, and awards (Doug Petruk later became long term chair) ; Ray Heck and Lloyd Levers, transportation; Marie Myrehaug, Dianne Johnson, Carol Roy, and Rita Giles, banquet; Randy Haugen and Dr. Arne Pedersen, medical; and Ray McIsaac, facilities (following Viking Cup '84). Others chaired various committees in later Viking Cups.

People Power

The overall strength of the tournament lay with the hundreds of volunteers who worked and hosted with enthusiasm and passion. An atmosphere of engagement permeated the community. Jeff Johnson, a Viking Cup player who later coached and became program co-coordinator in Viking '98, commented: "The focus was on community involvement— billeting and volunteering in so many ways. The long-term commitment of so many, this is what made the Viking Cup famous and the community stronger."

Jim Ofrim, a former Viking, captain of the U of A Golden Bears, as well as a retired principal of Camrose Composite High School, had two words to describe his memories of the Viking Cup: "Passion everywhere." Even the warmups seemed part of an all-out game, he said. "It was all high tempo!"

Joe Benadetto, beloved manager of Team US, observed in *American Hockey Magazine's* March 2004 issue, "The entire community rallied around it. Mention Viking Cup at Tim Hortons and a whole friendly conversation follows!"

Verlyn Olson, in charge of marketing, commented, "There are people who support and volunteer for the Viking Cup who aren't necessarily hockey fans. They want to be part of the experience."

It was common for many to arrange their holidays during the Viking Cup so they could be available to participate. Former students of Augustana would return from various parts of the province to volunteer their time.

After graduating from Augustana, Dan LaPlante would drive up from Lethbridge and meet fellow alumnus Lee Carter of St. Albert and the pair would spend their Christmas holidays helping out at the Viking Cup. "It was a homecoming with a new adventure each time," LaPlante said. "I was a team host. It was just fun to be there and I wanted to help those who had done so much for me."

Superfan Gary Gibeault was a Camrose city manager who always took his holidays during the Viking Cup. "I would much rather enter wholeheartedly into the games than find a warm, sunny beach to the south," he said. "The Viking Cup had everything I wanted and more!" He remembers his son's Viking Cup highlight was when his Pee Wee team was chosen to be the official hosts and cheerleaders for Team Sweden. One day at a Swedish practice, the Canadian boys were invited to lace up and join in. The Swedish players taught them many of the finer skills and, at the end of the session, the Swedish captain said, "Now we have taught you the Swedish way, it is time for you to teach us the Canadian way." The young boys looked at each other and didn't respond. The Swedish captain then said, "Well, can't you teach us how to fight?" That was the cue to a spirited "fun fight" between all the boys to end the practice session! Our boys cheered even louder for the Swedes at their next game!

When watching a Czech practice one day, Gary noticed a boy having difficulty with a broken (and well-worn) skate. After checking his size, he offered to scurry home to get his old "Tacks." The boy was all smiles as the fit was right, and the quality was a step up.

"I think we became friends for life when I told him to keep the skates at the end of the practice!"

> Our kids became more interested in hockey and skill levels reached new highs. What wonderful lessons for minor hockey and it was a cultural winner, too! The Viking Cup was very good for Camrose. The key was the international component. Nothing better than to see the Canadians playing the European teams; the different styles blended well. The NHL teams took notice with their many scouts in Camrose when the Viking Cup rolled around.

When Gary wasn't taking his holidays at the Viking Cup, he was always a forward-looking voice for the program around city hall. He was a steady hand in one of the great legacies of the Viking Cup—one of Alberta's best sports arenas, for events like the Viking Cup.

In the opinion of many, the Viking Cup was a powerful force in uniting the community and university in the Camrose region—an important outcome for major institutional growth and development to university degree-granting status as a campus of the University of Alberta.

At his retirement dinner, Dr. Allen Berger, dean of the Augustana faculty, University of Alberta, from 2011 to 2019, said, "The town and gown relationship is the best I have seen in my administrative career involving several universities. When I came to Augustana, there were no walls or fences to climb to reach the community! Half of our student body are involved in community learning positions and the citizens know our campus and programs well, especially through the joint performing arts centre on our campus and the city recreation centre."

Long-Serving Committee Chairs

Lorne Broen, thirty-seven years of service

"Much more than selling tickets"

Lorne Broen is a lifetime sportsman. For fifty-one years, he has held Edmonton Eskimos (Elks) football season tickets, and for over sixty years he played and was an active builder in the sport of hockey. His hockey-playing days—through high school, senior hockey with the Camrose Maroons, and "old timers" hockey—have left a few scars and trophies, but his years of long and dedicated service to the Viking Cup are among his most memorable.

Lorne was an original member of the CLC Vikings promotion committee in 1969 and he continued to serve college hockey on the Viking Cup steering committee as chair of ticket sales from the first Viking Cup tournament through to the last—the longest volunteer service of anyone. He accompanied the Vikings to Sweden in 1974–75.

To Lorne and Mary and his family of workers—mainly husband-and-wife teams—the job was much more than selling tickets. Lorne is quick to say, "We had a ball of fun welcoming people to the games. . . We loved the atmosphere. I had no problem finding recruits. I had a fantastic crew. We sure enjoyed the surprise pizza at the end of the day!"

For his outstanding service to Augustana and the community, the Augustana Alumni Association honoured Lorne with an Accolade Award in 1988.

Lorne does not hesitate to speak of the importance and legacy of the Viking Cup. "The Viking Cup put Camrose on the map … and not just a map of Alberta or Sweden, but a map of the whole hockey world. It certainly was a shot in the arm for the Augustana Vikings hockey program!" Lorne has been in the Viking Cup family long enough to know!

Verlyn Olson, twenty-six years of service

"To share the dinner table"

Verlyn Olson is a lawyer and a graduate of Augustana and the University of Alberta. He received the Augustana Distinguished Alumnus award in 2016. As a politician, he was elected to the Alberta Legislature to serve the Wetaskiwin-Camrose Constituency from 2008 to 2015. He was appointed minister of justice and, later, minister of agriculture. As leaders in the arts, Verlyn and his family founded the well-known Nordlys Film Festival of Camrose.

But more directly relating to the Viking Cup, Verlyn Olson is a sportsman. He is a former goaltender with the Vikings and was once a baseball pitcher and organizer. He was awarded the Bill Chmiliar Award of Merit for baseball leadership. Verlyn served as billeting chairman before chairing the marketing committee of the Viking Cup for many years. He chaired the steering committee for Viking Cup 2004 and led the Vikings on a European tour in 1994. Known for great hospitality, Verlyn and his wife, Mardell, loved the family living part of the Viking Cup. They regularly billeted players from Finland or Ukraine.

Verlyn was fond of saying "the Viking Cup is more than a hockey tournament." And, of course, it was. He once said, "There may be no other tournament in the world, in any sport, where players of this calibre compete at such a high level, then go home to share the dinner table with their adopted families."

The Viking Cup was like a kaleidoscope of Verlyn's many interests. And his talents matched a wide range of needs.

Ray McIsaac, twenty years of service

"A lot of work and a lot of fun"

Ray McIsaac joined the Viking Cup steering committee as chair of facilities for Viking Cup '86. Twenty years later, he was still leading his committee, through to the last Viking Cup of 2006. He was awarded the Augustana Alumni Citation Award for outstanding community leadership in 1999.

The Viking Cup 2000 Magazine states: "The success of the Viking Cup is due in large part to the atmosphere of the event and involvement of the Camrose community. Ray says it best: 'It's a lot of work, but it's a lot of fun.'"

Ray set an enviable tone for all to hear and follow. Following the end of the Viking Cup era, he continued to promote and serve sport as a volunteer with the Camrose Kodiaks junior hockey team, but a big part of his heart stayed with the Viking Cup.

Randy Haugen, twenty-six years of service

"No problem to get help"

In his down time from the Camrose Fire Department, Randy Haugen served as chair of medical services for every Viking Cup. He has lots of stories to tell, especially from the early days of Soviet involvement. He remembers a Russian doctor sitting beside three players and pulling out a syringe. "With the same needle, he injected each player's arm with medication from a bottle, one after another. Dr. Ninian got him a supply of needles for which he was grateful. We never knew how he used them."

Professional involvement from the local medical community was always enthusiastic and plentiful. "One day I looked up in the crowd where the medical staff sat and I saw four of our Camrose doctors. No problem to get help in the Viking Cup!"

Game Workers

Long-time game announcer and Radio CFCW news and sports figure Dale Smith is but one example of the hundreds of volunteer workers who were involved as hosts, ushers, security, sales, goal judges etc.

Dale Smith, twenty-plus years of service

"Spreading the good news"

Dale Smith knew the Viking Cup and he talked about it . . . a lot.

The Max McLean Arena, home to the Viking Cup, was notorious for its poor acoustics. But Dale's voice behind the mic united the crowds to the flow of the game. He spoke like the radio broadcaster he was for forty-seven years in Camrose.

Dale knew how to read a crowd. In spite of the language diversity of players who hailed from many different countries, the Viking Cup banquet was always a meaningful and memorable experience with Dale Smith as emcee. Dale's favourite in the lavish Scandinavian smorgasbord were "those tasty Swedish meatballs!" He served as announcer and scorekeeper for the Vikings and the Viking Cup for over twenty years, until 1994, when his son Curtis took over with much the same tone and clarity.

Jackie Rae Greening, general manager of Radio CFCW, may have best put her finger on the pulse of Dale's success. "He came from the school where broadcasters were taught to use proper English and clearly enunciate words," she said. "The thing I love about Dale is that he is so positive and so fun to be around. He brings energy every day to work."

As a broadcaster of varied experiences, Dale eventually chose to be a news director. "I like the news because it is always new," he once said. "And there is always that element of surprise, sometimes bringing a smile, other times a feeling of tearing up."

Dale never lost his love for sport, and has always been a close fan of college hockey. As for the Viking Cup, Dale says, "I loved the action, especially when the players came to the penalty box beside me. The hockey was unbelievably good. It sure gave me lots to talk about on radio the next day. The Viking Cup was a bonus that connected the international community to Camrose in a spirit of openness and excellence of competition."

Dale was in on the ground floor of the Viking Cup. In 1979–80, when it was first conceived, he and his wife, Diana, travelled to Sweden, Finland, and Russia with the Augustana Vikings. "We spent our best New Year's Eve in Stockholm, walking the narrow, cobbled streets of Gamle Stan, the Old Town, to gently falling giant snowflakes. Attired in casual team jackets, we strolled into a quaint restaurant with the Recknagles (parents of David, a Viking player), for a typical Swedish New Year's Eve supper. The place was full of Swedish couples dressed to the hilt for the celebrations. We felt so out of place. In no time, we were celebrating as one of their own—a highlight for us, for sure!

"The Vikings hockey trip was the window to Europe for Diana and me. It is a lasting legacy of the Viking Cup for us."

Back home, Dale took a week off to recover from their "holiday with the Vikings," a custom for him following every Viking Cup tournament. "After all those games and the sheer excitement of the Viking Cup, my voice was usually hoarse and in need of recovery before I read the news on CFCW radio," he said. "It was nice to just relax and reflect on the many great accomplishments and legacy of each Viking Cup. I am now retired, so I can do that every day!"

Reverend Allan Severson, 1927–2016

Reverend Allan Severson was a superfan, but much more. He was also a part of the team—many teams. For many years, he wrote a weekly article in the *Camrose Booster* newspaper for the Vikings hockey team, and he covered every game during the Viking Cup. He was a mainstay in the media room from morning till night, welcoming writers and guests. He served on the Viking Cup media committee and other committees over the years, as needed. And Allan was chaplain of the Vikings hockey team for many years.

No matter where he served, he brought a unique historical perspective to the game. People liked to talk to him. If you asked him a question about the 1940s or '50s Maple Leafs, he would pull out loads of scrapbooks and begin talking!

Don Cox

In 2016, Don Cox received a special award from Augustana Athletics for thirty-five years of volunteer service, which included dedicated service to all Viking Cup games. Don assumed responsibility for all game workers, including goal judges, penalty box assistants, security members, and the like, always relying on the many faithful volunteers like Jim Law, Bruce Enarson, and numerous others.

Tours to Europe

Following initial tours to Europe in 1974–75 and 1979–80, the Vikings toured Europe on alternating years throughout the '80s and '90s, until 2000–01. Beginning in 1982–83 until 1998–99, the Vikings visited and played a series of games in Czechoslovakia and the Czech Republic to fulfill an exchange arrangement with the Czechoslovakia Ice Hockey Federation (see Chapter 6 for details). Through the Viking Cup exchange program, the Vikings played in Europe on twelve different trips.

The European tours attracted numerous student athletes to Augustana and many played on European teams following graduation. Each tour gave twenty parents and fans the unique opportunity to travel abroad with the team. For example, on two occasions Frank and Agnes Lovsin accompanied the team when sons Mike and Ken were skating for the Vikings. As a well acclaimed businessman, Frank commented, "in our business ventures we always look for the pieces to come together for a perfect fit. Our family found that perfect fit at Augustana and those trips to Europe gave us a big bonus. We saw character development and words became reality especially behind the Iron Curtain. We are blessed."

Viking Cup Summer Language and Conditioning Program

Following the removal of the Iron Curtain, new opportunities emerged for young Czech, Slovak, and Russian players to play in the NHL. Few had been introduced to the English language during the Communist era. In 1993, the Viking Cup English Language and Conditioning Program was established in Camrose under the direction of Jeff Johnson. Randy Carlyle, who was the Winnipeg Jets' director of player development (and would later coach in Anaheim and Toronto), sent four of their recent drafts to the Camrose camp, including Nicolai Kaububolin of Moscow. After winning a Stanley Cup with the Chicago Blackhawks, Kaububolin later played with the Edmonton Oilers. Slovakian Martin Strbek of the Los Angeles Kings attended the program, too, along with many other prospects. The Kings' chief scout, Al Murray, commented: "It was certainly a worthwhile experience for any player hoping to make a career in North America." Several young Canadian players, including Shane Doan (Jets and Coyotes) and Josh Green (LA draft), attended the conditioning sessions. The program operated for four summers.

Billeting

The Viking Cup '81 *Wrap-Up Magazine* ran an article on family living entitled "Swedes Get Warm Kelsey Welcome." Had it been one year earlier, the title could have read "Canadians Get Warm Farsta Welcome." Hosts in Farsta, a Stockholm suburb, billeted several of the Camrose Vikings the previous year—a cultural bonus, for sure.

The Swedish experience and budget benefits led to the Viking Cup billeting program. In 1982, a groundbreaking billeting experiment occurred when Czechoslovakia, the first communist country team in the Viking Cup, cautiously entered Camrose homes. The details of the negotiations, eventual agreement, and longer-term outcome are featured in Chapter 6.

Billeting of the participating teams became an engagement and marketing strategy of the tournament. Well over a hundred families in the Camrose, Wetaskiwin and Millet areas supported the Viking Cup by opening their homes to players and team leaders. The media covered the games, of course, but they also picked up on the family living component of the tournament with major stories which proved to be a big factor in attracting large crowds to the games.

A farm in Kelsey? Of course!

An article in *Viking Cup '81* magazine tells the tale:

> It is a far cry from the tidy and compact suburb of Solna (Stockholm) and the two members of AIK Sweden billeted at the Blatzes' have relished the change. . . Certainly the Swedes aren't going to starve at the Blatzes. Awaiting them on the breakfast table are a dozen boiled eggs, a full pitcher of orange juice, and a mountain of toast. Jan and Mats, who speak excellent English, respond to questions about the night before with sly grins. . . Meanwhile, Ron Blatz is calling neighbours Al Kennedy and George Cunningham, who are also hosting Swedes, and moments later, Mats and Jan have excused themselves, donned their beloved cowboy hats, and joined four of their teammates outside by the snowmobiles.

> "They were hesitant at first," says Ron, "but once they got a taste of driving the machines, we had a heck of a time getting them off again." . . . The Kennedys, Cunninghams, and Blatzes compare experiences. They all agree it has been a most memorable New Year's and that they would definitely billet players again if the opportunity arose.

> "They have really grown on us. I've even told Mats and Jan that they are welcome to stay behind in Canada," says Janet Blatz, half in jest. Before leaving, I ask them if a farm in Kelsey is better than a hotel. They look at me as if I had left my brain in my coffee cup. Jan Eriksson, one hand on the steering wheel, the other on his cowboy hat, answers for them all. "Of course!" he shouts. Then he roars into the brilliant white distance.

Natural Lines of Communication . . . Proportions of Humour

The Czech players became a topic of endless debate amongst hosts and fans. "My little girl saw one of the boys in his underwear," Steve Yuha, of Rosalind, reports. "I told her not to get worried, that's how they do things in Europe." Despite the language barrier, there were natural lines of communication, especially amongst the teenagers. Situations, says Steve, easily took on humorous proportions. "Czech lads were convinced Gretzky was only as good as an average European hockey player while the Canadians argued he was the best in the world." The Czechs later saw an Oiler game and changed their minds about Gretzky.

"Better than living in a hotel as we usually do"

"The Viking Cup was my first experience in North America," said Dominik Hašek, who was with the Czechoslovakia national U18 Viking Cup in 1982. "We had a very good team and won in the final. We were spending time with families and we had fun. It was better than living in a hotel as we usually do."

Jim Brager, Hašek's billet said, "A couple of times (later), Dominik came during the summer with František Kučera, who stayed with the Johnson family. On one occasion, my son Warren and I took them out to the driving range to teach them some golf."

"What is most important is the close relations between the families and the players"

Miloš Broukal was general secretary of the Czech and Slovak teams for Viking Cup '92. In *Viking Cup '92 Magazine,* he said,

> The players have come to enjoy the chance to be billeted in a Canadian home, instead of staying cooped up in hotels as they do when travelling in Europe. . . It is a good experience for the players to live with families and learn another style of living and other non-hockey experiences. What is most important is the close relations between the players and the family, as you can see by the number of families who follow the players to other tournaments to visit. Some of the families are proud of the players who stayed in their homes. . . Not even differences in food detract from the visits to Camrose homes. I think every young player likes hamburgers, hot dogs, and Coke.

"Benefited the players psychologically"

"Czech teams have always felt welcome in Canada," said Viking Cup '94 Czech coach Josef Straka. "Family background [living] has benefited the players psychologically and helped them to overcome the burden of a long stay abroad and demanding tournaments."

"I'm talking about Camrose residents opening their homes and billeting all of these kids"

"Knowing tension between the Western world and some Iron Curtain nations can sometimes be tense, it was delightful to see the Camrose Lutheran College tournament be such a tremendous success," said Bruce Hogle, news and public affairs manager of CFRN-TV in a 1984 editorial. "And I'm not talking about hockey alone. I'm talking about Canadian and American kids able to mix with those from European nations. I'm talking about Camrose residents opening their homes and billeting all of these kids. . . They say that the future belongs to our young people and I couldn't agree more, because they don't have the distrust that has been built up in those older people now running the world."

"A community that is so involved"

"It's a tremendous undertaking for a small community," said Dave Tyler, USA Hockey vice-president and chair of Junior Council. "Nowhere else will you find a community that is so involved with the billeting and all the committees they've formed to put this on."

"Wonderful life experience"

Al Grazys from McGill University, Montreal was a coach in Viking Cup '90. "Fond memories from this tournament will stay with us for a very long time," he said, "Not only because of our success, but more so because of the warm and loving care that we experienced in our relationships with all your many volunteers and community . . . thanks for a wonderful life experience."

"Lifetime experience in Camrose homes"

"Probably the most amazing and impactful part of the Viking Cup was the opportunity for teams to stay with local Camrose families," said Mike Johnston, University of New Brunswick coach, Viking Cup '92 (and former CLC Vikings coach). "The one major hurdle would be the Eastern Bloc countries like Czechoslovakia and Russia. No one thought they would ever accept LeRoy's proposal, including our committee members. But they did, and for everyone involved, this became the legacy of the tournament. Lifetime friendships were made and, over the next twenty years, not only did the families and players keep in touch, but they often visited each other on a regular basis."

"We embraced them into our homes"

Cindy Trautman was billeting committee chair for the later Viking Cups. She and her husband, Pat, and their boys Justin and Jordan billeted a total of ten players, mostly from Finland. "Viking Cup billeting was one of the best experiences our family has ever participated in," she said.

> From the moment the players arrived in Camrose to the moment they left to return to their own families, we embraced them into our homes and, for two or three weeks every two years, we lived and breathed international hockey. Many of the families lived on farms, acreages, villages, and some in the city. Some of the special events we as families tried to do for the players were put on at least one potluck supper during their stay so that the whole team and coaches could be together and experience Canadian hospitality. The coaching team would always be amazed at how we could invite seventy people into our homes!
>
> Trust was a big part of the plan. They arrive in this strange city only to be sent off with a family they have never met, that would feed them and get them to the rink on time. Two weeks later, you would see these same players and billets standing outside in the cold of winter saying goodbye, giving lots of hugs to all the family members, children, moms, and some dads, some with tears in their eyes. That is when we knew our plan had worked.

"The Viking Cup experience was an integral part of my childhood"

"Every second Christmas my father and mother, LeRoy and Dianne, would open our home to a steady stream of foreign players, coaches, and dignitaries, who arrived in our little town from various parts of the globe," Dale Johnson remembers. "I'll never forget the friendships that were forged with players who were billeted at our home, many of whom have stayed in close contact with our family members to this day. My mother became a surrogate mom to all the young athletes she opened our home to. And, inevitably, there would be those moments when we had to remind my mother that our foreign guests would not miraculously begin to understand English just because she spoke it to them more loudly!"

"They just rubbed their stomachs and we knew what they wanted"

"Christmas to our family of seven was the Viking Cup," remembers Keith and Connie Stollery. "It was 24-7 for two weeks", said Keith. "I loved to drive the boys to practices and games and to sit and watch them perform. At home, we played on our garden rink with lights on and sometimes we would go in to the Armena rink. After that, we would have their favourite, a barbecued hamburger. They didn't speak English, but that was OK. They just rubbed their stomachs and we knew what they wanted!"

"It was a holiday at home"

"So many friends were together from Camrose and elsewhere and all were having a great time with our guests," remembers Liz Rolf. "Everyone seemed to want to help out. The Co-Op gave grocery hampers to the billets, the word got around quickly. The community is an ideal size for this undertaking."

"It was our holiday at home," remembers Rob Rolf. "The next year, we went to Winnipeg to the World Junior Games to see 'our boys' play. It was a great education on what sport can do to uplift people."

Many more billeting stories/experiences are featured in the chapters to follow, as they relate to each of the participating countries.

Smorgasbord

The banquet was a focal part of the Viking Cup experience, and was always planned to be an expression of comradery, excellence, and fine Canadian food. It was a vital educational component, where a representative of each team spoke briefly of the program in the country they represented. Some of the early guest speakers included: Scotty Bowman (Buffalo Sabres), Dr. Randy Gregg (Edmonton Oilers), Glenn Sonmor (Minnesota North Stars), and Anders Hedberg (Toronto Maple Leafs).

In the spirit of Viking Cup excellence, the banquet committee, often headed by Carol Roy and a crew of dedicated volunteers, sewed special aprons and other smart-looking apparel, which was always added a special touch. "The Western-themed banquet one year was a real hit," Carol remembers.

A special thanks is extended to the numerous members of the community who applied their expertise to menu preparations, decorating, and organizing memorable banquets. They always bolstered the theme on the tournament, "All things extraordinary!"

To billeting families, the banquet was a short break from the routine of hosting hungry hockey players to home-cooked meals. Always willing to be involved, the city and county of Camrose sponsored the banquet with assistance from the province of Alberta.

Scotty Bowman, banquet speaker Viking Cup '81

"I rarely come to Western Canada on a scouting mission, but this stop in Camrose has been full of pleasant surprises. The skating and passing skills of the European teams are exceptional." (*Viking Cup '81*)

Randy Gregg, Edmonton Oilers Stanley Cup Champions, Viking Cup '86 banquet

"More and more people are realizing it isn't the stronger, tougher players who perform best, but the smarter, more tactical, and better coached players, such as Jari Kurri and Igor Larionov and the brother act of Brian and Joe Mullen in Calgary."

Glen Sonmor, Minnesota North Stars, Viking Cup '84

"Anyone who wonders where we're able to find the talented players has only to come to a tournament like this. You must have fun—that's what it is all about."

Culture

Hockey is a good example of a sport that is both art and science. There are numerous expressions of beauty as the human body performs advanced skills and manoeuvres that collectively advance the quality of play. When the great Patrick Eliáš, Viking Cup '92 player, had his familiar jersey number twenty-six retired after twenty years with the New Jersey Devils, adoring fans described his performance as "poetry in motion."

In *Red Army*, director Gabe Polsky notes that the creator of Soviet-style hockey, Anatoli Tarasov, who studied chess and ballet and literature, made hockey more of a magical thing to watch, a deep expression of human creativity. It was a very fluid style; improvisational. "They were playing jazz on the ice."

The diversity of cultural traditions and backgrounds in the Viking Cup, on and off the ice, created unusual expressions of beauty and skill that were appreciated by spectators as well as participants. It broadened tournament appeal and put more people in the seats. With enthusiasm, longtime billet Yvonne Myrehaug spoke for many, "I liked the entertainment part of the tournament."

I once asked a lady musician in the community why she attended the games. She responded: "I arrive early to hear the national anthems in the different languages, I love the music and the atmosphere, I like the beautiful banners, happy people… the drama of it all."

I thought at the time, *it is nice to know* why *you are here, but it is more important* that *you are here.*

Experimentation in strategies of play and team dynamics supports hockey as a science. Viking Cup coach Perry Pearn commented: "It was a real-life laboratory setting to adjust to different styles and strategies from other countries, as well as testing one's own ideas."

The Viking Cup was played in a uniquely festive stadium with banners and flags tastefully adorning the spaces, music bouncing on sound waves, and mascots and other attractions entertaining the crowds. I often mused that we were ahead of our time in Canada but catching up to the American way of promoting school-related sports. It was with considerable scorn from some in the hockey world that the Edmonton Oilers introduced cheerleaders at their games in 2010. Now it is standard, in addition to so many other entertainment attractions. The lifeblood of sport at the advanced level is in the number of eyes watching the games, and the sporting world has become much more in tune to that reality in recent years.

Music

National Anthems

From previous trips abroad, we knew how important it was for players representing another country to hear the music of their national anthem. We went a step further.

Musicians in our town were commissioned to perform each national anthem in the mother language of each team. The group became known as the Viking Cup Trio, and were a mainstay throughout Viking Cup history. Their harmony was superb and, after so many performances before every game, pronunciation improved to near perfection, I'm told. "They even sang our national hymn in *our* language" was an oft-heard comment among the visiting players.

A Tribute to the Viking Cup Trio - a legacy.

Hockey players are not normally known for their musical talents, but the Viking Cup gave them an opportunity to showcase what they had.

Leader of the group, Carolyn Olson commented, "Mr Johnson heard us sing at a function and asked us if we would like to do the national anthems at the Viking Cup. We said sure, and from then we were a regular, for 24 years. But we weren't always alone. Players and their leaders increasingly joined in, proud to be singing their national anthem in their language on foreign soil."

Carolyn said that the players were especially respectful, and often sang with the trio, never leaving their position until they were finished. "I think they liked our three-part harmony—unusual for national anthems." The Edmonton Oilers later invited the group to sing at one of their games, when Paul Laurier, their regular, was not available. "It was a wonderful experience, all because of the Viking Cup."

Lloyd, a member of the group, commented, "Many coaches, managers, and players would come to us and say, 'Thanks for singing our national anthem in *our language*. We have never heard that before when travelling to other countries.'"

Singing was a family passion for the Olsons. Daughter Tova, now a professional musician, commented: "We learned all the

Viking cup Trio: Crystal Mackay, Lloyd Olson, Carolyn Olson

songs listening to our parents practise at home. Once when they couldn't be at a game, we sang for them, and Russian players told us we sang the words perfectly! We sure liked that."

Sister Kiva had other memories. "We were proud when kids at school would say, 'Oh, your parents are the ones that sing at the Viking Cup!' Some kids wore jerseys from players that were living with them . . . they were always looked up to. It was a big part of our growing up."

The Olson kids also had their opinions about the games. "We liked the hockey because players would play hard and still be friends."

Upon reflection, the Trio members commented: "We appreciated so much the music of the anthems. They are all beautiful—and especially the Russian national anthem!"

Game Music: "Playing the little tunes between whistles"

Live game music that coincided with play action accentuated game action and appeal. For several years, keyboardist Dale Johnson provided the music, and his band produced a special Viking Cup theme song that was unique to the Viking Cup and a hit with the crowd. "My role was very small in the tournament, and typically involved recruiting some hockey players as volunteers to assist in hoisting our family organ into a truck and carrying it up into the press box at the frigid Camrose arena," Dale recalls. "Playing little tunes between whistles to warm the audience and get their blood circulating… and, in turn, warming my frozen fingers with a space heater when the puck was dropped and play resumed. I remember thinking how luxurious it was when the arena finally installed plexiglass into the press box, allowing us to sit in warmth and comfort in the best seats in the house.

"I remember fondly my many chats with John Short, who would often sit next to my keyboard taking notes and preparing for his many articles written over the years about the tournament."

Intermission Entertainment

Viking Cup intermission entertainment was a part of an overall marketing strategy to draw more people into the arena and to enhance their experience.

Special guests often performed between periods of the games. Examples included: the Calgary Fiddlers, Edmonton Shumka Dancers, First Nations Hoop Dancers, Kurt Browning figure skating, Susan Humphries figure skating, local precisionaire skaters, various bands, abbreviated minor hockey games, etc.

Morley Dunlop (CLC Vikings 1973–76), who was a member of the awards committee, recalls the day that Kurt Browning, later to become a four-time World Champion figure skater and top Canadian athlete in 1990 (Lou Marsh Award), performed at the Viking Cup. "They asked me to take Kurt out for dinner between his performances in the afternoon and evening games. We had a good time but I had no idea I was with such a fine future celebrity. I guess that was typical of the Viking Cup."

Art

Recently (twenty-five years after his Viking Cup banquet speech), I called Anders Hedberg to glean some memories of his Viking Cup '96 visit. Here's what he told me: "It is very interesting that you called, because I am sitting in my office here in Stockholm, admiring a beautiful painting on the wall. It is a painting of two students walking down a lane with hockey bags and sticks over their shoulders (one with a red-and-white jacket and the other blue and yellow). I'm sure they are on their way to play hockey. I think it is the Camrose College at the far end of the lane because

World Champion figure skater, Kurt Browning provided in-between periods entertainment at one of the games in Viking Cup '88.

Kurt Browning

this is the painting you gifted to me at the banquet. The painting is by Glenda Beaver. Is she from Camrose, too?"

I knew, then, that it had been a good plan to feature a painting of a typical Camrose scene, commissioned by a well-recognized artist of our community, for each Viking Cup (after '92). Reprints of the painting became the standard gift to all team officials and honoured guests. The painting was the cover feature for all posters, programs, greeting cards, and other marketing initiatives. More important, it was a reminder that the Viking Cup ran on different but related tracks of interest—sport, culture, arts, and education.

Other Viking Cup paintings are featured throughout this book. Several businesses purchased the complete series and they're still on display in some locations. In earlier years, there were painting competitions in some of the schools for display in the arena at the games, and on two occasions, the Viking Cup was part of community New Year's Eve celebrations known as "First Night."

Education

In the early years of the Viking Cup, Hockey Alberta teamed up with Augustana to hold advanced coaching clinics in Camrose. Coaches of the Viking Cup teams were often guest instructors, and some even took the courses. Many other great hockey minds were in Camrose for the Viking Cup, and therefore available to supplement discussions. For example, Glenn Hall, Scotty Bowman, and Dave King made presentations. Important lessons are a big part of the Viking Cup legacy, and many are expressed throughout this book by participants.

"Who invented these educational values in learning and development?"

Finnish coach Juhani Wahlsten of the first Viking Cup championship team, recalls "learning at the Viking Cup."

> Winning the Viking Cup was a statement to us that, even under difficult circumstances, you can achieve something if you keep your mind on principles of success. Some of those principles that were stressed were initiative, self-improvement, enthusiasm, dedication, and, most important, love of the game. Who invented these educational values in learning and development? I don't know, but I do know that this is a highly competitive game that you Canadians invented. . . In a country like Finland, we are [raised] this way. But these things plus many others helped us to compete at the highest level, like in our gold-medal game with the Prince Albert Raiders.
>
> This may stay as one of the most thrilling games I have ever been part of. When one of us scored, the other tied: 1-0; 1-1; 2-1, 2-2, 3-2, 3-3, etc., until the score was 6-5. Then for the first time we had a two-goal lead, but very soon it was 7-6 again. The last nine minutes of the game we could experience what the hard Canadian forechecking was like. We practically could not come out of the zone. The final score was 8-6 (an empty net).

For me, learning to compete under tough circumstances is not only winning, it can also be losing after doing your best. Winning the Viking Cup was that special reward for doing our very best.

"It definitely had an impact on how and what I taught throughout my career"

There were many takeaways from the Viking Cup that contributed to enhanced instruction in other countries. The story of Pavel Geffert is one example.

Pavel was billeted with Walter and Dianne Nigh's family at Viking Cup '86, and the families are still in regular contact. After Camrose, Pavel played fifteen years in the Czech "Extraliga," mainly with HC Sparta Prague. He played for the Czech national team in the Lillehammer Olympics in 1994, and at the World Championships in Stockholm in 1995. From 2005, he worked for HC Sparta Prague as the chief of youth for fifteen years, where he was responsible for the methodology of training players, coaches, scouting, and foundation work. He led seventeen Czech hockey academies from all regions in the Czech Republic followed by two years of work for the Czech Hockey Federation.

> I lived my childhood and youth under a repressive Communist ideology, so my most important experience from Camrose was what the real life of freedom means, Pavel said. I saw how Canadian people love hockey and their enthusiasm and passion made a big impression on me. It definitely had an impact on how and what I taught throughout my career.

It was always rewarding for members of the Viking Cup steering committee to receive similar expressions from our own Augustana Vikings about learning, and the bonus of exposure to international competition and ways of life in other countries attracted many new students to the Augustana Vikings program. Those alumni can now reflect on dreams realized.

From Small College Town Alberta to Hockey Hall of Fame

Judge Bill Andreassen, who sits on the Alberta Provincial Court, was team captain for the Vikings' 1974/75 national champion season. "We started out as a bunch of student hockey players from a small college and small-town Alberta, and along our journey, we ended up in Alberta's Hockey Hall of Fame," Bill remembers. "Now, forty-five years later, we are a group of farmers, civil servants, a number of pastors, teachers, lawyers, tradesmen, businessmen. None of us became professional hockey players, but we became leaders, especially in sport, in our communities.

"I was involved in most Viking Cups after my playing days, first on the rules and awards committees, and later as a billet host. And when our guests played against the Vikings, I appreciated the athleticism and competitiveness of both sides. . . When I was young and playing hockey, I had a strong negative feeling toward the opposition. My involvement in the Viking Cup, especially the billeting, contributed to a more mature perspective."

"More than proud to be on the leading edge"

"The hockey tour was a dream come true," remembers Lorne Monaghan, Principal at Archbishop Jordan Comp High School, in Sherwood Park, Alberta, and a Vikings player in the 1979–80 season. "And the hard work, organization, and vision led to the (birth of the) Viking Cup. The Viking Cup had a long run as one the most successful international tournaments in Canadian history. Our group, the 1979-80 Vikings, is more than proud to be on the leading edge of this event, which has positively impacted so many over the years. Through the success of the Viking Cup, many players, families, and coaches had their first North American hockey experience through the great welcoming of the Camrose community and our country of Canada."

"My journey to the Olympics began in Camrose"

Ken Lovsin, who played under Tom Renney on Canada's Olympic hockey team in Lillehammer, and is currently a businessman in Stony Plain, remembers how his journey to the Olympics began in Camrose. There, he took his final year of high school at Camrose Lutheran College.

"I was a walk-on in the hockey tryout camp. I went to Europe with the Vikings in 1984–85, and played in Viking Cup '86. This opened my eyes to a more skilled brand of hockey that I wanted to play. It was fantastic! Soon, I had the opportunity to play in the Spengler Cup, the premier tournament in Europe. Through similar experiences, I learned what Olympic hockey was like, and I wanted to get there.

"Mike Johnston from Augustana helped me a lot. I was lucky that coaching was so upgraded at this time through university coaches such as Clare Drake and Dave King. They were open and willing to share their ideas/secrets for the good of the game. I played for the Olympic team from '89 to '94, three full years. This led to a tryout with the Washington Capitals and one year playing in Mora, Sweden. I played for two weeks with our Olympic team in Russia—Beef Stroganoff for fourteen days straight! I played in the Isvestia Tournament in Moscow. I remember seeing large photos of the Politburo up in the arena–Gorbechev was most prominent. I remember the Russian KLM line and Viktor Tikhonov, the coach. For me, it was all education plus."

From the Camrose Arena to London's Wembley Stadium

"I was a young kid from Sirois, Manitoba, so the opportunity of a European tour and a Viking Cup cinched it for me," said Terry Kurtenbach (CLC 1982–85).

When Terry left CLC, he had been chosen to the All-Conference ACAC All-Star team and was an all-star defenseman in Viking Cup '84, where his team won bronze. "My experience in Camrose whetted my appetite to play in Europe. After completing my degree at Brandon, Wayne Fleming of Winnipeg helped me to sign a professional contract to play in Nottingham, Great Britain. I played there and in Guildford professionally for thirteen years and then coached for eight years. In 1991, our Nottingham team won the British League Championship in Wembley Stadium, London—one of my greatest thrills. I was chosen to play on the British national team on three occasions. In 1994, we played in the A pool World Championships, in Bolzano, Italy. The Russians and Canadians beat us quite badly, but it was a great thrill to play against some of my NHL idols like Luc Robitaille, Rob Blake, and Paul Kariya. I scored our first goal against the Russians.

"Living in Europe is an education in itself. I have travelled and played in almost every country. Today, many years later, I remember the great time I had with the guys in Camrose—playing and travelling and getting my education at the same time. I got my start there because there was a Viking Cup."

"It was my inspiration"

Kevin Dickie (1982–84), Director of Athletics at Acadia University, NS, is happy to reminisce on his days in Camrose. "I thought; to play in the Viking Cup or to play hockey in Europe every Christmas season . . . no other university of College program had that bonus to offer . . . anywhere. And so, I came to Camrose. Looking back now, the place changed my life way beyond hockey, from life-long friends thru to it becoming my foundation to be a school teacher, hockey coach and athletic director. The Augustana experience was my inspiration and Coach Mike Johnston was my mentor." Kevin spent 18 years coaching junior, major junior and university hockey and assisted with Canada's National Junior Program before an administration career at UNB and Acadia.

"A pinnacle for me! I want people to have the same experiences"

Tyler Bellamy (2006 BA), founder of the Augustana Vikings Hockey Alumni Association, likes to talk about the magnet that attracted him to Camrose.

"I was a young boy from Revelstoke visiting my uncle in Millet. He and my dad took me to a Viking Cup '94 game. Mike Comrie was playing. I was so impressed with the atmosphere, the noise, the excitement. It was so cool and the hockey was amazing! We bought a Viking Cup jersey and I wore it to show off back home… at minor hockey events especially.

> I saw the gold game of Viking Cup 2002 on TV in Langley, where I was playing Junior hockey. My teammate was playing for the BC All-Stars against Augustana Vikings. Who are they? I soon found out. They won the Viking Cup! I realized then that college hockey in Alberta was good, so I enrolled in Camrose. Playing in the Viking Cup was all I had dreamed it to be—huge noisy crowds, passion, and unbelievable atmosphere…. Man, I had a good time! I loved everything about Augustana, and Camrose. Lifelong friends, the professors, the hockey program . . . and I met my wife! Our family is part of the Camrose Police department now. But I still found time to be an assistant coach with the Vikings!

"I was a contact in Europe"

"The Viking Cup enabled me to realize my goal of playing in Europe," said Pat Ryan, who had come from Nova Scotia to play with the Vikings (1984–86). Pat still holds the ACAC record for most goals in a season. "I was scouted at Viking Cup '86 by the Finnish team, and played three years in Finland. I travelled to Leningrad, Russia, in 1988, and saw first-hand the contrast in the life from what I was accustomed to growing up with in Canada. We played an exhibition game against a Russian top-league team and I wanted to trade a stick before the game and two different players got in an argument as to who was going to get my stick! They had really bad equipment and they looked like a hobby team—until the puck dropped! Later I played in Salzgitter, Germany and helped to make arrangements for the Vikings to play our team and a team in Hamburg."

Opened doors to play in Europe

WestJet pilot Pat Seeley had this to say. "A big part of my passion and respect for international hockey came from my Viking Cup experience and wealth of good memories. The Viking Cup helped to open doors to play in Italy, as well as a brief experience with the Canadian national team." Fellow Viking Rick Dietrich played with Pat in Italy, followed by stints in Austria and Japan. "I learned a lot in Camrose and it gave me a passport to play abroad." Rick continues to hold the ACAC scoring record of seventy-two points in twenty-four games.

Coaching in a World Championships after Graduating from Augustana

After CLC, Lloyd McKinney (1982–84) played in Denmark, Britain, and South Africa, where he became an assistant coach of the South African national team in Johannesburg. After graduating from Augustana, Jeff Johnson (1984–87) played in Australia and was hired to be an assistant coach of the Australian national team. What a coincidence that they coached on opposing teams at the World C-Pool Championships in Slovenia in 1993. Lloyd comments, "The Augustana Vikings gave me a fresh start in hockey and, down the road, there have been so many interesting stops and learning opportunities." Jeff says, "I like to support the Vikings hockey program. It gave me interesting opportunities, globally speaking."

"The atmosphere it brought to the whole town"

Sven Sandberg of Stockholm, Sweden attended Augustana and played for the Vikings in '83–84. "The first time I heard of the Viking Cup was in Stockholm, in 1982, after my two friends Dan Lindqwister and Ulf Hall came back after being part of the CLC Vikings in '81/82. The highlight of the season was for sure Viking Cup '84. I learned what hard preparation was. You could feel all the atmosphere it brought to the whole town and people around. The arena was sold out, and of course you knew even the scouts from the NHL were there. To me, it felt amazing that a small town like Camrose could get a great international tournament like the Viking Cup. We had nothing like it in Sweden!"

"It opened my eyes to the world. It opened our game to the next skill level"

Alberta RCMP Inspector Yvon de Champlain, CLC Vikings '82–84, reflects on his Viking Cup days. "The Viking Cup opened the door for Canadian hockey to become much more skill-based. It moved our game to the next skill level (e.g., five-man unit, defense in the offensive zone, etc.). It removed us from pugilistic hockey to a thoughtful, purposeful game. Personally, it changed my perspective. It opened my mind to other possibilities in life. It started me on my journey of learning. I became a student of all that I have done. I discovered that I had something to offer to people, especially the vulnerable, and so I went into the public service."

"It started me on my business career"

Don Lauweryssen, CLC Vikings '81–83 had a career working with Agrium (now Nutrien Ltd.) globally. "The Viking Cup was a trigger/stimulus for what became a deep curiosity about new cultures, ways of living, and doing business. Hockey was our ticket to fast inroads and connections with people in various countries—the ultimate ice-breaker, you might say. The Viking Cup was a seven-day event and the Europe trip was fifteen to twenty days. However, the positive memories from those days have lasted a lifetime."

"My son now plays with the Vikings"

"It was my opportunity to play at the highest level. We lived it—at home and in Europe," said Alan Skip (1979–83), Alberta businessman (Finning). "I remember the whistling by the fans when they disapproved. . . the national anthem sent chills. It was humbling to represent our country in this Communist land—a unique legacy for Camrose, and I was privileged to be part of it. My son, Curtis, just now graduated from the Vikings."

"Grandpa, I got to play in the Viking Cup!"

Dr. Lyle Hamm, CLC Vikings '84–87, assistant coach '89–91 and now a professor of education at UNB, discusses his good start.

"Travelling through Austria, Germany, and Czechoslovakia by bus with my teammates, seeing castles and finding the famous rivers, and tasting Pilsner beer in an ancient brewery, I realized there was a larger world to engage, be part of, and to learn about. I felt a long way from Flin Flon (Manitoba) in psychological terms, and from the outdoor skating rink where I began playing hockey on ice near the trailer court where I lived with my family. It felt very good. I wanted more.

"It's been thirty-three years since that semi-final game in the Viking Cup. Today, I am guided by questions in my research and teaching in the faculty of education at the University of New Brunswick.

"When I'm asked, 'What impact did the Viking Cup have on your life?' I have to respond that it was everything. Or nearly everything. If I didn't make that call to Mike (Johnston), on my grandpa's suggestion in 1984, I would never have attended college. I played in the Viking

Cup, travelled through Europe, and had contact with experiences I just couldn't imagine while skating on the chipped and broken ice near the trailer court. I am forever grateful for the opportunity I had to attend CLC and play on the Vikings, but my gratitude goes beyond that. I made lifelong friends, I benefited from unconditional mentoring from my teachers and coaches, and, yes, I got to play in the Viking Cup!"

"On my way to school"

Barry Dillon, teacher at Chester Ronning School and Viking Cup committee member, sees the Viking Cup through the eyes of his students.

"I was walking to school early one morning. It was snowing lightly. All of a sudden from a distance, I heard huffing and puffing and boots stomping on the fresh snow, like an army on parade. I looked up and thought I saw a herd of buffalo emerging from the darkness toward me. Then I realized it was the Swedish hockey team in training in that early, dark, snowy morning. I hadn't seen them play hockey yet, but when I did, I didn't want to miss a game. The atmosphere was tremendous! There was a poster competition in the schools and some of our students were on minor hockey teams that were the sponsoring team of one of the Viking Cup teams. Some of our families were billeting, so there was a lot of talk and enthusiasm. Sometimes, kids would miss school if their team was playing, as they were expected to cheer them on! That was acceptable, though—no problem. After all, it was Viking Cup time!"

Marketing

The product on the ice

The greatest strength of the Viking Cup was the product on the ice, and, like with Gordie Howe, the first year was its biggest selling piece. There were the usual marketing strategies and a strong effort to attract the attention of the Edmonton media, and word spread quickly about the quality and diversity of play.

However, for every noteworthy success, new problems arose. The first was the escalating crowds for playoff games. Regarding the final game between TPS Finland and the Prince Albert Raiders in the first Viking Cup, ticket sales chairman Lorne Broen said, "We had to hold the crowd back until game time to ensure that all who had bought advance tickets got seating. Not everybody was pleased! It was more than a complete sell-out!"

European junior involvement, being the novelty that it was, drew curious NHL scouts looking to discover a new rising star. And the public, in general, were introduced to a new class of hockey. Viking Cup '81 confirmed that our vision had found legs (and skates) and was in itself a strong product to sell. It quickly showed up on the radar screens of hockey. The Viking Cup steering committee was inspired by the quality of play and the excellent public response it had attracted, leaving no doubt that a Viking Cup '82 should follow.

In succeeding Viking Cups, many new marketing initiatives were introduced, but the greatest attraction was the array of stars . . . on the ice.

Some of the most noteworthy marketing strategies included the following.

"Skating" the Torch through Western Canada: A Win-Win-Win Journey

The Viking Cup was a New Year's holiday event in Camrose, but the teams typically made the city their home for a longer period of time. Participation agreements with European and American teams included a series of pre-tournament exhibition games in the four Western provinces. During Communist times, the Czechoslovakian and Russian teams were provided air tickets in exchange for the rights to sell and market exhibition game tours to interested hockey teams and towns. Within the agreement, each host team was to promote the Viking Cup in connection with each game.

The tours were like a "running of the torch," designed to hype interest and draw people to the Viking Cup.

The exhibition games fulfilled an important objective of the visiting Viking Cup teams: to improve their hockey programs by playing tough Canadian opponents. The Czechs and Slovaks, in particular, considered the exhibition swings vital to their development programs.

"The whole environment, tour across Alberta, wild broad nature, number of games, people around hockey, and fans—this all was very special to our development," said Slavomír Lener, of the Czech Ice Hockey Federation in 2020.

For the spectators, including scouts, the teams were well acclimatized and in top shape to perform at the Viking Cup following their pre-tournament tours. Camrose saw the players at their peak level of play!

The third win was for the host team of each exhibition game. With effective marketing strategies, the host team could raise its profile in its community and realize a financial gain. It was an opportunity rarely afforded a Canadian team to host and play a national team from a major hockey country. Communities became involved in the games, often providing community-sponsored dinners with both teams following the games. It was also a rare opportunity for game officials to referee games involving different styles of hockey.

The Viking Cup teams were our greatest ambassadors in the run-up to the tournament itself. The Czechoslovakian and Czech Republic teams alone played close to 100 pre-tournament exhibition games throughout Western Canada as part of their twelve visits to the Viking Cup.

The "Skating of the Torch" was a grueling program of many miles, especially for the Czechoslovakians and Russians. But it was win-win-win for all involved.

Every Team a Home Team—The Liberec Story

In sport, there is usually no problem to create a lively atmosphere when home teams play. The challenge in a tournament is to create the same atmosphere when two visiting teams are playing. Czechoslovakia gave us an answer in the Liberec story. It's detailed in Chapter 6 but, in summary, a Camrose minor hockey team was assigned as the official cheerleader and host for each Viking Cup team. They were given seating directly behind their team's bench, from where they would cheer on their team. An award was presented to the minor hockey team that did the best job throughout the tournament. Parents, grandparents, uncles, aunts, and friends of the young boys responded by coming to the games and lending their vociferous support. The same occurred with player billets and their families and friends, who also joined the cheering sections. The surroundings may have been unfamiliar, but the lively atmosphere spurred on every team as if they were playing in their hometown.

Russian player Sergei Gonchar, who had a lengthy NHL career, recalls his Viking Cup experience: "You know I had never seen such attention by the fans. . . And they cheered for us, too. As Russians, we were not used to that!"

A Festive Atmosphere

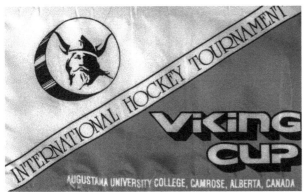
Viking Cup Flag

One of the very unique features of the Viking Cup was the carnival atmosphere created in the stadium. A large number of Viking Cup flags were produced and hung throughout the arena. They flew alongside large flags of all the participating countries and all the provincial flags. Special banners for each major sponsor were prominently and centrally placed above the ice surface. (We were fortunate that the Camrose arena had a high roof.) The auspicious display of flags and banners provided for a much better quality of sound throughout, and the music was choreographed to match the mood during play and intermission.

City officials requested that the colourful patterns adorning the stadium be left on display for the remainder of the season. We obliged, but with some consternation that the Viking Cup might lose some of its fresh shine at the next tournament.

Spectators entered Viking Cup games with a sense of awe and beauty. It was a neat and classy place to be! We also believed that the players performed better in an atmosphere of such high-spirited crowds and high standards of stadium decor. Most would agree that it worked. The Viking Cup was our magnet, and extraordinary initiatives determined the "field" around it.

Uddo and the Opening Ceremonies

Many Scandinavians immigrated to the Camrose area to settle the land, build a college, ski, and play hockey. But the biggest and tallest Viking ever to cross the seas to open the west with his axe was our mascot, Uddo. Once he tasted our soil and found his mate, he was convinced that Canada would be his home.

Uddo landed in Edmonton in 1927, axe in hand, as a young brushcutter from northern Sweden. He eventually chopped his way to the Camrose area, where he married a beautiful Norwegian girl from the neighbouring village of Bawlf, another Norwegian settlement. Uddo was a towering gentleman who was 6'11" (211 cm)—seven feet in boots and approaching eight feet to the tip of his helmet horns.

Uddo Johanson, Dianne & LeRoy Johnson

Uddo, our real Viking, was only too happy to officially open all early Viking Cups, welcoming players from or near his Viking ship, which Norwegian shipbuilder, Olaus Straumsnes, built for the seventy-fifth anniversary of Camrose Lutheran College. The ship is a true replica (half-scale) of the original Vikings' longship. It was on display in the Vancouver harbour during the 1986 World Fair (Expo '86) and is now on permanent display in the Camrose Chamber of Commerce Centre.

Uddo towered over all the hockey players, even when they had their skates on. It was a striking opening, and many thought our Viking was equipped with stilts. But he wasn't. Had Uddo been able to skate, the Vikings hockey team would surely have had him in its lineup!

In the later years of the Viking Cup, mascots Sven and Ole Uffda provided lively entertainment amongst the crowds during each game.

The feature of the closing ceremonies was the distribution of specially minted Viking Cup gold, silver, and bronze medals—and, of course, the Viking Cup, to the champions. All-star teams were announced and awards presented, including for the tournament's MVP (see Chapter 3). The ceremony was choreographed to appropriate live music (by Dale Johnson for many years), with announcements from famed long-time announcer, Dale Smith. But, for many years, Uddo was always there to conspicuously preside over the ceremonies.

Following Viking Cup '98, Big Valley Jamboree Enterprises was contracted to plan and run Viking Cup opening and closing ceremonies, with an emphasis on professional entertainment emanating from the famous Big Valley Jamboree in Camrose.

Viking Cup Magazine and Souvenir Supplement

A magazine with feature articles, lineups, and advertisements was produced for each Viking Cup. The commissioned painting was featured on the front cover and on tournament posters. Following the early Viking Cups, a souvenir supplement was produced as a memento for all participants and for a record of happenings. The *Camrose Canadian* produced a daily wrap-up supplement that was very popular for Viking Cups '96 and '98.

Wall of Fame and Championship Banners

NHL teams' drafting of Viking Cup players contributed to tournament credibility and status as the years progressed. For Viking Cup '86, a Wall of Fame with photos and information about all draftees who'd attained NHL game play was introduced in the arena's foyer. This became an important year-round marketing strategy and has also been significant in the recruiting program for Augustana Vikings hockey. There are currently seventy-two players on display in this selection. Unfortunately, the program was not continued after 2000.

Viking Cup '98 project coordinator, Jeff Johnson, introduced championship banners for each gold-medal-winning team of the Viking Cup. The banners continue to hang in the Max McLean Arena, where all Viking Cup games were played.

The Press

The radio, TV, and print media in Camrose and Edmonton were strong Viking Cup partners and supporters—and increasingly so with each successive Cup. Shaw Cable broadcasted

Viking Ship

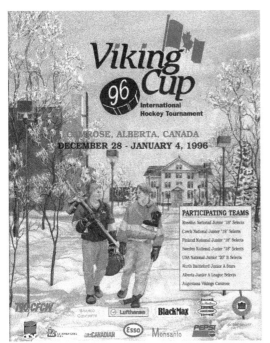

Poster and Magazine cover

live play-by-play coverage in the later years of the Viking Cup, even though the Max McLean Arena did not lend itself to good viewing. Edmonton sportscaster John Short was particularly effective in reporting the games and mobilizing the Edmonton media to cover the Viking Cup. Camrose reporters Murray Greene and Dan Jensen enthusiastically covered every tournament with interesting stories and photos.

Wall of Fame

A Tribute to John Short

"I liked the all-encompassing atmosphere"

Any sport . . . any time.

That theme may have made John Short a legend in sport, but his devotion to the objectives and achievements of the Viking Cup have made him a legend beyond sport.

"My favourite early memory is tied to that initial telephone call and a one-hour conversation on air the same night," John remembers, of the beginning of his Viking Cup journey.

"I promised LeRoy there would be plenty of time, if he could arrange to be in the studio by the 9 p.m. start time. His silence told me of his surprise that an Edmonton station, perhaps sixty miles from Camrose, would dedicate so much time to this idea. But Viking Cup was a perfect fit for the *Sports Talk* theme: 'any sport any time.'

"Right on time, LeRoy and Verlyn Olson showed up. They were loaded with facts and figures and details on how the tournament started and how communication had grown simpler and borders had virtually disappeared when all came to realize love of hockey and pride in Camrose were the major motivational factors.

"So impressive were they that I offered to help in any way I could to encourage Edmonton's larger population to fill the Camrose arena and be involved in pre-tournament exhibitions played all over the province of Alberta. To my great pleasure, the offer was accepted. I spoke whenever invited to service clubs and community groups for miles around. A few years later, *Sports Talk* moved to CFCW Radio in Camrose and the experience I'd gained in supporting the Viking Cup reflected itself in a comfort level with that community that has never shrunk—not in the slightest."

But who is John Short?

He was born January 31, 1937, on the kitchen table of his family home in Toronto and grew up on the tough streets of Detroit. In high school, when he was on the verge of going down the wrong path, the Globe and Mail newspaper gave him a shot to work as a copy boy from 7 p.m. to 3 a.m. It turned Short's life around, and sports fans are thankful he took the job.

John Short is a Canadian sports journalist and broadcaster. He formerly worked for the Canadian Press and *Edmonton Journal*, as well as the Edmonton Oilers as public relations director during the Peter Pocklington days. But John was best known for his sports-related radio shows.

Short is a member of the Alberta Sports Hall of Fame and Museum (inducted in 1988) and a recipient of the Chester Bell Memorial Award for excellence in sports writing, as well as the Fred Sgambati Media Award recipient for university sports coverage. John Short's wide knowledge of the Canadian sport scene was recognized when he was named to the selection committee for Canada's Sports Hall of Fame.

Jason Gregor, a sportscaster on Edmonton CFRN who was John's protégé in sport journalism and broadcasting, draws attention to his youth and the hundreds of other youth who followed John: "In the 1980 s and '90s, thousands of young northern Alberta teenagers shared a common bedtime routine. After washing their face, brushing their teeth, and kissing parents good night, they would hop into bed—but not all of them went right to sleep. Instead, they would pull the covers over their head and turn on their clock radio to listen to one of the greatest radio sports talk hosts we've ever heard, John Short."

"I love engagement," John has said. "I am a communicator." To that we can add, John is a storyteller with a fantastic memory. He has that unique ability to relate sport to life and the good of mankind . . . and to listen and talk to anyone of any age.

Short wrote numerous columns on the Viking Cup over the years, and he left little doubt where he stood. For example, he wrote:

"The effect of this tournament is evident everywhere. Entire families–Grandma, Granddad, Mom, Dad, sons, daughters, aunts, uncles, cousins—congregate in seats they have occupied for years. They're knowledgeable about the game, supportive of their team. Camrose has created an impressive community event that deserves to remain above the crass commerciality of much else in sport. Putting it simply, this has become an NHL scout's dream. The Viking Cup is one of the great memories of my life."

John Short made believers out of us. We went to John to sell our product, and he made us stronger believers in our own cause. He convinced us that we had a great thing going in the

Viking Cup. He gave us a stronger measure of assurance and confidence . . . and that may have been his greatest contribution to the Viking Cup.

Fans

"Knowledgeable and passionate people"

Chief Referee George McCorry was heard to comment: "The crowds at the Viking Cup were very knowledgeable hockey people. They knew and appreciated a better brand of hockey. They were better hockey people . . . and good to be around!"

These are indeed complimentary words for fans of the Viking Cup. Could it be a reflection of the quality of hockey in the tournament? Sport-loving people will travel great distances for A-quality performance. But it is also a reflection of an engaged community who chose to passionately be involved and to learn to appreciate and understand by seeing and touching the best that sport had to offer. The Viking Cup attracted knowledgeable hockey people, but it also raised the bar of understanding and passion in the whole community.

During the Vancouver Olympics, Coach Mike Babcock of Canada's Golden Hockey Team would deliberately walk amongst the attendees of every game with fellow coaches Jacques Lemaire and Lindy Ruff.

"I wanted to experience the excitement and energy of the people," he said in his book, *Leave No Doubt*. "It was fun. It energized us. People were alive. We fed off them. You could see and feel their passion. Their energy was awesome. They made us feel like they were part of our team. People were enjoying the moment. And so was I. It was great to be among them."

Unknowingly, Babcock, who coached in Viking Cup '90, was also describing the atmosphere around Viking Cup games. It was energizing to walk amongst the people of the community and sit amongst the lively crowds at the games. It was motivating for me and all committee members to be well prepared in our game responsibilities so that we could relax in our seats, enjoy the action …the engaged fans!

And what impact did the engaged fans have on the competing teams? Chris Topp, captain of the Viking Cup's 2002 gold-winning Augustana Vikings, recently commented: "I remember the full house for the championship game. Their enthusiasm energized our play. The crowd loved good hockey, and so did we!"

Publicity for Augustana and Camrose

Camrose knows only too well the power of sport attracting recognition and publicity to its community and college. As early as 1927, five of its sons, the Hansen brothers, journeyed to Augsburg College in Minneapolis to advance their education and play hockey for a fledgling hockey team (read their story in Chapter 1).

The Augsburg school newsletter of the time, *The Echo*, stated:

This tiny college, with but a few hundred students, suddenly shot into the national limelight. . . And their bid for international fame brought the school and the team, and especially the Hansen brothers, before the public eye in all the leading newspapers of America, as well as in many foreign countries.

More recently, local but internationally recognized cattleman (he's a member of the Alberta Agriculture Hall of Fame and the Canadian Agricultural Hall of Fame) and former Camrose County reeve and hockey referee, Bob Prestage, had this to say: "My ranching operation has taken me to many parts of the world, through many ports and countries. When I tell people I am from Camrose, so often they will say, 'Oh that is where they have the Viking Cup.'"

Alberta businessman (Freson Bros.) and Order of Canada recipient, Frank Lovsin, whose sons and grandson attended Augustana comments, "The College was given a huge boost in public exposure and recognition through the Viking Cup and hockey trips to Europe."

Many others have a story to tell about why Camrose and Augustana are much better known amongst people from different countries and provinces, near and far, because of the Viking Cup.

The Viking Cup defines an era of sport excellence in a small but active community in Canada. How long will its legacy endure? Long-time sports broadcaster Dale Smith comments, "The Viking Cup's legacy will have great longevity— it took place over many years and people remember meaningful and fun events for a long time."

Shadows from a Light, by Lindsay Leckelt (Viking Cup 2006)

CHAPTER 3

Hybrid Hockey . . . The Games

"Tournaments like the Viking Cup are beneficial in that they provide the players involved with a contrast in hockey styles. As well, the coaches gain benefit from seeing and evaluating different forms of tactics [and, in that regard], the Viking Cup was one of Canada's most successful international hockey tournaments. It evolved into an important event in the international hockey calendar."

—David King, coach of the Canadian national team (two Olympics and five World Championships, 1982–1992)

Dave King knows a lot about hockey. It's no wonder, then, that he is a member of the IIHF Hall of Fame and a recipient of the Order of Canada.

King began his amazing coaching career at the University of Saskatchewan. He coached Canada's national team for nine years, and in the NHL with Calgary, Montreal, Columbus, and Phoenix. He also spent several years as a head coach abroad—in Japan, Germany, Russia, and Sweden. He has been a mentor to numerous coaches, including Dave Tippett, coach of the Edmonton Oilers, who said of him in an *Athletic Weekly* interview: "He learned a little something from each international stop: discipline from the Japanese, order from the Germans, the importance of collective benefit from the Swedes, and skill from the Russians. I can't imagine there's anybody that knows the game tactically better than him in the world."

From his numerous encounters with Finland and Czechoslovakia, King could no doubt make reference to the resilience of the Finns and the passion for the game of the Czechs and Slovaks, which was so evident in their regular appearances at the Viking Cup.

The teams that came to the Viking Cup brought their sticks and pucks and protective gear, but they brought much more. They brought their training, skills, style of play, culture, politics, social norms, and family values. In the *Athletic Weekly* interview, Dave King, who attended Viking Cup '81, concluded: "All countries have something interesting to offer and their culture from their society permeates their game."

At the onset of the Viking Cup, the most dramatic hockey contrasts were seen in the North American and European game, played out in different levels of hockey—from junior, national, and club teams, to college and university teams. The era of hockey hybridization, the merging of the games, coincided with the era of the Viking Cup, and this may have been the tournament's most dominant and interesting feature.

James Patrick, an All-Star of Viking Cup '81, player of twenty-three years in the NHL, and regular international competitor, recently commented to me on the changes in hockey: "It has become a global game. The European influence has been enormous. International hockey used to mean differences in style and strategy. Not so now."

Russian player Sergei Gonchar, All-Star of Viking Cup '92, player of twenty-two years in the NHL, and regular international competitor, recently said "There was a big difference in hockey styles when I played in the Viking Cup. Now everybody learns from each other and we incorporate the best from all systems. . . Otherwise, hockey is the same all over; it doesn't matter where you are."

Diversity

The diversity of the team lineups—and therefore the heterogeneous nature of the Viking Cup—was predicated by a few realities.

First, the Viking Cup was owned and operated by a college, and therefore college/university teams were participants. The home team was always the Augustana (CLC) Vikings. Since there was a precedent of inter-league exhibition play between university and college teams, universities, on some occasions, were invited to play in the Viking Cup. One of the objectives of the tournament was to promote college/university hockey.

Secondly, unlike Canada, Europe has no comparable university or college hockey teams. Top-level European junior teams and U18 national teams were seen to be of a similar calibre to Canadian and American college and Canadian and US junior hockey.

Thirdly, North American junior teams were invited as strong competition and a good draw in the tournament. Their players' ages were more in line with the ages of the participating European players. Some teams, such as the powerful Prince Albert Raiders, relished the idea of something different: to test their skills with European and university/college hockey.

For the Europeans the differences in age was generally not a problem, as long as the refereeing was competent (and close) and the teams were roughly of the same calibre of play. The various European hockey federations sought tough competition on their Canadian tours, as this was considered the best way to improve their home programs.

When the younger national U18 teams of Europe began to participate in this diverse hockey scenario, it was viewed as an opportunity to improve their chances of winning the European Championships that followed later in the season. The plan bore some fruit, especially for the Czechoslovakian program.

Miloš Broukal, general secretary of the Czech and Slovak Ice Hockey Federation, commented in an interview at the World Junior Championships in Saskatoon in 1991.

> Our teams have had tremendous success after their return home. For the past two years, the teams that have played in the Viking Cup have become European champions. It helps them very much. It is especially good for the Czech Junior team to learn your style of hockey in your rink—the whole atmosphere in the rink, the selling of souvenirs, the number of spectators, the popularity of hockey is new to them. . . The players look forward to it.

Interestingly, the NHL scouts flocked to the Viking Cup, valuing the opportunity to see young high prospects playing in these challenging circumstances.

As quoted in *Viking Cup 2000 Magazine*, Edmonton Oiler scout Kevin Prendergast said, "The Viking Cup allows scouts a unique opportunity to see Europeans perform in the North American amphitheatre. It gives us a pretty good idea how they are going to react to the physical part of the game."

Calgary Flames scout Ian McKenzie agreed. "For the European prospects, adjustment is the key. Their style is different. We like to see how they adapt and how they fit in. I'm a great supporter of the Viking Cup for that reason."

Coach Gord Thibodeau, twice the head coach of the Alberta Junior League All-Stars at the Viking Cup and long-time Alberta junior hockey coach, commented:

> The differences in age at the Viking Cup didn't bother me. It was a great challenge for the younger players to show their stuff. The scouts loved it. It added a new dimension. We took a young team to Viking Cup '98, but Saskatchewan had an older team, with more twenty-year-olds. That was the choice. I enjoyed the challenge.

It should be noted that, while the U18 teams were actually seventeen years old as of December 31 (during the Viking Cup), almost all players had birthdays in the first few months of the new year—typical for a national junior team. This means that players on the U18 teams at the Viking Cup were all about to turn eighteen. Some even celebrated their birthdays at the Viking Cup in early January.

In the later years of the Viking Cup, the European national U18 teams seemed less competitive, as some of their best players were being harvested for league play by Canadian junior teams or higher-level senior teams at home. At the same time, the Canadian and American Junior All-Star teams were consistently strong and physical.

There is no doubt that the diversity of teams in the Viking Cup was a unique feature that led to its success. Even at that, some considered this strength to be a weakness. They would argue for a tournament of only U18 teams, but that would omit the home Vikings team and team parity would have become a problem as the weaker U18 national teams of the world were not competitive with the U18 teams of the major hockey countries. The Canadian U18 national team was not available to participate and Hockey Canada was about to develop their own plan for U18 international hockey.

In the end, there was a gradual movement for the Viking Cup to become a junior tournament (including U18 national teams), with the Augustana Vikings as the only college team and the overbalance of Canadian junior hockey teams may have led to the tournament's demise. Following Viking Cup 2002, the Canadian Junior Hockey League and Hockey Canada formed their own international tournament, named the World Junior A Challenge and provincial Junior All-Star teams withdrew from the Viking Cup, leaving a vacuum too large to fill. Without the Canadian provincia Junior All-Star teams, the Viking Cup became less attractive to European junior and U18 national teams. At the time, there was little interest in the Viking Cup changing directions to become a tournament of only North American college/university teams.

The life-long results of the tournament give some indication that a measure of team parity was achieved. The distribution of gold medals was as follows: National U18: 3; European Jr. Club: 1; USA Jr. All-Star: 1; Canadian Jr.: 2; Canadian College: 3; Canadian University: 3. All categories did not participate in all Viking Cups.

Hockey Canada (Canadian Amateur Hockey Association) Sanctions

International hockey became the new frontier for the CAHA following the lead of the Summit Series and Canada Cup competition in the late 70's and '80's. There was new ground to be broke and, to his credit, Murray Costello, elected as the CAHA first President in 1979, was understanding and complimentary to the Viking Cup which began in 1980.

Canadian participation in International competition was made more complex by the presence of two official governing bodies stemming from the creation of a National team program under Father David Bauer in 1964 (Hockey Canada) to get Canada back into medal contention on the world stage. Eventually the CAHA and Hockey Canada merged in 1994 to form the 'new' Hockey Canada under President Costello. The growth and development of the Viking Cup took place amid reorganization of the two governing bodies and the realization by the CAHA that it was time to become much more involved in International hockey. Teams were beginning to travel abroad.

Top Swedish and Finnish Junior teams participated in the first Viking Cup in 1980-81 and the Czechoslovakian National U18 team began a twenty-two-year era of Viking Cup participation the following year. Other European teams followed and the Augustana Vikings and other Canadian teams played in Europe.

When the CAHA realized the potential to make hefty profits from national team tournaments in Canada, starting with the World Juniors (U20) in Toronto/Hamilton/London in 1986, followed by Saskatoon in 1991, they began to look at other levels as well. Wikipedia describes the growing profile of the world Juniors in Canada as follows:

> The competition's profile is particularly high in Canada; its stature has been credited to Canada's strong performance in the tournament (it has won the gold medal seventeen times since its inception), the role of hockey in

Canadian culture, along with strong media coverage and fan attendance. As such, in recent years, nearly half of the tournaments have been held in Canadian cities…"

In 1986, the CAHA established the World U17 Hockey Challenge, formerly known as the Quebec ESSO Cup. Czechoslovakia was expected to attend, but by this time were a mainstay at the Viking Cup with their U18 national team. Suddenly in a financial squeeze, they almost pulled out of the Viking Cup until further assistance was found. It was clear though that the CAHA sponsored U17 tournament would take priority.

Although there was no U18 World Championship tournament at that time (only a European Championship), there were rumours that creating one would be the next step. In January 1989, Costello informed me of the following:

> I should explain to you that there is a movement afoot to confine the teams participating in invitational tournaments to club teams, as opposed to national teams. . . At our last congress . . . a lengthy discussion was held among the federations regarding the kinds of competitions that should be approved by each federation. It was agreed that, so long as club teams played against club teams and national teams against national teams, the system would work well and this is what we will pursue.

The European federations seemed to have no hesitation in sending their national U18 teams to the Viking Cup through the '90s and up to the final Viking Cup in 2006. It may have been a matter of semantics as the CAHA approved the teams as "Selects," and left to the various federations who would be chosen for their teams. Each of the National U18 teams of the Viking Cup continued to wear their national team jerseys . . . and chose the players that would play for their country in the European championships later in the season. They continued to send their best. That was evident by their number of players that were being drafted.

Costello was satisfied to see the Viking Cup continue. In his greeting in the *Viking Cup '92 Magazine,* he described the Viking Cup as "one that is fast becoming one of the most recognized holiday tournaments in Canada." In a letter to me in 1993, he expressed CAHA support.

> In that we are not involved in this area (U18) at the national level, we are in no position to take exception or express concern for what you are doing. Particularly, since you run such a fine tournament and the experience is a good one for all of the federations, which send representative teams.

It should be noted that the CAHA did not send the Canadian national U18 team to the Viking Cup. We understood that it would be difficult for the U18 national team to play at the same time as the U20 World Championships. Junior club teams would be missing too many of their players for regularly scheduled games over the Christmas/New Year break. It would also have created an inconsistency of policy for the CAHA.

The Viking Cup grew in stature and reputation throughout the '80s and '90s, and it was obvious that the major European hockey federations felt it was their best alternative to improve their U18 teams during the Christmas and New Year break. As such the Viking Cup became well known in European Ice Hockey circles. Following the 1994 CAHA-Hockey Canada merger Verlyn Olson (Viking Cup Marketing Chair) and myself met with Ron Robison who had been President and Head of Business Operations of Hockey Canada before the merger. (Later he became the commissioner of the Western Hockey League) Recalling his previous meetings with International hockey leaders his first comment was, "The Viking Cup sure is well known in Europe. The first item on our meeting agendas was the world championship, the second was the world juniors (U20), and then the Czechs and Finns and Russians (especially) wanted to talk about the Viking Cup. It seemed that it was high on the radar screens in Europe. They really liked to come."

More recently Robison, who continues to be the Commissioner of the WHL, recalled similarities between the Viking Cup and Canada's National team program under Father David Bauer, Dave King and others. "Both programs did a lot to develop hockey at the grass roots level. We used to travel to many smaller Canadian towns with Team Canada to play exhibition games with the Russians and others. The Viking Cup made a great contribution to Canadian hockey in the same way…and it definitely was in on the ground floor in the development of International Hockey. It was an amazing feat."

In May of 1996, I met with Murray Costello and Bob Nicholson (incoming Hockey Canada president) at the World Championships in Vienna to discuss sanctions for national teams coming to the Viking Cup, and how the Viking Cup might support Hockey Canada's plans for National U18 hockey. Later, I met with Nicholson in Calgary and he invited me to make a proposal for a National U18 program and Viking Cup to mesh in some way. He offered a few thoughts. I sent a proposal, but was elected to the Alberta legislature soon after and left the Viking Cup in other hands at Augustana.

Meanwhile, there was an U18 tournament developing in Europe known as the Nations Cup—later the U18 Junior World Cup and, finally, since 2007, the Ivan Hlinka Memorial Tournament, hosted by the Czech Republic and Slovakia. In January 2018 Hockey Canada announced an agreement with the Edmonton Oilers Entertainment Group and Czech and Slovak ice hockey federations that the tournament would now become the Hlinka Gretzky Cup and that it would alternate between Edmonton and the Czech Republic in August until at least 2022. This, appears to be Hockey Canada's solution for an U18 International tournament in Canada at the present time.

The first Hockey Canada-sponsored World Junior A Challenge tournament was held in 2006, the same year of the demise of the Viking Cup (see Chapter 10 for details). According to Wikipedia, "The idea behind the tournament was to showcase players from Canadian Junior A to Canadian Hockey League, National Collegiate Athletic Association, and National Hockey League scouts, while also exposing them to an international level and style of play."

From the small community of Camrose, the Viking Cup pioneered a new and lasting stream of international hockey competition at the junior level, and its legacy continues in international competitions today.

Professional coach Rob Daum, (UofA, Edmonton Oilers, Europe) who was also a graduate of Augustana said, "at the time, it was a one-of-a-kind tournament, and a precursor to all the international tournaments that are so commonplace today."

Looking back, Gord Thibodeau, who is today head coach and general manager of the Fort McMurray Oil Barons, comments, "The Viking Cup opened eyes. It was a trendsetter for tournaments and international hockey. It was good for hockey. Hockey Canada saw an opportunity to copy the idea and started the world Junior A challenge tournament."

John Short saw the Viking Cup as a leader in the revolution of international hockey in the '80s and '90s. In 2016, he wrote in the *Edmonton Journal,* "Believe it or not, the World Junior A hockey challenge and the Ivan Hlinka tournament that makes its temporary home in Edmonton probably got their start when the Viking Cup disappeared from little old Camrose in 2006, a year or so after its twenty-fifth birthday."

Hockey Alberta (Alberta Amateur Hockey Association)

"The Viking Cup brought international hockey to Alberta."

–Scott Robinson, Hockey Alberta Foundation

Hockey Alberta has a history of being fully supportive of the Viking Cup. Over the years, the various presidents have consistently participated in the opening ceremonies, banquets, and closing ceremonies and have given their enthusiastic support. There was never a problem in sanctioning the numerous exhibition games involving the international teams throughout Alberta, including referee clearance. Hockey Alberta worked tirelessly with Dean Dr Roger Epp of Augustana and Verlyn Olson of the Viking Cup committee in an effort to find a way for the Viking Cup to continue its long tradition of international hockey in Camrose and Alberta.

In the *Viking Cup 2006 Magazine,* Terry Engen, president of Hockey Alberta states:

> It's a great feeling for Hockey Alberta to be a part of an event that can lead to the success of so many hockey players and coaches. The Viking Cup is a world-class event that creates memories that will last a lifetime for everyone who is involved. . . Sit back and enjoy some of the best hockey from all over the world.

Coaches

Viking Cup coaches were quick to express intrigue over their challenge to adjust coaching strategies to different hockey styles. The comments of coaches in the Viking Cup can be found throughout the chapters of this book, especially Chapter 13. Some introductory comments from coaches follow.

"The international flavour of the tournament was a great addition and being able to experience first-hand thc high level of competition and sportsmanship made our squad an improved team."

Jean Pronovost, *McGill University coach (former Montreal Canadiens player)*

"The Viking Cup became an important event in the hockey calendar. It was a really good tournament for bringing recognition to our team and a good measuring stick for our team vis-à-vis the Europeans and colleges."

Terry Simpson, *PA Raiders coach; NY Islander, Philadelphia Flyers, Winnipeg Jets coach*

"It was the ideal way to measure our skillset against the upcoming young stars of Europe. It was a big deal—exciting and a fantastic opportunity for our team."

Mike Babcock, *Red Deer College, University of Lethbridge, Detroit Red Wings, Toronto Maple Leafs, Team Canada—two Olympic golds*

"The Viking Cup was one of the most prestigious tournaments in hockey anywhere, and one of the few tournaments in North America that rivaled some of the great European tournaments, including the Izvestia Trophy (now the Channel One Cup) and the Spengler Cup. . . The unique challenge of quickly adjusting my strategy to a different style made me a better coach and helped me advance in my coaching career."

Perry Pearn, *NAIT, two-time Viking Cup-winning coach and national coach; Ottawa Senators, NY Rangers, Montreal Canadiens, and Winnipeg Jets coach*

"Competing against a variety of European teams and also getting a chance to look behind the scenes as we visited each country allowed me to grow rapidly as a coach."

Mike Johnston, *CLC Vikings coach. UNB-winning coach, Viking Cup '92; NHL coach Pittsburgh Penguins, LA Kings, Vancouver Canucks*

"It was amazing. . . it is quite a story. Every coach would want to be there."

Clare Drake, *UofA Golden Bears and hockey's master teacher and coach*

Referees

Alberta referees and other officials gained valuable experience in international competition through tournament and exhibition games. Ernie Boruk, who was head referee on many Viking Cup games, said, "All the exhibition games arranged by the Viking Cup throughout Western Canada were a great help in our training program."

Experienced referees John Jacobs of Stettler (native to Camrose) and Bob Prestage of Camrose, were mentors to young officials gaining experience at the Viking Cup. Never to miss a game, John once commented: "We don't take someone who has never seen this calibre of hockey and throw them into the fray. The play here is a whole lot faster than they are accustomed to. It is a thrill to be a part of it. The tempo of these games is excellent."

John went on to point out that, considering the age differences in this tournament, the referees were instructed to call games close and keep to standards set before the contest.

Long-time Viking Cup referee-in-chief George McCorry credits the Viking Cup for "incredible experiences in international hockey." He points out that great officials like Lance Roberts, Roger Castle, Mike Rebus, and our own Todd Sverda of Camrose would not have reached their heights in professional and international hockey had it not been for their experience in the Viking Cup.

"Everyone wanted to do games in the Viking Cup—just to be a part of it," said Roger Castle, who officiated Edmonton Oiler games in 1979–80, and worked over thirty games in the Viking Cup, from 1981 through 1994.

> It helped numerous officials advance. It was the plum job, very prestigious. I was so proud of the Viking Cup crest on my shirt….It was about international relations. It was so crucial at an important time in history. It built character in players. When it comes to icons in sport, you don't want to overlook the Viking Cup.

The question about whether there should be referees from other countries, in tune with the hybridized nature of the event, was posed often. This never occurred except in the very first Viking Cup, when a referee accompanied the TPS Finnish team and worked games as a linesman. As the tournament evolved, the next step would surely have involved international referees.

A Tribute to George McCorry

For George McCorry, the Viking Cup was a home base and a springboard . . . and for the Viking Cup, George McCorry was the backbone of officiating.

George grew up in Camrose, where he played his minor hockey and one year of college hockey with the hometown Vikings. Even then he didn't hesitate to throw on a referee's sweater when occasions were presented. Soon, he made

Edmonton his home and began to climb his ladder of achievement in the worlds of work and officiating hockey.

For those who knew George, it was not a surprise to see his rapid advancement in officiating. He had the necessary qualities and temperament and, as a player, had even experienced his share of time in the penalty box! He understood and had a feeling of the game from all perspectives—player, coach, parent, and fan.

George's first game of the Viking Cup was in 1982 as a level-five referee, and it spurred his interest in international hockey.

In 1984, he went to Montreal to successfully challenge for level six, the highest status possible. In 1985, he was selected to officiate the Pravda Cup in Leningrad, Russia. In 1988, he worked six games in Czechoslovakia in an U18 tournament. In 1989, he was off to Japan to officiate the World Junior B-Pool Championships in Sapporo and, the following year, to Anchorage for the World Junior A Championships. Then, finally, George achieved his dream. In 1992, he was selected to officiate games at the Olympics in Albertville, France, the top rung of his remarkable officiating climb.

All this occurred while George established himself as a distinguished referee back home in Canada. He refereed numerous games for Canada's national teams at various levels, the CIAU (university) national championships (seventeen times in final and semi-final games), and final games in the Centennial Cup (now RBC), Hardy Cup, Allan Cup, and Viking Cup.

George was right at home in the Viking Cup. He officiated at eight Viking Cup tournaments and served as the referee-in-chief for seven of them. He shares his knowledge and skills with numerous young officials of the game. For twenty-five years he was an instructor, and for thirty-eight years he was a supervisor of officials in Alberta.

He has served for the past twenty years on the provincial executive of the referees' association, and since 1999 he's been vice-president of the Alberta Junior Hockey League in charge of officiating and league discipline.

George McCorry has received numerous accolades and awards in recognition of his exemplary career. At the top of this amazing ladder is his induction into the Hockey Alberta Hall of Fame, an award he so well merits.

And what does George McCorry have to say about his long-time love of the Viking Cup? "It was my springboard in international hockey! This is where I received my initial experience and inspiration to realize my Olympic dream . . . and I was given that opportunity right here at home!"

George has a wealth of memories of the Viking Cup. Unlike other officials, George remembers each game and likes to relive the action. He had that special interest.

He remembers one of his first games when he was sure a tough Finnish team was intent on settling an old war with Russia, challenging their biggest player. We all remember how George re-established the Iron Curtain, which separated them at the time . . . a masterful job for sure!

He recalls the player agents looking for new clients in the back halls of the arena and hanging around the referees' room, trying to glean information about the best players—something he wanted no part of.

He understood and applied the objectives of the Viking Cup. He understood the importance of entertainment in satisfying the crowds at the games. He understood the importance of satisfying the NHL scouts. He understood the importance of exciting game flow and control. And he understood the importance of applying common sense to decisions.

I remember an incident involving the MVP player of the tournament that could have warranted disqualification. George agreed with a one-game suspension. He understood the application of reason in the circumstance and the importance to the tournament as a whole. "You have to understand the purpose of the event."

George was fair. He assigned referees to give each the opportunity to do a feature evening game along with the day game assignments. "Everyone wanted to do the Viking Cup games, even from other zones and provinces. We understood the financial constraints of the tournament, so usually chose our best referees from northern Alberta."

George wanted referees to have an inclusive experience in the Viking Cup. When official Viking Cup crests were sewn on each player's jersey, George asked if there were extra crests to sew on the referee sweaters. He pointed out later the battle with his association as some considered the idea too revolutionary for officials. Some referees felt more comfortable keeping their distance from the players. But George won the day and some officials kept Viking Cup crests on their sweaters for the rest of the year! "Why shouldn't we be a part and show our support," he said.

George loved the atmosphere of the Viking Cup . . . and he was right at 'home' in that crowd!

The Hockey Scouts

If you were wondering where to locate the scouts at the Viking Cup, you needed only look to the top row of seats. There, you would find the trench-coated hockey gurus charting every move of the game stars on their pads of secret reflections.

Augustana Vikings star player Jim Jones (1980–82) comments, "I remember Scotty Bowman sitting with a toque on . . . and an overcoat in the top row, scouting. He was the guest speaker at the banquet."

Randy Haugen, chair of the medical committee, likes to tell his story about Claude Ruel, scout and former coach of the Montreal Canadiens.

"He asked me, "How tall are you?"

"I responded 5'10"."

"OK," Ruel said. "Go stand by the wall where all the players will be walking by. I want to see what their true heights are. Most of the recorded heights on my list are inflated; I think they were sent in by their mothers!"

Between games and periods, scouts quickly migrated to the cushy furniture in the curling rink media lounge, where team information and game statistics were conveniently available. Curling activities were cancelled as the whole community focused on the Viking Cup.

Earl Berry, who was often in charge of the media lounge, comments:

"We sold packages with all the information for about $350 in the latter Viking Cups, and that included food and refreshments. Most NHL teams made the purchase. Some teams purchased more than one to help out while others shared information. Most were very focused and there for one purpose."

Meanwhile, members of the sports media fed in the latest results to the various networks. The place was abuzz. The local *Camrose Canadian* newspaper presented a daily news summary of the previous day's activity and results. Long-time sportswriter and broadcaster John Short was sure to be there, promoting the Viking Cup and gathering information for his next broadcast of *Sports Talk*. The Edmonton media—the *Journal*, the *Sun*, radio, and TV—all covered it. Some scouts were new visitors, but others were long-time participants, like Elmer Benning of the Montreal Canadiens, Dennis McIvor of the Buffalo Sabres, and Al Murray of the LA Kings and later the Tampa Bay Lightning.

"The Viking Cup Was in a Class of Its Own" – Elmer Benning, Montreal Canadiens

Elmer lights up when you mention the Viking Cup—but then, he knows a lot about it. He became a part of it . . . and he promoted it.

When the scouts rolled in for the Viking Cup, the question on faithful workers' minds was *not* "Is Elmer coming this year?" but was "Is Elmer here yet?" Elmer had been a scout for the Montreal Canadiens for fifty years, and had covered well over a million miles travelling to all types of arenas throughout Western Canada.

And his voice was listened to.

In 2005, he highly recommended that the Canadiens draft goaltender Carey Price, and they did!

Back home, he and his wife, Liz, raised four hockey-playing sons, including Jim, now GM of the Vancouver Canucks, drafted sixth by Toronto in 1981; Brian, drafted twenty-sixth by St. Louis in 1984; Mark, a Harvard graduate; and Craig, a graduate of St. Francis Xavier in Nova Scotia. Grandson Matt, with the Edmonton Oilers, was drafted six years ago, and sister Abby stars with the U of A Pandas. The Benning family is well known and respected in hockey circles.

Elmer likes to talk about his Viking Cup experiences.

> The Viking Cup was in a class of its own. To me, it was a can-do experience. Youngsters would see the stars of the future and say, CAN DO that, too. The players were there to show they could achieve their dreams . . . a little community can host the world.

> The organization of the tournament was an example to the rest of the hockey world and it was a source of inspiration to others, including myself . . . the little details were always covered. Playing against other countries was the key to gaining the interest from the scouting world. It was a bonus for me as a

Western Canada scout to see the Europeans play here. For one who likes desserts, it was icing on my cake!

Where else could I meet all my colleague competitors from other NHL teams and have a friendly game of curling between hockey games or relax in a comfortable lounge with refreshments supplied? It was always a totally positive experience—and I never missed it.

Elmer always brought a Montreal Canadiens jacket for the MVP of one or more games. But the Canadiens' greatest gift to the Viking Cup was Elmer Benning.

"If They Tell You the Sun Shines, Take a Look . . . in Camrose" – Dennis McIvor, Buffalo Sabres

Dennis was one of the originals . . . and he never missed a Viking Cup.

Many remember the visit to the first Viking Cup of Scotty Bowman, who was general manager of the Buffalo Sabres; but few may remember that he was accompanied by Dennis McIvor, his Western Canada scout.

McIvor was always in search of "character players" for the Sabres. "I was in the people business," he would say. "You get to be a good judge of character and trust. . . I have always prided myself with my gift of assessing people. It served me well in my scouting endeavours." Dennis would then say, "Your Viking Cup leaders were easy reads . . . resulting in instant trust and friendship!

"One year you put me at the head table at the banquet, I still remember that. You always made me feel like it was important that I was there."

And it was . . .

Dennis was one of our good ambassadors, spreading the good news of the Viking Cup to others in his profession and helping out in myriad ways at the tournament. He's now well past his retirement year, and I visited him as a friend one more time in his home in Red Deer. When I returned home, I had an email from Dennis.

It read: "I hope you could sense how pleased I was to see you once again after all the years."

During our visit, he had commented: "Where else could you see so many good players and have a good time with great people?"

In the end, Dennis said, the important thing was how you played the game, not whether you won or lost. He believed all Viking Cup games were well played—on and off the ice. He made many trusting friendships there.

In his own frank way, Dennis said, "In the scouting business you have to assess for yourself in a world of secrets, rumours, stargazers, and hunches. . . And you can't make too many mistakes! If they tell you the sun shines, take a look!"

Dennis came for a look at the very first Viking Cup, and the sun shone for the rest!

"The Best Prospects from Europe were there"
– Al Murray, Tampa Bay Lightning and LA Kings

Al Murray knows where to find talent. That is why you could always find him at the Viking Cup.

He has spent the last nine seasons as director of amateur scouting with the league-leading Tampa Bay Lightning. He leads the Lightning at the draft table each year now. But first, he spent eighteen years directing the scouting program of the LA Kings. During that time, the Kings won the Stanley Cup in 2014. Between his time in LA and Tampa, Al directed the selection process for Hockey Canada's national team programs at all levels with great results, including earning a Canadian Olympic Gold in Vancouver.

"I always included the Viking Cup in my schedule because I knew the very best prospects from the European nations would be there," Al said. "I always marvelled that the Viking Cup drew the very best from Europe and I liked to see the best from Europe playing with tough Canadian opposition, even the university and college teams. That was unique to the Viking Cup—a good format."

Al knew university hockey, as well, having coached at the University of Regina from 1985 to 1988.

While attending the Viking Cup, Murray mostly had his eyes on the hockey games. But he did notice other features of the event. "I always came to the games in time to hear the Viking Cup Trio do the national anthems in the language of the country. That was really special. I could even pick out the singers on the teams. And those fries and gravy at the concession? Well . . ."

Posterity

It would indeed be unusual to find a hockey arena that did not in some way feature its glory days. I always stop to take a look—it's like reading a chapter in the community story. Banners hang in Rogers Place in Edmonton to remind people of the Oilers' great Stanley Cup dynasty, and a bronze statue of Wayne Gretzky greets all visitors. Twenty-four Stanley Cup banners of the Montreal Canadians dominate the wonderful atmosphere of the Bell Centre. The Gordie Howe statue in Little Caesars Arena tells the story about a dynasty in Detroit. Every team and every community have their way of telling their sport history.

This book is but another chapter in the sport history of the many communities that it touched – the home community and others, near and far. It carries stories that contribute in a significant way to the history of hockey in our own country and in the arenas of international hockey. The forces and streams came together in different ways and places but nowhere was it more evident than on the ice where the game was played and where champions were declared.

The Champions . . . Gold, Silver, Bronze . . . The All-Stars

Viking Cup '81

Participating Teams in Placement Order

Team	Locale	Coach
TPS Juniors	Turku, Finland	Juhani Wahlsten
Prince Albert Jr Raiders	Prince Albert, Saskatchewan, Canada	Terry Simpson
Red Deer College Kings	Red Deer, Alberta, Canada	Al Ferchuk
Centennial College Colts	Scarborough, Ontario, Canada	Neil Osborne
AIK Solna Juniors	Stockholm, Sweden	Andres Jacobson
Camrose Lutheran College Vikings	Camrose, Alberta, Canada	Joe Voytechek

Tournament MVP

Player	Team	Position
Hannu Virta	TPS	Defense

Tournament All-Star Selections

Player	Team	Position
Jouni Rokama	TPS	Goaltender
James Patrick	Prince Albert	Defense
Peter Anholt	Prince Albert	Defense
Rob Dyck	Red Deer College	Forward
Mats Hessel	AIK Solna	Forward
Teppo Virta	TPS	Forward

Viking Cup '82

Participating Teams in Placement Order

Team	Locale	Coach
CSSR (Czechoslovakia) Junior Selects	Czechoslovakia	Vladimír Šustek, Julius Kovac
Prince Albert (Junior "A") Raiders	Prince Albert, Saskatchewan, Canada	Terry Simpson, Rick Wilson
Västra Frölunda Juniors	Gothenburg, Sweden	Ronny Andersson
Camrose Lutheran College Vikings	Camrose, Alberta, Canada	Joe Voytechek
Southern Alberta Institute of Technology (SAIT)	Calgary, Alberta, Canada	Bob Moore
Revelstoke (Junior "A") Rockets	Revelstoke, British Columbia	Charles McGeehan

Tournament MVP

Player	Team	Position
Petr Klima	Czechoslovakia	Forward

Tournament All-Star Selections

Player	Team	Position
Dominik Hašek	Czechoslovakia	Goaltender
Robin Bartel	Prince Albert	Defense
Dale Pilon	Camrose Luth. College	Defense
Peter Elander	Västra Frölunda	Forward
Lumir Kotala	Czechoslovakia	Forward
Jiří Poner	Czechoslovakia	Forward

Viking Cup '84

Participating Teams in Placement Order

Team	Locale	Coach
Northern Alberta Institute of Technology (NAIT)	Edmonton, Alberta, Canada	Perry Pearn
CSSR (Czechoslovakia) Junior Selects	Czechoslovakia	Zdeněk Šindler, Břetislav Guryča
Camrose Lutheran College Vikings	Camrose, Alberta, Canada	Mike Johnston
St. Paul Vulcans	St. Paul, Minnesota, USA	Kevin Hartzell
IFK Juniors	Helsinki, Finland	Kari Malinen
St. Albert Junior Saints	St. Albert, Alberta, Canada	Doug Hicks

Tournament MVP

Player	Team	Position
Cleo Rowein	NAIT	Goaltender

Tournament All-Star Selections

Player	Team	Position
Ivo Čapek	Czechoslovakia	Goaltender
Terry Kurtenbach	Camrose Luth. College	Defense
Rudolf Paryzek	Czechoslovakia	Defense
Franco Disciglio	NAIT	Forward
Brian Hermanutz	NAIT	Forward
Petr Rúčka	Czechoslovakia	Forward

Viking Cup '86

Participating Teams in Placement Order

Team	Locale	Coach
Northern Alberta Institute of Technology (NAIT)	Edmonton, Alberta, Canada	Perry Pearn
Camrose Lutheran College Vikings	Camrose, Alberta, Canada	Mike Johnston
CSSR (Czechoslovakia) Junior Selects	Czechoslovakia	Pavel Soudský
Kärpät Juniors	Oulu, Finland	Pekka Karjala
AIK Solna Juniors	Stockholm, Sweden	Ove Stafström
Notre Dame (Junior "A") Hounds	Wilcox, Saskatchewan, Canada	Barry MacKenzie

Tournament MVP

Player	Team	Position
Mark Schultz	NAIT	Forward

Tournament All-Star Selections

Player	Team	Position
Radek Tóth	Czechoslovakia	Goaltender
Petr Pavlas	Czechoslovakia	Defense
Jamie Bartman	NAIT	Defense
Pat Ryan	Camrose Luth. College	Forward
Martin Hrstka	Czechoslovakia	Forward
Ari Klint	Kärpät, Finland	Forward

Viking Cup '88

INTERNATIONAL HOCKEY TOURNAMENT

1988 CHAMPIONS

University of Alberta Golden Bears

Edmonton, AB

Participating Teams in Placement Order

Team	Locale	Coach
University of Alberta Golden Bears	Edmonton, Alberta, Canada	Clare Drake
CSSR (Czechoslovakia) Junior Selects	Czechoslovakia	Rudy Tomanek
USSR Junior Selects	Soviet Union	Gennady Tsygurov
AIK Solna Juniors	Stockholm, Sweden	Jan Back
Camrose Lutheran College Vikings	Camrose, Alberta, Canada	Dave Clement
Red Deer College Kings	Red Deer, Alberta, Canada	Al Ferchuk
TPS Juniors	Turku, Finland	Kari Kauppila
University of Arizona Ice Cats	Tucson, Arizona, USA	Leo Golembiewski

Tournament MVP

Player	Team	Position
Brent Severyn	University of Alberta	Defense

Tournament All-Star Selections

Player	Team	Position
Roman Turek	Czechoslovakia	Goaltender
Sergei Zubov	USSR	Defense
Parie Proft	University of Alberta	Defense
Pavol Zůbek	Czechoslovakia	Forward
Dan Baker	Red Deer College	Forward
Roman Kontšek	Czechoslovakia	Forward

Viking Cup '90

INTERNATIONAL HOCKEY TOURNAMENT

1990 CHAMPIONS

McGill University Redmen

Montreal, QUE

Participating Teams in Placement Order

Team	Locale	Coach
McGill University Redmen	Montreal, Quebec, Canada	Al Grazys, Jean Pronovost
CSSR (Czechoslovakia) Junior Selects	Czechoslovakia	Pavel Sirotek, Pavel Beránek
USSR Junior Selects	Soviet Union	Vladimir Kamenev
University of Lethbridge Pronghorns	Lethbridge, Alberta, Canada	Dave Adolph
Red Deer College Kings	Red Deer, Alberta, Canada	Mike Babcock
Camrose Lutheran College Vikings	Camrose, Alberta, Canada	Bill Luke

Tournament MVP

Player	Team	Position
Jamie Reeve	McGill University	Goaltender

Tournament All-Star Selections

Player	Team	Position
Jiří Podešva	Czechoslovakia	Goaltender
Darius Kasparaitis	USSR	Defense
Ivan Droppa	Czechoslovakia	Defense
Martin Raymond	McGill University	Forward
Konstantin Korotkov	USSR	Forward
Marek Zadina	Czechoslovakia	Forward

Viking Cup '92

Participating Teams in Placement Order

Team	Locale	Coach
University of New Brunswick (UNB) Red Devils	Fredericton, New Brunswick, Canada	Mike Johnston
CIS (formerly USSR) Junior Selects	Commonwealth Independent States	Vladimir Bogomolov
Northern Alberta Institute of Technology (NAIT)	Edmonton, Alberta, Canada	Perry Pearn
CFSR (Czechoslovakia) Junior Selects	Czechoslovakia	Edward Giblick
Färjestad Elite Juniors	Karlstad, Sweden	Claus Silfers
Augustana University College Vikings	Camrose, Alberta, Canada	Gary Snydmiller

Tournament MVP

Player	Team	Position
Sergei Brylin	CIS	Forward

Tournament All-Star Selections
TEAMS MISSING

Player	Team	Position
Chris Somers	UNB	Goaltender
Mike Cavanagh	UNB	Defense
Libor Procházka	Czechoslovakia	Defense
Greg Geldart	NAIT	Forward
Trevor Boland	UNB	Forward
Alexey Loshkin	CIS	Forward

Viking Cup '94

Participating Teams in Placement Order

Team	Locale	Coach
Russia National Junior "18" Selects	Russia	Jan Kamenetsky
Dauphin (Junior "A") Kings	Dauphin, Manitoba, Canada	Guy Vestby
Mount Royal College Cougars	Calgary, Alberta, Canada	Scott Atkinson
Västra Frölunda Juniors	Göteborg, Sweden	Ulf Labraaten
Czech National Junior "18" Selects	Czech Republic	Josef Straka
Augustana University College Vikings	Camrose, Alberta, Canada	Gary Snydmiller
Finland National Junior "18" Selects	Finland	Jorma Kurjernmaki
Augsburg College Auggies	Minneapolis, Minnesota, USA	Ed Saugestad, Mark Wick

Tournament MVP

Player	Team	Position
Sergei Luchinkin	Russia	Forward

Tournament All-Star Selections

Player	Team	Position
Anton Zelenov	Russia	Goaltender
Joel Dyck	Mount Royal College	Defense
Thomas Jonasson	Västra Frölunda	Defense
Lars Mølgaard	Dauphin	Forward
Per-Johan Axelsson	Västra Frölunda	Forward
Patrik Eliáš	Czech	Forward

Viking Cup '96

Participating Teams in Placement Order

Team	Locale	Coach
Finland National Jr "18" Selects	Finland	Kari Jalonen
USA National Jr "20" B Selects	United States of America	Mike Hastings, Tony Curtale
Augustana University College Vikings	Camrose, Alberta	Gary Snydmiller, Len Frankson
Alberta Junior "A" (AJHL) Selects	Alberta, Canada	Bruno Baseotto, Fran Gow
Czech National Jr "18" Selects	Czech Republic	Petr Míšek, Pavel Hynek
North Battleford (Jr "A") North Stars	North Battleford, Sask, Canada	Blaine Gusdal. Jeff Johnson
Sweden National Jr "18" Selects	Sweden	Lars Öberg, Christer Höglund
Russia National Jr "18" Selects	Russia	Vladimir Shadrin, Sergei Gimaev

Tournament MVP

Player	Team	Position
Olli Jokinen	Finland	Forward

Tournament All-Star Selections

Player	Team	Position
Jani Riihinen	Finland	Goaltender
Dale Donaldson	AJHL	Forward
Niko Kapanen	Finland	Forward
Jeramie Heistad	AJHL	Defense
Josh DeWolf	USA	Defense
Jason Collins	Augustana Univ. College	Forward

Viking Cup '98

Participating Teams in Placement Order

Team	Locale	Coach
Saskatchewan Junior "A" (SJHL) Selects	Saskatchewan, Canada	Blaine Gusdal, Doug Hedley
Alberta Junior "A" (AJHL) Selects	Alberta, Canada	Gord Thibodeau, Brett Cox
Finland National Under 18 Selects	Finland	Jukka Rautakorpi
Slovakia National Under 19 Selects	Slovakia	Miroslav Kimijan
Sweden National Under 18 Selects	Sweden	Mats Emanuelsson
Czech National Under 18 Selects	Czech Republic	Vladimír Bednář
USA National Under 18 Selects	United States of America	Steve Pleau
Augustana University College Vikings	Camrose, Alberta, Canada	Gary Snydmiller

Tournament MVP

Player	Team	Position
Mark Hartigan	SJHL	Forward

Tournament All-Star Selections

Player	Team	Position
Rob Schrader	SJHL	Goaltender
Jesse Cook	AJHL	Defense
Ossi Väänänen	Finland	Defense
Christian Berglund	Sweden	Forward
Mike Comrie	AJHL	Forward
Greg Classen	SJHL	Forward

Viking Cup 2000

Participating Teams in Placement Order

Team	Locale	Coach
USA National Junior "19" Selects	USA	Mike Hastings
Alberta Junior "A" (AJHL) All-Star Selects	Alberta, Canada	Brett Cox, Jeff Truitt
Sweden National Junior "18" Selects	Sweden	Tomas Thelin, Gorn Lindblom
Manitoba Junior "A" (MJHL) All-Star Selects	Manitoba, Canada	Ken Pearson, Doug Stokes, Don McGillivray
Saskatchewan Junior "A" (SJHL) All-Star Selects	Saskatchewan, Canada	Larry Wintoneak, Wade Klippenstein
Augustana University College Vikings	Camrose, Alberta, Canada	Gary Snydmiller
British Columbia Junior "A" (BCHL) All-Star Selects	British Columbia, Canada	Troy Mick
Czech Republic National Junior "18" Selects	Czech Republic	Stanislav Berger
Finland National Junior "18" Selects	Finland	Timo Tuomi
Slovakia National Junior "18" Selects	Slovakia	Miroslav Kimian

Tournament MVP

Player	Team	Position
Rick Gorman	USA	Forward

Tournament All-Star Selections

Player	Team	Position
Brent Zelenewich	AJHL	Goaltender
Craig Strain	AJHL	Defense
David Hale	USA	Defense
Shawn Mamane	SJHL	Forward
František Lukeš	Czech Republic	Forward
Rick Gorman	USA	Forward

Viking Cup 2002

Participating Teams in Placement Order

Team	Locale	Coach
Augustana University College Vikings	Camrose, Alberta, Canada	Gary Snydmiller, Doug Fleck
British Columbia Junior "A" (BCHL) All-Star Selects	British Columbia, Canada	Mike Vandekamp, Mark Holick
Alberta Junior "A" (AJHL) All-Star Selects	Alberta, Canada	Gord Thibodeau
Manitoba Junior "A" (MJHL) All-Star Selects	Manitoba, Canada	Doug Stokes
USA National Junior Selects	USA	Bliss Littler
Saskatchewan Junior "A" (SJHL) All-Star Selects	Saskatchewan, Canada	Bob Beatty, Doug Hedley
Czech Republic National Junior "18" Selects	Czech Republic	Břetislav Kopřiva, Pave Marek
Finland National Junior "18" Selects	Finland	Jukka-Pekka Annala
Sweden National Junior "18" Selects	Sweden	Johan Schillgard, Magnus Hävelid
Slovakia National Junior "18" Selects	Slovakia	Igor Tóth

Tournament MVP

Player	Team	Position
Jeff Tambellini	BCHL	Forward

Tournament All-Star Selections

Player	Team	Position
First Team		
Marc Leclerc	MJHL	Goal
Joel Anderson	AJHL	Defense
Jonathon Sitko	SJHL	Defense
Jeff Tambellini	BCHL	Forward
Jade Gallbraith	AJHL	Forward
Greg Rallo	USA	Forward
Second Team		
Glenn Fisher	AJHL	Goal
Brad Farynuk	BCHL	Defense
Danny Richmond	USA	Defense
Justin Williams	AJHL	Forward
Jamie Muswagon	MJHL	Forward
Lonnie Granley	Augustana	Forward

Viking Cup 2004

Participating Teams in Placement Order

Team	Locale	Coach
Finland National Junior "18" Selects	Finland	Harri Ahola
USA National Junior Selects	USA	Jim McGlynn
Slovakia National Junior "18" Selects	Slovakia	Jindrich Novotny
Czech Republic National Junior "17" Selects	Czech Republic	Marcel Stasa
Augustana University College Vikings	Camrose, Alberta, Canada	Gary Snydmiller
Switzerland National Junior "18" Selects	Switzerland	Charly Oppliger
Germany National Junior "18" Selects	Germany	Jim Setters
Norway National Junior "18"Selects	Norway	Arne Billkvam

Tournament MVP

Player	Team	Position
Tuukka Rask	Finland	Goaltender

Tournament All-Star Selections

Player	Team	Position
Alexander Salák	Czech Republic	Goaltender
Kyle Klubertanz	USA	Defense
Andrej Sekera	Slovakia	Defense
Tim Green	Augustana	Forward
Matt Hartman	USA	Forward
Julien Sprunger	Switzerland	Forward

Viking Cup 2006

Participating University Teams in Placement Order

Team	Locale	Coach
University of Guelph Gryphons	Guelph, Ontario, Canada	Jeff Reid
Augustana Vikings, University of Alberta	Camrose, Alberta, Canada	Dan Peacock
University of Lethbridge Pronghorns	Lethbridge, Alberta, Canada	Greg Gatto

Participating Junior Teams in Placement Order

Team	Locale	Coach
AB Jr. "A" Hockey League (AJHL) N. Div. Selects	Alberta, Canada	Mark Howell
AB Jr. "A" Hockey League (AJHL) S. Div. Selects	Alberta, Canada	Boris Rybalka
USA National Junior Selects	USA	P. K. O'Handley
Switzerland "18" National Junior Selects	Switzerland	Roger Bader
Finland "18" National Junior Selects	Finland	Rauli Urama
Slovakia "18" National Junior Selects	Slovakia	Jozef Fruehauf
Germany "18" National Junior Selects	Germany	Jim Setters

Tournament MVP   *Tournament All-Star Selections Unavailable*

Player	Team	Position
Patrick Ouellette	Augustana	Defense

Breakaway, by Karl Skaret (Viking Cup 2002)

CHAPTER 4

Ice . . . Swedish Connections

The "Swedish Express" sailed into Canada in 1974. The news soon became a flagship for hockey fans searching for an upgraded style of Canadian hockey. Anders Hedberg and Ulf Nilsson signed with the Winnipeg Jets and were joined by Bobby Hull to form one of the most skillful and prolific scoring lines ever in Canadian hockey. They are remembered as the "hot line" of hockey. Earlier, Börje Salming had signed with the Toronto Maple Leafs.

In the same season, the Camrose Lutheran College Vikings Hockey Club skillfully skated to the first-ever Canadian college hockey championship in an ice storm on the eastern Nova Scotia shore city of Sydney. In both of these hockey milestones, Sweden played a vital role.

In December of that year, Sweden was the destination for the Vikings in their first-ever tour of Europe, and their first stop was the eastern Baltic coastal town of Nynäshamn, hometown of Ulf Nilsson. In a rainstorm on an outdoor rink, the Vikings matched the host team in their play and spent breathers between shifts breaking dripping icicles from their helmets—their introduction to Swedish ICE hockey!

But Nynäshamn was not the only connection to the "Swedish Express." Camrose was another.

Some twenty years later, Anders Hedberg was the guest speaker at the Viking Cup '96 smorgasbord. At that time, he was scouting for the Toronto Maple Leafs, searching for young, exceptional players, which the Leafs needed badly at that time.

Hedberg's career in Winnipeg lasted for four years, until he joined the Herb Brooks-coached New York Rangers of the NHL for seven more years. In the 1976–77 season, he scored an amazing seventy goals and sixty-one assists in sixty-eight games for Winnipeg. While with the Rangers, he was a regular thirty-plus goal scorer. His outstanding career in North American hockey netted him 856 points in 751 games, an unbelievable feat by any standard. Reflecting on his outstanding career in a recent call, he commented to me:

> It was unbelievable how three players as total strangers to each other—I from northern Sweden, Ulf from the Stockholm area, and Bobby from a farm in Ontario—could gel so quickly on one line. If you have the basic skills and you love the sport, it is amazing how quickly a successful unit can be formed!

"If you have the basic skills." Remember that statement!

It is no surprise then that Hedberg is considered one of the best to come from the blending seam of European and North American styles of hockey in the '70s and '80s.

Hedberg, having graduated from the Stockholm Phys Ed University, is a well-spoken man. His banquet speech to the young players of eight Viking Cup teams from six different nations (some not understanding English) was as "all-star" as his hockey career had been.

> We come from different parts of the world but we are here because we are the same. We have the same interests—we all love hockey! We are here because we are from northern countries and we like snow—and ice. We are all here because we like the cold temperatures that give us ice . . . and snow . . . and HOCKEY! We are here because we have gelled as line-mates and good teams. We have learned how to be winners. We are here because we like and respect the good competition and skills that they bring to our ice. We all have that in common. We are here because we are much more the same than we are different. We all love to play hockey together in this place at the Viking Cup. It is here that we feel good about ourselves—and about each other. And that makes our world better.

Anders Hedberg, guest speaker at Viking Cup '96
(Photo provided by Anders Hedberg)

Ric Graumann, a regular billet of Swedish players, heard Hedberg speak at the banquet and then met him later at the arena.

"Hedberg and other scouts were sitting in our seats," he remembers. "We didn't want to move them. Hedberg, noticing the surprised look on my face, asked if he was in my seat. He then autographed my young son's program and asked what he wanted to be. My son said 'Ole Uffda,' the mascot that was running around the arena. Hedberg and his friends sat next to us. Others were asking for his autograph."

Over the years, Ric and Janice Graumann could have received autographs from several stars of Swedish hockey. "My work boss, Murray Roy, who was a host and tireless worker with the Viking Cup, invited me to start billeting Swedish hockey players at the Viking Cup," Ric said. "Janice and I said sure, and for the next nine Viking Cups, we really got involved. We sure enjoyed the boys."

One year several Swedish players gathered at the Graumanns' to watch a Toronto Maple Leafs game on their TV. Of course, their main interest was in watching Swedish star, Mats Sundin. "I pretended that I had never heard of Mats Sundin." Ric laughed. "They brought me up to speed in a hurry—or at least they thought they did. Then I pulled out a Sundin card and told them he was my favourite player, too!"

Per Hallin and Daniel Rafner stayed with the Graumanns in '98. As Ric recalls, Per's father, Mats, had played for the New York Islanders, but Per had never seen his dad's hockey card. The Graumanns gave him one from their collection. After Daniel returned to Sweden, he sent them a note asking them to send flowers to a girl he had met in Camrose.

"Henrick Lundqvist stayed with us . . . we could tell he would be drafted"

"Goaltender Henrik Lundqvist stayed with us in Viking Cup 2000. It took five overtime periods for Sweden to win the Bronze over Manitoba. We could tell then that Henrik would be drafted, but what a bargain for the New York Rangers when they took him in the seventh round!"

Following his outstanding rookie year with the Rangers, the New York media dubbed Lundqvist "King Henrik" and the name has stuck. For sixteen years he has been the all-star goaltender of the Rangers while setting many records including the most wins for any European goaltender in the NHL. From 2006–07, for five consecutive seasons, he was declared the MVP of the Rangers, and in 2012 he won the Vezina Trophy as the best goaltender in the NHL. He led the Swedish national team to the gold medal in the Turin Olympics in 2006.

Henrick and twin brother, Joel, played together in Viking Cup 2000 and, on December 14, 2006, they played their first game against each other in the NHL. It was only the third time that identical twins had played against each other in the NHL. Joel was drafted by the Dallas Stars in the third round following his Viking Cup experience but played most of his professional career with Frölunda HC in their home city of Göteborg, Sweden.

Janice Graumann gave a special gift to Ric for his fiftieth birthday. "I sent him to Montreal to watch King Henrik and the Rangers play the Canadiens." Déjà vu of the Lundqvist final bronze game in Viking Cup 2000.

"We made up Swedish jerseys for our family to wear at all the games"

Henrik Zetterberg (Viking Cup '98) and Henrik Lundqvist had things in common beyond their native country. Both were drafted in the seventh round and therefore were, at best, long shots to make the NHL. "King Henrik" and "Hank," as Zetterberg was known in Detroit, both had outstanding careers in the NHL. Detroit scout, Jim Nill, who later became GM of the Dallas Stars, had noticed one simple thing about Hank. "He always seemed to have the puck. He was small then, but later had a growth spurt, so he learned to protect the puck because of his size."

Zetterberg has the distinction of being a triple crown winner in 2006: the Stanley Cup, World Championship, and Olympic gold when he served as captain of Team Sweden. He scored 960 points in 1,082 games in the NHL and was captain the Red Wings in the final six years of his fifteen-year NHL career. He is the fifth-leading scorer in Detroit Red Wing history.

Taylor and Graham Leibel, Henrik Zetterberg, '94

Henrick Zetterberg, Detroit Red Wings Captain
(Photo courtesy Dave Reginek)

Graham and Taylor were ten and eight when Zetterberg stayed with the Leibel family at Viking Cup '98. Over twenty years later, Graham recalls, "He was like a brother to us. He was just a lot of fun to be around—he was the favourite. He played street hockey with us, and then when he got on the ice, you could tell he would go places." Taylor remembers, "He sent us a letter when he got home. In it, he said, 'I am practising six times a week. It's "tuff," but I have to be good so I can play in the NHL and visit you and all others in Camrose.'"

Lavona and Mark Leibel commented, "We made up Swedish jerseys (yellow with three crowns) for our family to wear at all the games to support our Swedes over the years of the Viking Cup."

"Your house is much smaller now"

Christian Bäckman was Hank's teammates at Viking Cup '98. St. Louis drafted the 6'4" defenseman from Gothenburg in the first round following a superior performance at the Viking Cup. His career in the NHL included St. Louis (five years), the NY Rangers, and Columbus, after which he returned to play with Frölunda in the Swedish Elite League (now SHL). He won gold playing for Sweden in the 2006 Olympics. Christian, now retired, recently reflected on his Viking Cup experience.

> I learned a lot from the Viking Cup. It was my first visit to Canada. For sure it was an important step in my journey to the NHL. This was the only time I stayed with a family in my hockey travel and it was great. We felt like Donna and Dave Tomaszewski and their kids loved having us there.

Dave commented: "In 2007 when St. Louis was playing the Oilers in Edmonton, Christian came to Camrose to visit us. When he walked into our house, he said, 'Your house is much smaller now.' I said, 'Compared to your new house in St. Louis after signing your new contract, I guess so!' Backman wanted to come back for Donna's wonderful tacos, and to his Camrose home . . . again."

The Tomaszewskis billeted numerous Swedish hockey players over the years, including Kristian Huselius (Viking Cup '96), who played eleven years in the NHL with Florida, Calgary, and Columbus. In 2002, Robert Nilsson, who later played for the Islanders and Oilers, also stayed with them.

Robert's father, Kent, who previously had an impressive career with the Flames and Oilers, was scouting for the Edmonton Oilers at the time and enjoying the Viking Cup games high in the stands.

One day, Dave and Kent were sitting together watching the Swedish team play. Dave told Kent that he had asked Robert what he wanted to be when he grew up. Robert had replied, "a DJ." When Dave relayed the conversation to Kent, he lowered his head and said, "Really?"

The next spring, Robert was drafted in the first round by New York Islanders.

Don Meehan, Robert's agent, was also at that Viking Cup. Through the billeting arrangements for Robert, Don and Dave Tomaszewski became casually acquainted—enough that Dave likes to share this story about Meehan.

> He had rented a car at the airport. At the arena, he called on me for help when his keys wouldn't open the car door, which he assumed was frozen because of the cold weather. I asked him, are you sure you are using the right keys? Meehan then realized that he was using keys from his pocket for his car

back in Manitoba! Don said to me, "Don't you dare tell anyone. I will never live this down amongst my friends." Of course, I never told anyone!

Of their many years of billeting at the Viking Cup, Donna says, "It was a life experience we will never forget. [As soon as one was over], we were in anticipation for the next Viking Cup. They were all great kids to have around. We keep in contact."

"We spent three weeks in Sweden . . . our son met Peter Forsberg"

Judy and Regan Bergstrom billeted Swedes from '96 to 2002, and Swiss players in 2004. Judy talks enthusiastically about the interesting times they have had together.

> Once, we spent three weeks in Sweden. We stayed with some of the boys who'd stayed with us. Because of our Viking Cup connection, our son got to meet Peter Forsberg and spend two days at the rink with him during summer training. He was thrilled. Our daughter Angela has often heard players say, "Oh, so you are from Camrose. I've been there. I played in the Viking Cup." It's amazing how well it was known and how many people it touched. Our involvement with the Viking Cup led us to billet Camrose Kodiaks for seventeen years. We met our son-in-law, Nick Holden (Las Vegas Golden Knights) that way.

While Judy talked of how the Swedes liked chocolate milk (they put it on cereal and other food) and how rewarding it was to see the boys get to the next level, Regan was anxious to show me the wide collection of hockey memories in their rumpus room. "You know, the boys were so interested in Canadian hockey history, and so are we."

On a whim, the Bergstroms drove through a blizzard to the World Juniors in Winnipeg in '99.

> We started at five in the morning because the Swedish boys from Viking Cup '98 were playing and their team had made the medal round. They were phoning to see why we weren't there. Since they were in Western Canada, they were assuming that Winnipeg must be close to Camrose, like on a Swedish map.

The Bergstroms sat with the Swedish supporters even when the Swedes were playing the Canadians. "One player who was playing for the Swedes, Christian Berglund, was suspended in the game after playing for just five minutes. When he saw us after the game, he said, 'And you drove fourteen hours just to watch me play for five minutes? Amazing!'"

"Anna is like a daughter to me – her kids call me Grandma"

When Kris McClennan billeted Swedish equipment managers Rolf Eriksson ('86 and '88) and Tommy Berglind ('88), she didn't realize that she was becoming part of the Berglind family. This, then, is an example of another Viking Cup extended family.

Kris explains, "All the Swedish leaders came to my place for supper one night at Viking Cup '88. It was such an enjoyable evening. Tommy was a Swedish referee and his son Johan was playing for AIK Stockholm in the Viking Cup."

Through the Viking Cup experience, Tommy's daughter Anna lived with Kris for a year while attending the Camrose Composite High School.

> Anna is like a daughter to me. Now her kids call me Grandma. They have been back to see me many times and I have been to the Berglinds [sic] in Stockholm three times. They take me on their large sailing boat in the Baltic—oh, so enjoyable! The Berglind kids have stayed with me while attending summer hockey school in Camrose. It has been such a positive relationship for our families.

"Lots of networking moments"

Doug and Anne Fleck billeted Swedish hockey players through five Viking Cups, but that was only part of their involvement. Doug was an assistant coach of the Vikings and, later, a coach for the Camrose Kodiaks.

"The Viking Cup opened many doors," Doug says. "I was a guest coach of a hockey school in Sweden through the Viking Cup. We spent one month in Sweden while visiting our boys and their families—the ones that stayed with us at the Viking Cup. After that, the father of Ronnie Kristensson (a Viking Cup '94 player) came to Camrose to go hunting with me."

Anne added, "We have lifelong friendships with the families on both sides of the ocean. The cultural growth of our own kids was so important."

Player Development Programs

Sweden is well known for its many hockey players who have come to North America to do very well in the NHL, including many who started at a Viking Cup. Ulf Hall, a former Augustana Viking player who's now working with the Swedish Ice Hockey Federation, refers to the Viking Cup as "a window for Swedish players to enter the NHL."

Swedish coach Mats Emanuelsson, who has mentored great players like the Sedin twins and Mikael Backlund (Calgary Flames) through his Swedish Hockey Institute in Uppsala, knows all about the Viking Cup. He attended Viking Cup '96 as an assistant coach of the Swedish national U18 team and Viking Cup '98 as the head coach of the Swedish national U18 team. Through his close ties with Camrose and Viking Cup host Terry Ofrim, Team Sweden U17 trained in Camrose while playing in the U17 World Challenge in Red Deer in 1997. The well-known Sedin twins of Vancouver Canuck fame played on that team.

> The experience was good for Swedish ice hockey players," Emanuelsson recalls of his visits to Camrose. "The players really liked to play on the smaller ice surface. The game was faster and more exciting. In Camrose, there were big crowds, even cheering for us! The community was really involved. That

doesn't happen in Sweden, where there are fewer volunteers [than in the Viking Cup]. The Viking Cup really helped Swedish players get contact with Canadian and NHL opportunities. It was interesting to travel to the various arenas in the area. Once we played in a little town called Viking. We walked right through the kitchen to get to the ice! But my better memory was when I bought a 50/50 ticket from the mother of the famous hockey-playing Sutters—pretty special from such a famous lady, especially for a Swede like me in Viking, Alberta!

Reminiscent of the seven Hansen brothers of Camrose in earlier times, the Sutters are a family of seven young hockey stars, six of whom had NHL careers.

The most important part of the experience, Emanuelsson recalls, was the family living component in Camrose. They had meetings in their dressing room in which each player would share stories of their billets and home life. He remembers lots of laughs and an expressed love for their families. "Our equipment manager made Swedish coffee for us in the dressing room. The billets of our players were lined up just outside for a cup of strong, three-kroner coffee. The Swedish way, you know."

After Viking Cup '98, the players all pitched in and bought a ticket for their Canadian host, Terry Ofrim, to come to the U18 European Championships in Sweden. They said it was their gift for making them feel so welcome in Camrose.

Early Hockey Exchanges with Sweden

Sweden is known as a welcoming country that's rich in hockey exchanges. In 1972, the Malmo district in Edmonton (a Swedish connection, I'm sure) hosted a Swedish Midget team from Malmö for a series of games. The organizer, Dick White, approached me about the possibility of playing a game in Camrose with the local Midget team. It was thought that a first-time Swedish team visiting Scandinavian-infested Camrose was sure to be a hit!

It was. The arena filled to capacity and an invitation was extended to the Camrose team to return the visit to southern Sweden.

Meanwhile, Camrose Mayor Rudy Swanson (who was of Swedish heritage) suggested that if the Vikings were to go to Europe, it would be a good incentive for the younger Midget players to play college hockey someday. It was also a time when the Vikings had just entered the competitive ACAC league.

Determined people set sail to recruit players, raise funds, organize, and prepare the way. On December 15, 1974, our Vikings, along with several of their most loyal fans, returned to the original land of the Vikings, landing in historic Stockholm. We did not realize then that a fresh new stream was beginning to make its way for a Camrose international tournament to follow within a few short years.

Augustana (Camrose Lutheran College) has a history tied very closely to the Norwegian immigrants who settled in the Camrose area around 1900. Plans therefore included a visit to Oslo for Christmas celebrations. There was another reason, too.

The CLC concert choir, not to be outdone by a hockey team, were also touring in Scandinavia and likewise planning to be in Oslo for Christmas. We never knew for sure, but later we kidded Vikings Dennis Dunn and chorister Barb Anderson that the tours criss-crossed solely for their benefit. You see, he had bought a special souvenir in Stockholm, a diamond ring, and gave it to Barb in Oslo that Christmas night! That was the souvenir that took the cake—a wedding cake! I think it was planned in advance, but hockey tours can have their surprises for unsuspecting leaders.

Prior to the Oslo detour, the entourage played games in Nynäshamn, Örebro, Västerås, and Strömstad and visited the interesting sites of Stockholm including Gamla Stan (Old Town).

After thrashing the Västerås team 6–1 and still having energy to burn, some of the players had their first encounter with the game of bandy on the adjoining stadium. Bandy is a little-known sport to Canadians, but it attracted our boys' special interest because of its resemblance to ice hockey. It was being played by very fast skaters on what was apparently a soccer field completely covered in ice—eleven players on each side with a bowed stick chasing a small ball. It reminded me of my early days of learning how to play hockey on a slough or lake of ice extending on and on and on. We learned that it was called "Russian hockey" in its earliest days due to its popularity in Russia prior to World War II.

Although the Europeans seemed to concede that hockey originated in Canada, some say that bandy influenced the development of the game and led to what is referred to as "European ice hockey." We were told that bandy players make very good hockey players. This was just an example of so many learning moments and connections in Sweden, and it certainly gave us a better understanding of the great skills of hockey in that country.

Back home, there was much interest and daily reporting of our tour. Mona Iverson, manager and faithful operator of Mona's Coffee House at Augustana for forty-two years, was one who was following our journey. She had emigrated from Västerås but was now a true Canadian, cheering for the Vikings of Camrose even when playing in her Swedish hometown.

Our first game in Denmark was in Ålborg. The Danish national team, hearing of the strength of the Canadian Vikings, brought in Johan "Honken" Holmqvist, former Swedish national team goaltender and IIHF Hall of Famer, for the game. Even so, they were no match for us Canadians.

"Honken talked to me afterward and offered me a scholarship to come to Stockholm University to study medicine, free ride," our player, John Danko, later commented. "I still have the letter. Should have taken them up on it. [But] I was happy in Camrose."

Our outstanding goaltender Svend Green also helped to lay our journey's path. Svend and his family were from Ålborg, Denmark. Needless to say, we were well received by the many relatives of Svend and Knud Jensen (a fan accompanying our team), with home-cooked Danish meals and baking following our successful games there. Our captain Bill Andreassen and defenseman Lee Cumberland were the last to leave the dressing room and unfortunately missed the bus. They settled for hot dogs at the arena, I think!

The Vikings' journey was complete after visiting Copenhagen, Tyringe, and Malmö, Sweden—home of our first Swedish visitors to Camrose.

Malmö has since built a beautiful new arena, where it was my pleasure to attend the World Junior Hockey Championships in 2014, with Sven Sandberg of Stockholm. Sven attended Augustana and played with the Vikings during the 1983-84 season, and was a graduate of the Stockholm Phys Ed University, Andres Hedberg's alma mater.

Svend commented, "It brings back great memories when I am talking or meeting with you or coach Mike Johnston, or former teammates from the Vikings now in Camrose or Stockholm or Malmö or other places in the world."

The Vikings' first trip to Europe was followed quickly by a visit to Camrose by the Farsta (a suburb of Stockholm) Club, through contacts made in Stockholm.

In 1979-80, the Vikings travelled to Europe for a second time with the assistance of the Farsta Club, who billeted our players while in the Stockholm area. One of the four games in the Stockholm area was with the Swedish Junior National champion team (AIK) in Solna, another Stockholm suburb.

We were now playing against the best juniors in Sweden and were quite pleased with the outcome. I later invited this same team to the first Viking Cup tournament in Camrose for the following year. We knew the Swedish style of play would always be a hit in Camrose.

By this time, AIK had contributed to the intriguing Swedish style in the NHL. Three of their graduates—Ulf Nilsson (Winnipeg and NY Rangers), Thomas Gradin (Vancouver Canucks), and Kent Nilsson (Oilers and Flames)—were making their mark in North America.

Following that first Viking Cup, AIK's Mats Thelin was the first Swedish player of the Viking Cup to be drafted by the NHL. Mats, a heavy-hitting defenseman, was drafted by the Boston Bruins and he played three seasons in Boston before completing an impressive sixteen-year professional career with AIK of the Swedish Elite League. Thelin played for Sweden in the '82 and '83 World Championships, the '84 Olympics, and the '84 Canada Cup.

By the early 80s, team exchanges with Sweden were well established, giving individual players a new opportunity to enhance their educational experience in a different country. International education at Augustana was beginning to take root.

The Vikings–Sweden exchange took on new meaning when four of the Vikings—Rick Webster, Dan Wilson, Rory Rost, and Jim Gotaas—returned to Sweden to play with the Farsta team in Stockholm in 1981-82. Later, the exchange continued with Ulf Hall, Dan Lindqwister, and Sven Sandberg attending Augustana and playing with the Vikings.

Vikings player Rob Fisher, of Consort, Alberta, met up with Lindqwister, Hall, and Mats Hessel, a star with AIK in Viking Cup '81, in Stockholm, during the Vikings' European tour of 1982-83. "Mats was driving as the four of us cruised the streets of Stockholm," Rob remembers. "I said, 'Aren't you driving pretty fast?' He said, 'If I get stopped, I will say we are hockey players. That way we will only get a warning!' I wasn't sure if he was kidding, but to me it was another message that hockey is pretty important in Sweden!"

Hard-hitting defenseman Johnny Johnson was on the same tour and had played in Viking Cup '82 with teammates Hall and Lindqwister. "I remember as a kid receiving a Swedish jersey from my brother Harley for Christmas," Johnny said. "He had just returned from Europe and had played for the CLC Vikings in 1974–75. For me, it was special to play in the Viking Cup as, wouldn't you know, my first game was against Sweden. Those iconic Swedish jerseys still bring back memories of playing in the Viking Cup whenever I see Sweden play on the international stage."

AIK must have brought back good reports on their Viking Cup '81 experience, as there was a quick commitment to send a leading junior team, Västra Frölunda, from their second-largest city, Göteborg, for Viking Cup '82. The city, on their west coast, is known for good universities and manufacturing Volvos, but in hockey circles its most famous product is Daniel Alfredsson, who played and captained the Ottawa Senators for seventeen years before his last NHL season with Detroit. Västra Frölunda played well in Viking Cup '82, taking home the bronze medal. The Buffalo Sabres drafted Mikael Andersson, who played well in the tournament, in the first round. Andersson had an impressive seventeen-year career with Buffalo, Hartford, Tampa, Philadelphia, and the Islanders. He played for Team Sweden in the '98 Olympics, and several World Championships.

Following Viking Cup '81, the assessment of Swedish play was summarized in the post-tournament magazine as follows: "And though the Swedish system fell short of perfection during the Viking Cup, anyone who watched Mats Alba thread a perfect pass to a breaking forward, or Mats Hessel rocket by a helpless defenseman, or Dan Pettersson do his magic act with the puck, knows that the AIK tradition of excellence lives on."

And so does the long tradition of skillful hockey in all of Sweden.

The Swedish Stream in Ice Hockey

Sweden has been a member of the IIHF since 1920, and has held its own on the world stage of elite hockey. Today, about 10 percent of NHL players come from Sweden, in spite of its small population of nine million—certainly much less than 10 percent of the total population of the other major hockey countries.

Anders Hedberg's comment about the importance of individual skills in the formation of the famous Winnipeg "go line" aptly applies in all hockey. Swedish players are known for their well-developed individual skill, and they have therefore done very well in winning positions on NHL teams and, in many cases, providing excellent leadership. Who could forget players like Börje Salming and Mats Sundin in Toronto, or Markus Näslund and the Sedin twins in Vancouver, or Nick Lidström and Henrik Zetterberg in Detroit, or Daniel Alfredsson in Ottawa?

However, during the era of the Viking Cup and into the new century, the Swedish national team's success on the world stage, although commendable, didn't measure up to its own expectations.

Tommy Boustedt, elite team coach of Frölunda in Göteborg, was appointed to head up a review of the system in 2002. (The Frölunda junior team had competed twice in the Viking Cup.) Boustedt later became the general secretary of the Swedish Ice Hockey Association.

In a 2011 article on NHL.com, he said, "The proof came at the 2003 World Junior Championships in Halifax. The Swedes went 1–4 in the round robin and were forced to play in the relegation round. They finished eighth and survived, but the result was an embarrassing wake-up call heard across the country.

> Everyone saw the problems. We always had the knowledge about what was important if you wanted to develop players but we didn't co-operate in Swedish hockey.
>
> The big difference from fifteen years ago is that we started to co-operate. We are a small country worldwide, so to be successful and have a little chance to compete with the big countries, we need to be more efficient because we don't have the [enrolment] numbers like the big countries. The best way to be efficient is to work together.

On a different scale, the Swedish lessons were much akin to the Augustana and Viking Cup story. Problems of small enrolment can be turned into strengths when everyone works together for maximum efficiency.

Boustedt goes on to relate hockey style and development to the political and social realities of the people of Sweden and how hockey has changed in Sweden in the past fifteen years.

> Let's face it, the word "compete" was obsolete in this country—we haven't been in a war in 200 years and we have a classic social democratic system that built this society, and to "compete" has historically been a bad word.

Today, having that competitive spirit in everything associated with Swedish hockey is what has changed most, according to Boustedt.

> The word 'compete' is a good word again in Swedish hockey," he said. "Our message to the kids is what they need to do to become an elite hockey player, but society and sport are very intertwined in Sweden. It's like you can't have one without the other. In many communities, the ice hockey rink served as a community gathering place, another expression of the symbiosis between state and society characterized by Sweden's social democratic *folkhemmet*.

In the Viking Cup, the best success of Swedish teams was three bronze medals over their ten years of participation. During all Viking Cups, however, Sweden was a very popular team due in part to "high-bar" skills and, I suppose, the strong Scandinavian heritage of the Camrose area.

It is clear, however, that the Swedish style was a reflection of the political and social history of Sweden. In international competition, the Swedes have always been able to put a strong team together, mainly with players from the NHL, where competition is at its highest level. In 2006, they won both the World Championships and the Olympics, with players well-schooled in the NHL style of play, including the five Swedish players with the Detroit Red Wings, who won the Stanley Cup that year—triple gold winners! This feat was considered so spectacular it was declared story number eight in the IIHF list of the 100 most famous hockey stories of all time. The list was announced on the IIHF's 100th anniversary in 2008.

Sweden—The Original Partner in the Viking Cup Exchange Program

Swedish ice hockey is embedded in the origins of the Viking Cup. It was to Sweden that the Augustana Vikings journeyed on their maiden voyage to Europe, and AIK of Stockholm was a founding participant of the Viking Cup in Camrose. The Swedish style of play, characterized by a high skill level, was an admired stream in the mix of hockey traditions in the Viking Cup. And for the Swedish teams, the Viking Cup was an opportunity to advance their competitive skills.

The Viking Cup is an example of Sweden's contribution to a better brand of ice hockey globally. They have contributed in numbers of elite players beyond their size and proportions to the highest levels of hockey, including the NHL. And many, in demonstrating outstanding skills, started that climb at the Viking Cup in Camrose.

SWEDEN

VIKING CUP PARTICIPANTS WHO PLAYED IN THE WINTER OLYMPICS (AS OF THE CONCLUSION OF 2018 GAMES)

Name	Viking Cup Team	Year(s)	Olympic Team	Year(s)
Mikael Andersson	Västra Frölunda	1982	Sweden	1988, 1998
Per-Johan Axelsson	Västra Frölunda	1994	Sweden	2002, 2006
Christian Bäckman	Sweden	1998	Sweden	2006
Tobias Enström	Sweden	2002	Sweden	2010
Mats Hessel	AIK Solna	1981	Sweden	1984
Mathias Johansson	Färjestad	1992	Sweden	2002
Henrik Lundqvist	Sweden	2000	Sweden	2006, 2010, 2014
Joel Lundqvist	Sweden	2000	Sweden	2018
Mats Thelin	AIK Solna	1981	Sweden	1984
Mattias Weinhandl	Sweden	1998	Sweden	2010
Henrik Zetterberg	Sweden	1998	Sweden	2002, 2006, 2010, 2014

VIKING CUP PARTICIPANTS SELECTED IN NHL ENTRY OR SUPPLEMENTAL DRAFTS

Player	Viking Cup Team	Year(s)	Selected By	Draft	Round	Overall Selection
Erik Andersson	AIK Solna	1988	Los Angeles	1990 Entry	6	112
			Calgary	1997 Entry	3	70
Mikael Andersson	Västra Frölunda	1982	Buffalo	1984 Entry	1	18
Johan Asplund	Sweden	1998	New York Rangers	1999 Entry	3	79
Per-Johan Axelsson	Västra Frölunda	1994	Boston	1995 Entry	7	177
Christian Bäckman	Sweden	1998	St. Louis	1998 Entry	1	24
Christian Berglund	Sweden	1998	New Jersey	1998 Entry	2	37
Johan Björk	Sweden	2002	Ottawa	2002 Entry	4	125

Patric Blomdahl	Sweden	2002	Washington	2002 Entry	9	272
Josef Boumedienne	Sweden	1996	New Jersey	1996 Entry	4	91
Niklas Eckerblom	Sweden	2002	Minnesota	2002 Entry	7	204
Johan Eneqvist	Sweden	2000	Montreal	2000 Entry	4	109
Patric Englund	AIK Solna	1988	Philadelphia	1990 Entry	8	151
Tobias Enström	Sweden	2002	Atlanta	2003 Entry	8	239
Tim Eriksson	Sweden	2000	Los Angeles	2000 Entry	7	206
Johan Forsander	Sweden	1996	Detroit	1996 Entry	5	108
Jonas Frögren	Sweden	1998	Calgary	1998 Entry	8	206
Johan Hägglund	Sweden	2000	Tampa Bay	2000 Entry	4	126
Patrick Haltia	Färjestad	1992	Calgary	1994 Entry	6	149
Pierre Hedin	Sweden	1996	Toronto	1999 Entry	8	239
Johan Holmqvist	Sweden	1996	New York Rangers	1997 Entry	7	175
Peter Högardh	Västra Frölunda	1994	New York Islanders	1994 Entry	8	203
Kristian Huselius	Sweden	1996	Florida	1997 Entry	2	47
Fredrik Johansson	Sweden	2002	Edmonton	2002 Entry	9	274
Mathias Johansson	Färjestad	1992	Calgary	1992 Entry	3	54
Pierre Johnsson	Sweden	2002	Calgary	2002 Entry	7	207
Lars Jonsson	Sweden	2000	Boston	2000 Entry	1	7
Gabriel Karlsson	Sweden	1998	Dallas	1998 Entry	3	86
Jens Karlsson	Sweden	2000	Los Angeles	2001 Entry	1	18
Mikael Lindman	AIK Solna	1986	Montreal	1985 Entry	12	239
Henrik Lundqvist	Sweden	2000	New York Rangers	2000 Entry	7	205
Joel Lundqvist	Sweden	2000	Dallas	2000 Entry	3	68
Anders Myrvold	Färjestad	1992	Quebec	1993 Entry	5	127
Mattias Nilsson	Sweden	2000	Nashville	2000 Entry	3	72
Robert Nilsson	Sweden	2002	New York Islanders	2003 Entry	1	15
Jonas Nordqvist	Sweden	2000	Chicago	2000 Entry	2	49
David Nyström	Sweden	1998	Philadelphia	1999 Entry	8	244
Marcus Paulsson	Sweden	2002	New York Islanders	2002 Entry	5	149
Pontus Petterström	Sweden	2000	New York Rangers	2001 Entry	7	226
Jan Sandström	Sweden	1996	Anaheim	1999 Entry	6	173
Mikael Simons	Sweden	1996	Los Angeles	1996 Entry	4	84
Jonas Soling	Sweden	1996	Vancouver	1996 Entry	4	93
Peter Ström	Västra Frölunda	1994	Montreal	1994 Entry	8	200
Mats Thelin	AIK Solna	1981	Boston	1981 Entry	6	140
Dragen Umičević	Sweden	2002	Edmonton	2003 Entry	6	184
Andreas Valdix	Sweden	2002	Washington	2003 Entry	4	109
Rickard Wallin	Sweden	1998	Phoenix	1998 Entry	6	160
Mattias Weinhandl	Sweden	1998	New York Islanders	1999 Entry	3	78
Daniel Widing	Sweden	2000	Nashville	2000 Entry	2	36
Henrik Zetterberg	Sweden	1998	Detroit	1999 Entry	7	210

Hockey on the Farm, by Martin Giesen (Viking Cup '92)

CHAPTER 5

Sisu . . . Finnish Connections

Scotty Bowman knows a great hockey player when he sees one—and he was always looking. Small wonder then that he walked into the Camrose arena for the very first Viking Cup—Viking Cup '81.

There were several players to watch in that tournament, and ten were chosen in the June NHL draft held at the Montreal Canadiens' Forum. Bowman, however, had his eyes fixed on one player, a versatile Finn who was selected MVP of the tournament, defenseman Hannu Virta. Bowman secured Virta in the second round for the Buffalo Sabres, the first of sixty-six Finnish players, and the first European, to be drafted by the NHL from the Viking Cup in the years to follow.

There could not have been a better introduction to Finnish hockey than through Virta, the epitome of a complete hockey player with skills well beyond his young age of seventeen in the Viking Cup. On defense, no one got around him, and on offense, he was the quarterback of the team, anchoring a dynamic power play. Virta was a picture of intensity and focus and a coach's dream for a team leader.

Virta made his mark with the Sabres over the next five years, after which he returned to his native Finland.

In Finland, he was a stalwart with TPS Turku of the Finnish Elite League for the next eight years. He played on the Finnish national team in seven World Championships and the 1994 Olympics in Lillehammer, Norway. Virta turned to coaching after his outstanding playing career.

Viking Cup '81 was not the last that we in Camrose saw of Virta. In 1990, while playing a series of games in Finland and other European countries, the Vikings were guests of TPS Turku, playing in an "elite league" game. Along with courtesy game tickets, there was a requirement that we choose the game's three stars. That was easy: we chose Hannu Virta as MVP.

Reflecting on his illustrious career two years later, Virta gave the Viking Cup his own "valuable experience" award. "It was a good experience. It really helped me become more familiar with the Canadian style of hockey. What I really learned was to be ready all the time and expect a hit. Not only were there differences at the hockey rink, but at the homes where the Finnish players were billeted. I think all the boys would say the people took good care of us, they looked after us very well. It was a bit surprising to win the tournament and be named MVP. It was tough to win because there were a lot of good quality teams and players in the tournament. It was really good hockey!"

More recently, in retirement, Virta was asked if the Viking Cup was an important part of his illustrious career. The answer came quickly: "Of course."

The TPS Turku junior team of '81 was not an ordinary hockey team. They were Finnish League champions the previous year and they brought one of the great hockey minds of Finland as their leader and coach, Juhani Wahlsten whose son, Jali played on the team.

Wahlsten had been an elite-level player in Finnish hockey, mainly with TPS Turku, and he had played and coached in Austria, Switzerland, and, later, Germany. He played on the national team for eleven years and was captain when he retired in 1972. Later, he was inducted into Finland's Hockey Hall of Fame and the IIHF Hall of Fame.

Being a part of the first Viking Cup was a perfect fit for Wahlsten.

By this time, he had established an organization called the "World Sports Friendship Exchange Program." This non-profit organization arranged international trips for young athletes with a goal of achieving better understanding through sport. The Viking Cup not only brought youth from different countries together, but provided competition at the highest level, where Wahlsten had been for most of his life.

At this time, most of our Finnish visitors had limited command of the English language. Wahlsten, however, spoke five languages, and his English was all but perfect.

Whether it was Scotty Bowman, the other coaches, journalists, or plain folks from Camrose, his audience was eager to hear what he had to say in his deep, resonating voice. "Hockey is relatively new in Finland," he told a journalist for a story in the *Viking Cup '81* souvenir booklet.

> The present generation is the first to have knowledgeable coaches, people who have grown up with the game. We are lucky though in that we are exposed to different hockey philosophies. We can learn from the Swedes and Russians on either side of us, and also from the Czechs. Hockey is too organized and, as a result, the spirit is disappearing. In Finland, all young hockey players belong to a club. We don't 'cut' anyone; each boy is assigned to his own level. However, teams are only together as a unit for a small part of the time, since the secret to mastering skills is not found in organized drills, but in unsupervised skating and play on the outdoor rinks.

> But as far as North American hockey is concerned, you always play differently. Because of the smaller ice surface, you have to be quicker. The centre does not open up for clearing passes as it does in Europe, and you cannot make as many passes in the offensive zone. So, to those who debate endlessly which style of play is better, I say each is good for certain conditions.

Why do I like hockey? Because it is a great sport, and because you learn about life at the same time, about accepting responsibilities and working with other people. You in Canada forget, I think, what a great gift you have given to the world. Thirty-two countries now play hockey, including places like Spain and Australia. And remember, if it were not for hockey, none of us from Finland, Sweden, Prince Albert, or the rest would have come to Camrose!

Wahlsten was an educator, a networker, always anxious to learn from others. Following his satisfying experiences in Viking Cup '81, his World Sports Friendship Exchange organization, along with the Finnish Ice Hockey Federation, organized their first International Hockey Experts Coaching Symposium, in July 1982, in his home city of Turku, as a part of the city's 750th anniversary (Alberta celebrated its seventy-fifth anniversary at the same time). Juhani extended me an invitation to participate, and it was through this inspiring week in Finland that I met many hockey people of the world. This was an opportune time to promote and plan for future Viking Cups and hockey trips to Europe.

Interesting participants included the great "Red" Story, Scotty Bowman, Pat Quinn, Ralph Mellanby, Phil Myre, Red Berenson, Pierre Page, and numerous leaders and legends of European hockey such as Sergei Makarov of Russia.

It was at this time that I met Rudi Killias of Switzerland, who was the head coach of the Austrian national team and lived near Vienna. Killias was also a leader in the Spengler Cup in Davos, Switzerland, which soon became an example for Viking Cup development (see Chapter 9).

Launching Pad

Finland was the northern buffer nation to the Soviet Union (at the time), and to the CLC Vikings, Helsinki was a launching pad to the other side of the Iron Curtain.

On their first and only journey (1980) into Leningrad (now St. Petersburg), the Vikings departed on a Russian train from Helsinki on the rails of Finland to the border city of Viborg, where Russian authorities thoroughly searched all their belongings. A few years later, in 1983–84, Finnair departed Helsinki, delivering the Vikings to Prague on their first of several journeys to Communist Czechoslovakia.

The Russian train stopped on a bridge over the eastern fringe of the Gulf of Finland at Viborg. We soon realized we were on the border—the Iron Curtain.

The story of player Rick Sikorski spreading the false rumour within earshot of the Russian soldiers that Dan Wilson and Rick Webster should remove a Swedish men's magazine from their hockey bags is generally understood to be the reason for the long search of all hockey bags. Both Wilson and Webster maintain (to this day) that no such magazine was ever found in *their* bags!

Player Rory Rost was clutching his passport securely. In his rush to board the train, he discovered he'd left it in the taxi that had delivered him to the Helsinki train station. Just when the decision was made to leave Rory behind, the taxi driver, responding to a message from its headquarters, sped to the station with a special delivery for Rost. "Whew," he said after the fact. "To think I almost missed the Leningrad experience."

The remaining part of our first trip on the other side of the "red line" was rough and slow, but we eventually arrived at the Leningrad hotel. There, we were told that we could walk the streets if we had a passport. The hotel immediately confiscated all passports for safekeeping!

It was a "hot" time in the Cold War while we were in Leningrad.

The Russians decided to invade Afghanistan to prop up the ailing Communist government challenged by the mujahideen rebellion. The US, of course, supported the mujahideen. Our families back home were much more concerned (fearing a hostage situation, I guess) than we were. We had no news while we were there and, if we did, who of us understood Russian? Goaltender Allan Skip stayed close to me throughout, as he had overheard a Canadian embassy official bid us goodbye at the Helsinki train station with the words, "If you don't come back, we will come looking for you."

We did have a memorable time in Russia, but as the train crossed that red line into Finland on our return, our whole group let out a chorus of relief. We are home, but we were in Finland. Finland has so much in common with Canada, and it really did feel like "home" at that moment.

More significant than the two excellent games played in Leningrad (fast hockey, no penalties, as I recall) was the discussion on the train about establishing an international tournament in Camrose to bring teams from East and West together for friendly games (see complete story in Chapter 8). The seeds were sown that day and the Viking Cup became a reality the following year.

I often wonder whether the Viking Cup actually launched in Helsinki, Finland, the buffer between East and West. Or in Russia where, somehow, we wanted our people back home to see, first-hand, the great skills in the Russian game. Maybe the idea was germinating right on the border as our bags were searched.

We played our final game on the trip with the Helsinki IFK juniors. How could one forget it? Players Don Flowers and Dave Recknagle had gone for a short walk while in Leningrad, and noticed a man walking on the other side of the street with a bundle of Titan hockey sticks. They thought at the time that it was strange to see Finnish hockey sticks in Russia. Upon returning to the hotel, they learned that our remaining Titan sticks (Finnish hockey sticks were the best) had been stolen from the storage room. All that remained were the Russian sticks that several of our players had traded as souvenirs after the last game in Leningrad. Our guys called them "banana sticks" because of their unusual shape. Forty-one years later, Don Flowers and Dan Wilson still have banana sticks stored in their garages as souvenirs.

With our banana sticks and the loaner Finnish sticks from our IFK Helsinki Club friends, including Edmonton Oiler Esa Tikkanen's father, we "finn-ished" our tour with a final great game in Helsinki. The Finnish players, however, were reluctant to accept our banana sticks for the streamlined Finnish sticks as a final souvenir of Canada!

We spent our final night in Helsinki at the beautiful Presidential Helsinki hotel, a couple stars up from what we'd experienced in the previous days in Leningrad. Across the street, the boys noticed a large outdoor skating rink. Player Randy Stollery described it thus: "It appeared to be a soccer field covered with awesome ice surrounded by a speed skating oval… on a beautiful clear-moon night."

The boys grabbed their skates and the few sticks that remained and began to play old-fashioned shinny on one end while figure skaters and others occupied the rest of the unending ice. Randy reminds me that, soon, Coach Joe Voytechek was standing on the nearby snowbank with a whistle in hand, directing one of his intensive stop-and-go practices. "We thought, and wished, that Coach Voytechek was finally enjoying a break in his first-class room!"

Finnish Hockey Development and Style

The development of ice hockey in Finland is especially informative to any student of the game and the Viking Cup provides some clues to the phenomenal success of this small northern country of five million people. There is little doubt that their skillful, hard-hitting style of hockey reflects Finland's history, climate, and strategic location.

Early domination by Sweden was replaced by Russian rule early in the nineteenth century after which Finland struggled to gain its independence in 1917, just a century ago. During WWII, the Finns fought twice against the Russians to defend their independence. Miraculously, Finland was the only country bordering the USSR in Europe that kept its independence after WWII. Its first century as a democracy has been dominated by tension with Russia while maintaining a positive relationship with the free world. During the Cold War, Finland was the strategic buffer lying along the Iron Curtain, always in a state of readiness for the possibility of Russian aggression.

Finland joined the European Union in 1995, but because it wishes to maintain some neutrality toward Russia, it is not a member of NATO—even though it has built up its defences to compare with NATO countries. An important part of its defense is a massive tunnel bomb shelter system under its cities that could accommodate its entire urban population in the event of emergency such as a Russian invasion. The subterranean granite city beneath Helsinki has enough space to serve as shelter for 750,000 residents, more than the population of Helsinki. There are ice hockey arenas, swimming pools, field houses, and other public facilities down there.

On one occasion, the Vikings were scheduled to play in a stadium in Hervanta, near Tampere. As the Finnish bus stopped to drop the team at an enclosure barely large enough to accommodate our group, I asked our guide "Where is the stadium?" He said, "Just step in the elevator."

Down we went, several stories into a huge cavern buried in Finnish granite to a stadium free of any encumbrance above ground. It was a new experience for sure, and it brought us face to face with the geographical and political realities of Finland.

The Finnish players encountered new and unexpected experiences in Canada, as well, even some we took for granted. On an exhibition game swing to the town of Wainwright shortly after arriving in Camrose the night before, Finnish players crowded to the front of the bus as the driver began to drive east down the "correction line" road. I couldn't imagine what they were capturing on their cameras.

I thought: *Is there an accident ahead, maybe a stray moose on the road?* No, they were taking photos of the long, straight road, something new to Finns, who travel through a countryside largely on curvy roads around lakes, rock, and through vast forests. How boring, I thought. They said, "This is exciting." Really?

The Finnish people are much more than defenders of their land and freedom. They are also builders of a great society. This is also reflected in their hockey and other sports.

Today, Finland has one of the highest standards of living in the world. Their parliamentary democracy is geared to free-market capitalism that diverts substantial spending to social safety nets and public service. The country is one of the wealthiest in the world and is environmentally clean. Business and industry are efficient and profitable. For many years, the national air carrier, Finnair, served as the official carrier of Viking Cup exchanges to levels of satisfaction higher than the clouds over which we flew.

Finland's literacy rate is ranked number one in the world, and they have been ranked at the top for their education system for some years now. Amongst the OECD countries, they have been ranked number one in science education and number two in reading and math. Their university system is ranked third worldwide. Finland places a high emphasis on healthy people and, consequently, sport activity remains a high national priority.

Ice hockey seems a perfect fit for this northern nation, which is ever ready to triumph over harsh conditions. The winter ice on its numerous lakes gives all young Finns the opportunity to perfect basic skills and well-trained coaches advance those skills in their "ice halls," which are well distributed throughout the country.

It's no wonder that Finland has one of the most advanced international sport-training centres in the world, at Vierumäki, north of Helsinki. The Augustana Vikings were privileged to be hosted by the Finnish Ice Hockey Federation at Vierumäki, for training on their European tour of 1985. On a country-wide basis, Finland has 274 indoor "ice halls"—more per capita than any other European nation. (Canada has double that number of arenas per capita.)

Over the years, the Augustana Vikings have trained and played many games in Finland and have always learned much and been well received. We have marvelled at their ability to adapt to a North American style and merge the best qualities of European and Canadian hockey to suit any size of ice surface. As far as I'm concerned, of all the Viking Cup participants, the Finns were best able to combine high skills, aggressiveness, and discipline in their play on a consistent basis.

When the Vikings played games in Finland, it was the same style of hockey: tough and competitive and always a great learning experience. After the game, a nice warm sauna was almost always there to relax the muscles.

Viking player Todd Voshell was billeted with some teammates in the Finnish home of a doctor, and remembers the experience well. "We were welcomed into this beautiful home and then shown to a large sauna. When we were all relaxed in the hot steam, the doctor opened the door to announce that his wife was about to bring wine and refreshments."

Where were the towels? Chalk it up to another cultural learning experience about life in Finland.

When Todd enthusiastically told me of this special international stay, it brought back memories of my first visit to a Finnish cabin in the woods on a lake shore. It was from the hot sauna into the frozen lake through a hole chopped in the ice . . . and back to the hot sauna. The dramatic experienced seemed normal to my Finnish friends.

The Finns never lost their appetite for learning about Canadian hockey and the ways of the Viking Cup. For the last seven Viking Cups, the Finnish Ice Hockey Federation sent its national U18 team to participate and, before that, the TPS Turku junior team participated twice (winning the first time), and the IFK Junior Helsinki and Kärpät Junior from Oulu participated once. In addition, the Federation sent representatives, including manager Marita Leskinen and national coach Erkka Westerlund (later to become national team head coach), to observe and garner ideas for tournament play in Finland. They are masters of their game but, like their fine education system, are also in a state of readiness to improve and learn more.

The Finns were never short of good hockey players, yet the prospect of a few Canadians playing amongst their own was good strategy for understanding the Canadian system.

Following Viking Cup '86, CLC Viking Pat Ryan was recruited to play in Forssa, Finland. The Finns were good judges of talent. Pat was an all-star forward in Viking Cup '86, and he still holds the ACAC record for most goals in one season: thirty-six (in a twenty-four-game schedule).

"I was scouted at this tournament by the Finnish team and then played three years in Finland," Pat recalls. "I was twenty-two and my team, Imatra Ketterä, were playing against the Helsinki Jokerit when they brought this kid up from Junior who I was told would be a superstar in the NHL. His name was Teemu Selänne and he was only sixteen! I was honoured to play against him and so many of the great stars of Finland and other European countries."

Others from Camrose played in Finland as well, such as Ken Lovsin, Josh Green, and Karl Stollery as well as former Viking Dan Wilson's son, Jared Wilson.

The Finns are students of the game, but they are also teachers, and they have taught us much. In 1987, I attended the U18 European Championships, hosted by Finland in the city of Jyväskylä, again with great facilities and a well-known university next door. It was one of the many tournaments in Europe I attended to garner new ideas for future Viking Cups. The mother of Teppo Numminen (Winnipeg, Phoenix, Buffalo) was an official of the university and introduced me to their fine programs in the physical education department. Finland sport relates closely to their education system.

Fifteen years after Wahlsten and Virta led the Turku, Finland team to gold in the first Viking Cup, the Finnish national U18 team, led by Coach Rauno Korpi and MVP Olli Jokinen, won gold at Viking Cup '96 with an amazing, well-balanced team of skill and toughness.

A Rising Star: Olli Jokinen

Talented players adapt to different situations with ease and Olli was one who made the adjustments. "It was the first time I ever played in North American rinks. The rink in Camrose is very small—one of the smallest I ever played on—but I liked playing there."

The Viking Cup also afforded the Kuopio, Finland, native the chance to experience life in a north american home. "It was pretty nice. I didn't speak English that well. I learned English in LA (Kings). I also stayed with a family. I have only good memories of the Viking Cup. It's a fine tournament."

After Viking Cup '96, Olli participated in the 1997 World Junior Championships before being taken in the first round by the LA Kings (third overall) in the 1997 entry draft. After becoming the first Viking Cup participant to be drafted in the top three, life was a blur for the Viking Cup '96 tournament MVP.

> It went fast. We won the Elite League in Finland. Then we won the World Junior Championships and finished second at the World Championships. Then I was in the NHL.

> Olli has a fondness for northern Alberta. "It's nice to come to Edmonton. I saw my first NHL game when I was here for the [Viking Cup] tournament. My heroes were Jari Kurri and Esa Tikkanen. They played there."

Finnish people are loyal to their country and their teams. It was not uncommon to see Tikkanen, Kurri, or other Finnish players with the Edmonton Oilers, supporting their home country team at the Viking Cup.

Olli Jokinen had an amazing career with seven different NHL teams, finally retiring as a Florida Panther in 2017. He played in numerous World Championships and Olympic Games as a leader with the Finnish national team.

Viking Cup '96 coach, Rauno Korpi, had a distinguished coaching career in the Extra Liiga, primarily in Tampere. He became head coach of the national team in the '96–97 season and coached the national team in the '98 Olympics. He was chosen coach of the year in the Finnish Extra Liiga on two occasions and was inducted into Finland's Ice Hockey Hall of Fame in 2004–05.

Coach Korpi had this to say in his greeting in the *Viking Cup '96* magazine: "The Viking Cup is one of the main preparatory tournaments for our national U18 team. For most Finnish players, this cup is going to be the first experience with hockey in Canada. Talented Finnish youngsters are highly motivated to play in a Canadian-size rink, and especially against the home teams of good calibre. The whole Finnish team is eager to show its strength in your famous Viking Cup. Each of us wants to learn to play better hockey and to become familiar with other cultures. We want to show the spirit of courage and fair play as the right image of the whole international hockey family. Many warm greetings from Finland and thousands of thanks for your invitation to have the possibility to play in the homeland of great hockey!"

Cultural Environment

Camrose became part of the international hockey family at the Viking Cup, and Team Finland was always valued members. It was never a problem to find billets for the Finnish teams and succession billeting (repeats) was the norm. Many great stories of family living experiences at the Viking Cup are still being told on both sides of the ocean. Verlyn Olson, chair of the original host committee, reflects on those days. "We and our visitors lived together in a state of sport and Canadian cultural immersion . . . and we enjoyed the experience."

"Hi, mom, it's me!"

Cindy and Pat Trautman first billeted for Viking Cup '98. Everyone had been encouraging them to try it, so they decided 1998 would be a great time. Their boys Justin and Jordan, aged nine and five, were the right age. They were assigned two players from Finland, Ossi Väänänen and Marco Ahosilta. The following year, their family drove to Winnipeg for the 1999 World Juniors with the John Brown family (also billets) because Ossi was playing at the tournament and his parents had made the trip from Finland, as well. They were staying in the same hotel as the team and spent a few evenings with the coaching staff, sharing stories and getting to know them. Most of the staff had been to the Viking Cup in Camrose the previous year.

For Viking Cup 2000, the Trautmans billeted Kari Lehtonen and Mikko Kankaanperä. At Viking Cup 2002, they billeted Hannu Toivonen and Jaakko Viljanen, and at Viking Cup 2004, Petteri Wirtanen, Vesa Kulmala, and Miika Lahti. The final tournament in 2006 brought the family two goalies: Niko Hovinen and Riku Helenius, Cindy Trautman recalls.

> Every player we billeted gave us lasting memories and we enjoyed every one of them. The friendships lasted much longer than the two weeks they spent with us. Pat and I visited Finland in 2003, we spent time in Hämeenlinna, Finland, with Hannu Toivonen and his family, then travelled to Helsinki and spent time with Ossi Väänänen's parents. Hannu was drafted twenty-ninth by the Boston Bruins in 2002. We made a couple trips to visit him during the hockey season in Boston. Many times, I would answer my phone to hear his voice at the other end saying, 'Hi, Mom, it's me'!

Hannu returned to the Trautmans' home for a week-long visit one summer, and they took him on a quadding trip. He said, "I really need to buy one of these machines when I get back to Finland." And he did, Cindy remembers. He bought two for his cottage!

Ossi made sure the family could come to the Oilers games when he played with the Phoenix Coyotes, by whom he was drafted in the second round. He played in the NHL for nine years—Phoenix, Colorado, Philadelphia, and Vancouver.

The Viking Cup's 2006 magazine has a feature article on Kari Lehtonen—the touted goalie of Viking Cup 2000. Kari was the highest-drafted European goaltender in the history of the draft, being the number-two draft by the Atlanta Thrashers in 2002. He played thirteen seasons in the NHL, nine of which were with the Dallas Stars. On the international scene, he was the top goalie in the 2007 World Championships, and he played for Finland in the Sochi Olympics in 2014.

Kari comments: "I was talking to a few scouts before, but after the Viking Cup, there was more attention." The best goaltender in the 2002 World Junior Championships made his NHL debut on March 19, 2004, against Florida, "It was an amazing feeling … one dream come true."

"He was quiet and shy," Cindy remembered. "We definitely saw where he was going when he stepped on the ice!"

Living on a Canadian farm was a new experience for Kari. "It was fun on the farm," he said. "I had never seen anything like it; it was a new thing for me. I had no exposure to rural life. On our 'farm,' the pets are inside."

The Trautmans had a dog, cats, cows, and horses, and Kari enjoyed them all. Kari is from Helsinki, where the weather is like Vancouver in the winter—cloudy and misty. "They are just amazed at how blue our skies are and how much sunshine we get during the winter time," Cindy said. "Most of the players didn't speak English well, especially when they first came. Then they warm up and try. At the end, I told Kari, 'You speak better English than you thought you did.'"

Kari had nothing but kind things to say about his stay in Camrose. "It was a great experience for us," he said. "There are great fans and competition at the Viking Cup. I have a lot of good memories of my time in Canada [at the Viking Cup]."

Through the years, the Trautmans have watched Kari mature and develop. "When we went out for supper after a Dallas Stars game in Edmonton, and he was much more open and talkative than he was before. That is the icing on the cake," noted Cindy.

Finnish Hockey Players or Christmas Presents

Dave and Rita Giles have billeted players from several countries on eight different occasions, including Finnish players Mikko Koivu (Minnesota), Jani Rita (Oilers) and Valtteri Filppula (Detroit).

> The very first time we gave our kids a choice: we will either have Christmas presents OR billet Viking Cup players. Our kids Kelly 8, Chris 10, and Lisa 13 at the time, all chose to billet!" It was a great choice - We all enjoyed it so much! ... I still have my Finnish Jersey…RITA #22.

Mikko Koivu was drafted sixth overall by the Minnesota Wild in 2001. His home club in Finland is TPS (Turku), the same team that won the first Viking Cup. He is the brother of Saku Koivu, former long-time captain of the Montreal Canadiens. Mikko played for the Wild for sixteen years and became captain in 2009. He played for Team Finland in six World Championships and two Olympics and was captain when Finland won gold at the Worlds in 2011.

Jani Rita was drafted thirteenth overall by the Edmonton Oilers in 1999. He spent six years in the Oilers organization and one year with Pittsburgh before returning to play in Europe.

Valtteri Filppula was drafted in the third round by Detroit in 2002. He has played nine seasons with the Red Wings, four with Tampa, two with Philadelphia, and one with the Islanders.

The World Came to Visit

Liz and Rob Rolf billeted three times and they all had lots of laughs. "We are so happy for our kids to be a part of this. Lifetime friendships developed. It was our holiday at home!"

Guests of the Rolfs were: '02: Ville Mäntymaa and Jarkko Immonen; '04: Teemu Laakso, Jarmo Jokila, and Henri Heino; and in '06: Robert Nyholm and Jaako Pellinen.

"Ville [Anaheim draft] was gregarious; Jarkko [Dallas draft] enjoyed the social experience; Teemu [Nashville draft] was the best defenseman in the tournament. They all had their unique personalities and skills. They jokingly called Kelly, our daughter '*Kilipukin*,' which means billy goat! Ville made a small poster and put it on her door. We still have the cowbell with Finnish logos that we took to every game to cheer!"

"They were really dedicated to their training and meals/food schedule. But when one boy said he was allergic to fish, he meant he didn't like fish!"

"The coach's training plan was to run at 5 a.m. He obviously didn't know conditions in the country as the roads were pitch dark at that time. They ran anyway, with coyotes howling and cattle bawling as they ran by!"

"One dressed up like Clint Eastwood."

Barb and Bruce Stroh delayed their Christmas celebrations so that we could include their billets. They had Finnish kids at four different tournaments. "Since we had two girls about the same age, it was easy to keep them occupied! One dressed up like Clint Eastwood for a New Year's celebration. They left a Finnish jersey for us. One cried when he left. We so enjoyed them."

"Now was the time to celebrate."

Tuukka Rask, premier goaltender of the Boston Bruins, stayed with Dr. John Stuart and his family at Viking Cup 2004. He was crazy for John's special spaghetti sauce recipe, and ate a lot of it. He was very competitive, dedicated, feisty, and always wanted to win. And they did!

"Tuukka was so focused on the games at hand, but when the final buzzer sounded and the Finns won gold, he turned to me," John recalled. "I was standing behind the net, and he victoriously pumped his arm in the air. The message was: we, together, had won. He knew I was there. Now was the time to celebrate! Tuukka was the tournament MVP—a real winner, he is!"

Toronto drafted Rask in the first round in 2004, but before ever playing with the Maple Leafs he was traded to the Boston Bruins in a very lopsided trade that favoured the Bruins. He recorded a 4–2 victory over the Leafs in his very first NHL victory, and in his 500th game with the Bruins he recorded another 4–2 victory over the Leafs (October 2019). Tuukka and the Bruins won the Stanley Cup in 2011, and he won the Vezina Trophy as the top goaltender in the NHL in 2014. He holds the goaltending record with the Bruins for most games played, most wins, and most shutouts. He won bronze with Team Finland in the 2014 Olympics.

Finnish Hockey Leaves Its Mark on the Viking Cup

Finland won the Viking Cup three times, more than any other country or team. In 2019, Finland won gold at both the World Junior and World Senior Ice Hockey Championships, an unbelievable achievement. On the world scene, Finland can always be counted on to have a team worthy of gold. They maximize the potential of every player by playing exceptionally well as a team. They have grit and they never fade. That is what they proudly call "Finnish Sisu."

Finnish ice hockey leaves a high mark of respect and appreciation on the Viking Cup era in Camrose. The quality of play was always superb and the young players adjusted quickly and admirably to their newly adopted Canadian homes. The Finnish people have enjoyed a hard-earned century of independence through resilience, toughness, adaptability, and preparedness. That is the way they play their hockey—and who in the Viking Cup arena would want it any other way?

Finland is the little country that learned how to stand up to giants . . . and win. The Augustana Vikings can identify with that!

Special Recognition

Scotty Bowman may have been the first to scout the Finns at the Viking Cup, but he was not the last. It became normal for every NHL club to send their team of scouts to the Viking Cup and, in the end, they drafted a total of sixty-six players from Finland who'd called Camrose home during their Viking Cup performance.

I recently thought to call Juhani Wahlsten, the legendary coach of the first team to win the Viking Cup, to wish him a happy eightieth birthday. His son Sami provided a contact number but indicated that his dad now had dementia and likely would not remember Camrose. He did say that the TPS organization in Turku had honoured him recently at a game, and that his good friend Scotty Bowman, whom he met at the Viking Cup, brought greetings via the Jumbotron.

Juhani answered the phone in his deep, baritone voice and proceeded to talk Finnish nonstop with noticeable enthusiasm. I said, "I only understand English," but he continued, not appearing to absorb my message. After ten or more minutes of solid Finnish, I managed to say, "Juhani, it has been nice talking to you, but I must go now!" It was then that he said in perfect English, "And how is Simpson?"

Terry Simpson was the coach of the PA Raiders in that final Viking Cup '81 game, and the two rival coaches had become good friends in Camrose. The memories of the Viking Cup were as strong as ever, thirty-nine years later, for this International Hockey Hall of Famer. Juhani Wahlsten is but one of many who still light up with thoughts of the Viking Cup, whether in good or ill health. It is good therapy to relive good memories.

Weeks later, Juhani's son Sami Wahlsten sent me a translation of his father's comments in my last telephone call to him. His last words were: "I am so very happy to be part of Viking Cup history."

Two weeks later, Hannu Virta, MVP of the first Viking Cup, phoned to inform me that Juhani Wahlsten had passed away while riding his bike.

A Tribute to Juhani "Jusso" Wahlsten, 1938–2019

Juhani Wahlsten was a sport teacher by profession. He taught and coached in Finland and abroad, sharing his knowledge and valuable coaching material. He had a vast international network.

Juhani Wahlsten

Juhani Wahlsten played top-level ice hockey in Finland from 1957 to 1971, and in 200 games racked up 219 points. He spent most of his years as a player and coach with TPS Turku, where his number, eight, was retired. He contributed immensely to youth hockey development in his home city of Turku.

As an international player, he represented Finland in 115 international games (thirty-three goals, sixty-two points). In his last playing years in the late '60s, he was captain. He represented Finland in three Olympic Winter Games and five World Championships. After his playing days, he coached abroad, in Austria, Germany, Switzerland, and Spain.

He was inducted into the Finnish Hockey Hall of Fame in 1986, and entered the IIHF Hall of Fame in 2006.

His two sons, Jali and Sami, also played top-level hockey in Finland. Both represented the country at World Junior Championships and they won one championship together, with Jokerit Helsinki, in 1992. Jali played on his father's team, which won gold in Viking Cup '81. Wahlsten met and became lifelong friends with the dean of NHL coaches, Scotty Bowman, at the Viking Cup in Camrose.

Sami Wahlsten on His Father

"My dad would say that the Viking Cup had an important impact in Finnish hockey player development, especially when competing against Canadian teams in a smaller ice surface. Meeting Scotty in Camrose was, for 'Jusso,' a special moment, as they got along with each other—not just professionally but also as humans. My dad's gold medal at the first Viking Cup meant a lot to him."

FINLAND

VIKING CUP PARTICIPANTS WHO PLAYED IN THE WINTER OLYMPICS (AS OF THE CONCLUSION OF 2018 GAMES)

Name	Viking Cup Team	Year(s)	Olympic Team	Year(s)
Valtteri Filppula	Finland	2002	Finland	2010
Jarkko Immonen	Finland	2002	Finland	2010, 2014
Olli Jokinen	Finland	1996	Finland	2002, 2006, 2010, 2014
Niko Kapanen	Finland	1996	Finland	2006, 2010
Joonas Kemppainen	Finland	2006	Finland	2018
Miikka Kiprusoff	Finland	1994	Finland	2010
Mikko Koivu	Finland	2000	Finland	2006, 2010
Kari Lehtonen	Finland	2000	Finland	2006, 2014
Antero Niittymäki	Finland	1998	Finland	2006, 2010
Tuukka Rask	Finland	2004	Finland	2014
Tuomo Ruutu	Finland	2000	Finland	2010, 2014
Ossi Väänänen	Finland	1998	Finland	2002, 2006, 2014
Hannu Virta	TPS	1981	Finland	1994

VIKING CUP PARTICIPANTS SELECTED IN NHL ENTRY OR SUPPLEMENTAL DRAFTS

Player	Viking Cup Team	Year(s)	Selected By	Draft	Round	Overall Selection
Timo Ahmaoja	Finland	1996	Anaheim	1996 Entry	7	172
Marko Ahosilta	Finland	1998	New Jersey	1998 Entry	8	227
Kristian Antila	Finland	1998	Edmonton	1998 Entry	4	113
Tommi Degerman	Finland	2994	Anaheim	1997 Entry	9	235
Valtteri Filppula	Finland	2002	Detroit	2002 Entry	3	95
Juha Gustaffson	Finland	1996	Phoenix	1997 Entry	2	43
Riku Hahl	Finland	1998	Colorado	1999 Entry	6	183
Tommi Hannus	Finland	1998	Los Angeles	1998 Entry	7	190
Riku Helenius	Finland	2006	Tampa Bay	2006 Entry	1	15
Niko Hovinen	Finland	2006	Minnesota	2006 Entry	5	132
Harri Ilvonen	Finland	2006	Minnesota	2007 Entry	6	170
Jarkko Immonen	Finland	2002	Dallas	2002 Entry	4	110
Martti Järventie	Finland	1994	Montreal	2001 Entry	4	109
Jesse Joensuu	Finland	2004	NY Islanders	2006 Entry	2	60
Mikko Jokela	Finland	1998	New Jersey	1998 Entry	4	96
Janne Jokila	Finland	2000	Columbus	2000 Entry	7	200
Olli Jokinen	Finland	1996	Los Angeles	1997 Entry	1	3
Jan-Mikael Juutilainen	Finland	2006	Chicago	2006 Entry	6	156
Mikko Kalteva	Finland	2002	Colorado	2002 Entry	4	107
Markus Kankaanperä	Finland	1998	Vancouver	1999 Entry	8	218
Niko Kapanen	Finland	1996	Dallas	1998 Entry	6	173
Ville Kentala	IFK	1984	NY Rangers	1984 Entry	9	182
Miikka Kiprusoff	Finland	1994	San Jose	1995 Entry	5	116
Toni Koivisto	Finland	2000	Florida	2001 Entry	7	200
Mikko Koivu	Finland	2000	Minnesota	2001 Entry	1	6

Risto Korhonen	Finland	2004	Carolina	2005 Entry	5	159
Arto Kuki	Finland	1994	Montreal	1994 Entry	4	96
Teemu Laakso	Finland	2004	Nashville	2005 Entry	3	78
Arto Laatikainen	Finland	1998	NY Rangers	1999 Entry	7	197
Joonas Lehtivuori	Finland	2006	Philadelphia	2006 Entry	4	101
Joni Lehto	TPS	1988	NY Islanders	1990 Entry	6	111
Kari Lehtonen	Finland	2000	Atlanta	2002 Entry	1	2
Joni Lindlöf	Finland	2002	Washington	2002 Entry	7	209
Tero Määttä	Finland	2000	San Jose	2000 Entry	2	41
Tuukka Mäkelä	Finland	2000	Boston	2000 Entry	3	66
Ville Mäntymaa	Finland	2002	Anaheim	2003 Entry	9	280
Ilkka Mikkola	Finland	1996	Montreal	1997 Entry	3	65
Antero Niittymäki	Finland	1998	Philadelphia	1998 Entry	6	168
Mika Noronen	Finland	1996	Buffalo	1997 Entry	1	21
Kai Nurminen	TPS	1988	Los Angeles	1996 Entry	8	193
Robert Nyholm	Finland	2006	Columbus	2006 Entry	5	129
Esa Palosaari	Kärpät	1986	Winnipeg	1986 Entry	3	50
Tuomas Pihlman	Finland	2000	New Jersey	2001 Entry	2	48
Juuso Puustinen	Finland	2006	Calgary	2006 Entry	5	149
Tommi Rajamäki	Finland	1994	Toronto	1994 Entry	7	178
Tuukka Rask	Finland	2004	Toronto	2005 Entry	1	21
Jani Rita	Finland	1998	Edmonton	1999 Entry	1	13
Tuomo Ruutu	Finland	2000	Chicago	2001 Entry	1	9
Timo Seikkula	Finland	1996	Pittsburgh	1996 Entry	10	238
Markus Seikola	Finland	2000	Toronto	2000 Entry	7	209
Niko Snellman	Finland	2006	Nashville	2006 Entry	4	105
Eero Somervuori	Finland	1996	Tampa Bay	1997 Entry	7	170
Hannu Toivonen	Finland	2002	Boston	2002 Entry	1	29
Miikka Tuomainen	Finland	2004	Atlanta	2004 Entry	7	204
Ossi Väänänen	Finland	1998	Phoenix	1998 Entry	2	43
Tomek Valtonen	Finland	1998	Detroit	1998 Entry	2	56
Timo Vertala	Finland	1996	Montreal	1996 Entry	7	181
Hannu Virta	TPS	1981	Buffalo	1981 Entry	2	38
Teppo Virta	TPS	1981	NY Islanders	1981 Entry	7	147
Jari Viuhkola	Finland	1998	Chicago	1998 Entry	6	158
Juha Vuorivirta	Finland	1994	Los Angeles	1995 Entry	7	163
Jali Wahlsten	TPS	1981	Minnesota	1981 Entry	2	41
Max Wärn	Finland	2006	Dallas	2006 Entry	5	150
Petteri Wirtanen	Finland	2004	Anaheim	2006 Entry	6	172

Ice Ages, by Keith Harder (Viking Cup 2000)

CHAPTER 6

Open the Curtain . . . Czechoslovakia (Czech Republic and Slovakia) Connections

In 1946, Winston Churchill coined the term "Iron Curtain" to describe the division of Europe into a Communist East and a free West. This marked the beginning of the Cold War, which dominated the world for the next four decades. During this time, the course of ice hockey in Czechoslovakia was reset.

It is not this chapter's purpose to discuss political developments behind the Iron Curtain in any detail, but a few guideposts will help give some understanding of the close connection of ice hockey to a political system of turbulence and rigid control. More importantly, it will provide a pathway into Czechoslovakia ice hockey's unique partnership in the Viking Cup.

Ice Hockey in Czechoslovakia: Pre-Cold War

In December 1986, the Augustana Vikings were guests of the Czechoslovakia Ice Hockey Federation in a series of games in and around České Budějovice (the original home of Budweiser beer), near the Austrian border.

While the Vikings were in a training session at the city ice stadium, I walked back to our hotel (Gomel), accompanied by Miro, our capable host and interpreter. As we walked near a playground and tributary to the Vltava River, he said to me, "That is where the first hockey game with Canada was played. I think it was about 1924, and Canada won, 23 to 0. Canada taught us how to play hockey. Now Canada is back to our city."

I noticed that there was ice only around the edges of the river, so said, "They must have played on thin ice."

He said, "Our winters are much shorter than yours. Sometimes, there is no ice. You can be sure, wherever there is ice, Czechoslovaks will be playing hockey. They love the game. It is a big part of our culture. It stems from bandy, which was once our most popular game. Some young hockey players play both sports." In English, bandy hockey, a game which may have originated in England, was sometimes also called shinny.

I asked Miro about his regular job. He said, "I am an English teacher, but I have no students. That means I can be with a Canadian hockey team today. Now, all students must take Russian." This was to affirm Soviet control.

Later, in Prague, central to Czechoslovakia, I learned that natural ice seldom lasts more than a few weeks at a time in a normal winter and that the first artificial ice arena was built there in 1930, to host the World Ice Hockey Championships in 1933.

By comparison to other world hockey powers in pre-war days—Canada, Russia, Sweden, and Finland—Czechoslovakia is the only central European hockey power with this diminished possibility for hockey development on natural ice. They have relied heavily upon their few ice hockey indoor arenas, now 271 (Czech Republic and Slovakia; Canada has 3,300), human resources and a close government-sport partnership that has sent them into the elite circle of world hockey powers.

Where the remarkable American victory over Russia in the Lake Placid Olympics of 1980 is known as the "Miracle on Ice," Czechoslovakia ice hockey achievements should then surely be considered even greater: "the miracle without ice."

The Czechoslovakia Ice Hockey Federation was a founding member of the IIHF in 1908. It was not long before the Czechs were strong competitors, winning the European Ice Hockey Championships in 1911, 1912, and 1914.

The Czechs and Slovaks have always looked to Canada with admiration and appreciation when it comes to hockey. In pre-WWII war years, Canada made significant contributions in leadership to upgrade their level and style of play, and the Czechs have never forgotten.

Canadian Leadership: Mike Buckna, Trail Smoke Eaters

In 1934, Mike Buckna of the BC Trail Smoke Eaters visited his parents' homeland and ended up in the dual role of playing and coaching LTC Praha and the Czechoslovakian national team. He led that team to European Championships in 1938 and 1939. Thereafter, he returned to Trail due to German occupation and was offered a contract with the Chicago Blackhawks, but chose to resume his career in Trail instead.

In 1946, Buckna returned to post-war Prague to direct the entire Czech hockey system. He resumed his head coaching position with the national team and led them to gold at the World Championships in Prague in 1947, and in Stockholm in 1948. That same year, they won silver in the Olympics, losing only to Canada.

Buckna was inducted into the BC Sports Hall of Fame in 1989, and the IIHF Hall of Fame in 2004, in the builder category. In 1978, Buckna was introduced as the "father of Czech ice hockey," when he was a guest of the Czechoslovakia Ice Hockey Federation" (Trail Historical Society). Indeed, Trail was pivotal in Canada's great contributions to Czechoslovakia's hockey ascent to a position of number two in the world by mid-century.

What a thrill it was then for the Czechoslovakian U18 national team to visit Trail in 1990, as part of their pre-Viking Cup tour. Even more significant, the outstanding goalie of the 1956 Trail Smoke Eaters, who had won gold in Prague, the "masked marvel," Seth Martin, was there to welcome the team. Martin had developed a fibreglass mask and he became the first goaltender in international competition to wear that piece of equipment. Glenn Hall, Mr. Goalie, with the St. Louis Blues was wearing a Martin-made mask when Bobby Orr of the Boston Bruins scored his famous winning goal in the 1970 Stanley Cup playoffs.

Seth Martin was inducted into the IIHF Hall of Fame in 1997.

Don Falk and Petr Mirejovsky, Viking Cup hosts for the touring Czechoslovakians, recall the thrill of the visit to Trail and the reunion with Seth Martin.

> The coaches of the Czech team recognized Seth Martin and were ecstatic. As young men, the coaches had seen Seth Martin in Czechoslovakia, where he was the first goalie to wear a mask. They recognized him as the "masked marvel." Sadly, they did not get to meet Mike Buckna, who was still living in Trail at the time.

Inspired by Canadian hockey and a unique love of the game, Czechoslovakia dominated ice hockey in Europe during the first half of the twentieth century.

Even today, Czechoslovakia has participated in more ice hockey World Championships than any other nation. Participation ceased during Nazi occupation until 1945, but following WWII, ice hockey played an enormous role in helping Czechoslovakia weather turbulent storms on the "other side" of the Iron Curtain.

New Settlements Post-WWII

Shortly after crossing the Czech–German border on our trip to Europe in December of 1993, the Augustana Vikings hockey team entered the Czech city of Plzeň. There, we were met by members of the Martin Straka family, who invited Darryl and Ruth Phillips in our group to visit their home near Plzeň the next day. The Phillips had billeted Martin in Camrose at Viking Cup '90, and the Pittsburgh Penguins had drafted Martin that spring in the first round.

We met Martin's grandfather and he shared some of his memories of the war. After all those years, it seemed that the memories were still crystal clear. "We were just inside the American zone when the war ended," he told us. "The Russian forces had advanced within a few kilometres up the road. Occasionally, we would take cookies to the American soldiers in their camp just beside our farm, but only if it was a quiet day on the front. We were just on the line separating the Americans from the Red Army (the Karlovy Vary–Plzeň–České Budějovice line) when the liberation from Nazi rule took place on May 9, 1945."

Of course, the curtain was not built on that line, but along the German border, leaving all of Czechoslovakia in the Russian-controlled zone. The Strakas lamented about being assigned to the eastern side when they thought they would be part of the West.

What started out as a barbed-wire fence was fortified over and over and heavily controlled by soldiers and guard dogs, making an escape to the West next to impossible. On each of many trips across this border, the Augustana Vikings came face to face with the reality of the Iron Curtain and what it meant to be locked on the other side.

Vikings coach Mike Johnston recalls his most indelible experience in crossing the Iron Curtain.

> We were to cross the Czech border late at night from a small German town. We had issues with our bus and had been later leaving [the Frankfurt airport] than originally anticipated. When we arrived at the 'check point' or border crossing, I will never forget the players' expression as they looked out the window. There was a row of barbed-wire fencing as far as we could see on both sides of the bus. Walking along the fence were armed guards with dogs. We were told by our guide that they would shoot immediately if anyone came within fifty yards of the fence.
>
> There was about a foot of snow covering the ground, and you could see the footprints of the dogs and guards who had walked the line over the course of the day. Just in front of the bus were two guards, who approached and asked for our papers and passports. There was no casual conversation—their faces were stone cold as they told everyone to get off the bus and wait in the holding room. Well, from what I remember, this was a concrete room with benches along the walls and it was as cold inside as out. After about forty-five minutes, I became impatient and was worried because our guys seemed nervous and scared. I asked our guide what he thought. He just motioned to be patient and said there was nothing he could do, which now made me really nervous.
>
> In the end, we got back on the bus after what seemed like hours and, to a man, we were so thankful that we lived in a free country and were not bound by walls and barbed wire.

The Communist takeover of Czechoslovakia and the people's recourse through ice hockey is described by John Soares in an article entitled "Complexity in Soviet-Czechoslovak Hockey Relations," in *The (Inter-Communist) Cold War on Ice*:

> After a short-lived effort at self-government with substantial communist participation after World War II, Czechoslovakia was reduced to a single-party dictatorship in February 1948. What the West denounced as the "Czechoslovakia coup," the Prague regime celebrated as "Victorious February." Hockey, though, offered a number of indicators that many Czechoslovaks shared the Western view. Because it was hard to penetrate genuine public opinion in closed societies, embassy observers looked for a variety of ways to understand what the Czechoslovak people were thinking. And a sport of such importance in the country was one means of doing so.
>
> Czechoslovakian hockey fans manifested their unhappiness in many ways.

Czechoslovakia won the first post-war World Ice Hockey Championship, which took place in Prague. Canada did not participate. In 1949, Czechoslovakia won again, in Stockholm, but this time Canada did play. It was the first time a European team had won the World Championships with Canada as a participant. Players were hailed as national heroes on their return to Prague. It looked like another golden age for Czechoslovakian ice hockey was about to begin.

The situation, however, was quite different a year later, when the World Championships were scheduled for the United Kingdom. The Communist regime had experienced defections in other sports and there were rumours of possible defections in the high-profile sport of ice hockey, which offered the possibility of professional employment in the free world.

The story of what followed was deemed of such significance that it was included in the top 100 hockey stories of all time as part of the centennial celebrations of the IIHF in 2008. It also serves to give Viking Cup followers some context and understanding of why there was never a Czechoslovakian player defection at the Viking Cup during those Cold War years.

The gripping story, #48, is recorded as follows:

Czechoslovakian Team Jailed for Treason—An Entire Generation Lost

March 11, 1950 – Prague, Czechoslovakia

Czechoslovakia was the best national team in the world in the years following World War II. The team won the 1947 and 1949 World Championships and lost the 1948 Olympic gold to Canada only on goal differential.

But it was their own people, driven by conspiracy theories in Stalinist Czechoslovakia, who prevented this great team from defending its title at the 1950 World Championship in London, England. Just before the national squad was about to board the plane for Great Britain, on March 11, 1950, the players were handcuffed by the national state security police (KNB, Czechoslovakian forerunner to the KGB) and taken to jail.

Seven months later, on October 7, the players appeared in court accused of attempting to defect and were charged with treason. The security police presented "intelligence information" about plans to defect in Great Britain during the World Championship. The main argument was the information that, in December 1948, the players of LTC Praha (most of whom played for the national team) had discussed the option of defecting in Switzerland after the annual Spengler Cup tournament in Davos.

Yes, there had been earlier defections by Czechoslovakian hockey players to the West, but none of the accused players had ever seriously considered taking this step, although they had their chances. They could have stayed in Sweden after the 1949 World Championship or in Vienna, where they prepared for the 1950 event in London. The players, of course, pleaded not guilty.

Needless to say, their fate was pre-determined by authorities who ruled the totalitarian regime, and twelve were sent to jail. The players were labelled "state traitors".

Goaltender Bohumil Modry was sentenced to 15 years in prison; forward Gustav Bubnik to 14 years; forward Stanislav Konopasek got 12; Vaclav Rozinak and Vladimir Kobranov each got 10; and, Josef Jirka got six years. Six other players were given sentences ranging from eight months to three years: Mojmir Ujcik, Zlatko Cerveny, Jiri Macelis, Premysl Hajny, Antonin Spaninger and Josef Stock.

Modry, the best goaltender in Europe of that era, died in 1963, at the age of 47, from prison-related complications. Most of the players were released after five years, but their lives and families were shattered. So was a great hockey team. Czechoslovakia would have to wait 23 years, until 1972, before they won another World Championship.

The first golden generation of Czechoslovak hockey thus ended up in uranium mines at Jáchymov.

In an interview years later, star player and fan favourite Gustav Bubník was asked the question: What was it like in prison? Could you summarize what comes to mind when you hear Jáchymov?

"A huge amount of suffering of the best people who were Czechoslovakians, or people who followed their convictions and belief took place here. They were people who knew what Communism was and fought against it. I think that Jáchymov was the suffering of a nation that can never be forgotten."

Upon their release from prison in 1955, Bubnik and Roziňák were scheduled to play in a non-league game, where 2,000 spectators would normally be expected. When 7,000 showed up, officials panicked and disqualified the two players from the game.

The "little lion" of international hockey and the pride of the country had been tamed by a hostile government of fear and mistrust. What better way to establish the police state than to use high-profile ice hockey players to forcefully set the consequences of non-compliance?

The messaging was clear; the crown (coin) had landed with the tarnished side up.

After the fall of Communism, Augustin Bubník was elected to parliament. He was also directly involved in welcoming the Augustana Vikings to the Czech Republic in the late '90s. Augustana Vikings team leader of the 1994–95 tour Verlyn Olson enthusiastically remembers his time with Bubník. "He invited me to his home for New Year's so I got to meet his family, see all kinds of interesting keepsakes, and hear his amazing life story. What a great time."

During this tumultuous time, a young boy named Petr was growing up in Prague, trying to make sense of the fearful messages coming his way. There were Communist propaganda announcements on the streets about enemies of the state, their confessions and concentration camp/jail terms, playground chatter about star hockey players in uranium mines, and kitchen-table talk with his father (pastor), mother, and brother.

"Where is my favourite hockey team? And my favourite players like Modry and Bubník? Why did they not play in the championships?"

Like other children of this harsh, secretive era, Petr grew up in a strong family unit. He was guarded from the rest of society for fear of secretive police state informers where fate was so often that of recrimination. Later, in the Prague Spring, as we shall see, Petr pursued a crack in the daunt-ing Iron Curtain as so many longed to do.

Verlyn Olson and Gustav Bubnik

Petr recalls his "growing up" days in Czechoslovakia.

Canada from the Outside, by Petr of Prague (today)

I imagine many of you know much more about Canada than I do, and you may even know more about how the rest of the world looks from here. However, you may not have seen this country the way I saw it when I was a young boy—from the outside, and from quite aways away.

From Czechoslovakia, where I was growing up, Canada looked pure and unspoiled, perhaps a bit on the cold side, and very, very far away. Certainly, far from the problems that plagued our daily lives. For me, Canada then was the land of the great silent wilderness, populated by Indigenous people, hunters, prospectors, and other exciting characters, and all those wonderful wild creatures described so well by Ernest Thompson Seton, James Oliver Curwood, and Jack London in their gripping tales of adventure. For Czech speakers, it was also a land characterized by a peculiar sense of humour. In Czech, a "Canadian joke" is the same as a practical joke. I do not know why, and trying to figure that out would take us somewhere we do not want to go anyway. Besides, other than the land of the wolf hunters, Canada was, for me and for most of my friends, the land of hockey.

Many Czechs and most kids my age loved hockey, as well. We all played it, mostly on natural ice. As a result, given the climate in our part of the world, even before the onset of global warming, we tended to have not one but several hockey seasons each winter. Most of us, myself included, were not very good, but we played with enthusiasm. The high point of the hockey season was always the World Championship. Ever since the 1950s, the lineups were generally the same: the Swedes, the Soviets, Czechoslovakia, of course, as well as America and Canada.

We rooted for the home team. It was easy, as it tended to do reasonably well much of the time. Television was still young then, few people had TV sets at home, the screens were small and the picture lousy. Most of us followed the games on the radio anyway. It trained our imagination. Losing against Sweden or America was tough, as was losing to Canada, but, hey, we all knew even then that it was Canada's game! But the games against the Russians were a different kettle of fish. That is where emotions and passions, both pure and impure, became involved—big time! Officially, we were of course assured that the Soviets were Czechoslovakia's best friends and protectors. In private, however, most had strong doubts on that score. As a result, the games against the Soviets were invariably grudge matches. Certainly, for us little fans, for our parents, and, apparently, for the players, as well.

By that time, the Soviet national teams were good. Indeed, they were very good— excellent, even! But in the heat of the battles on the ice, few of us were ready to notice it, let alone admit as much.

I do not think I ever knew anyone who had actually been to any of the champion- ship games. Travelling to games played abroad was not an option. Very few people in Czechoslovakia were allowed to travel, and the games played at home were out of my reach, as well. The tickets were hard to get, and very expensive to boot. I did get to go to a few of the regular hockey league games; they were then still played in a stadium, which was only about two or three stone throws from where we lived—but World Championship games might as well have been played on the far side of the moon. However, I do remember the moment when I first saw the team representing the Land of the Maple Leaf! They were hard to miss.

I was walking along one of the main streets in Prague when, suddenly, I noticed a group of men wearing absolutely outlandish coats. They were white with black, yellow, red, and green stripes! Who in their right mind would ever think of putting something like that on! And in public! Then someone told me that they were

Canadian hockey players, and that their team was called Trail Smoke Eaters. It was only much later that I realized their coats were made from Hudson's Bay blankets, and that they probably also helped to make sure that no one got lost in what for them certainly might have appeared to be a dangerous place populated by Communists. At the time, I figured some of that smoke they ate must have affected their fashion sense.

The Trail Smoke Eaters were in Prague for the Hockey World Championship of 1961. They beat Czechoslovakia, which was tough, but we could take it, because our team beat the Soviets. There was a three-way tie for the gold. Czechoslovakia lost out, but in the final game, the Smoke Eaters trounced the Soviets 5-1, which made many of us very, very happy.

Trail Smoke Eaters were the last Canadian club team to represent Canada in hockey World Championships. After that came the national teams put together by Father Bauer. Nothing against Father Bauer, but I missed those club teams with their unique, extravagant, and, for us kids in faraway Czechoslovakia, ever-so-exotic names.

Little did I know that, in a few years, I would get to see the smoke coming out of the huge Cominco smelter in Trail in person, so to say, and that, a few years after that, thanks to the Viking Cup, I would get to go to a game in the Trail Smoke Eaters arena, and get to see Seth Martin and his goalie mask that our hockey announcer back home in Prague had talked about so much. And that it was the home of Mike Buckna, the man so admired by those of us growing up in Czechoslovakia in the 1950s, who had done so much for hockey in my Old Country.

Prague Spring 1967–69

While the Czechoslovakian team had been weakened and relegated to lower standings behind the powerful Russians of the '60s and '70s, the Czech people never lost hope that someday their national team would return to glory. To a Czech, that meant defeating the Russians whom many regarded as invaders.

Following the death of Josef Stalin in 1953, there was a glimmer of hope that Russian leaders might soften their clutch on power. In 1968, Alekander Dubček, the reformist Czechoslovak leader, came to power under the mantle "socialism with a human face." However, Moscow considered the proposed changes too radical and, after "reading the riot act," removed Dubček and other reformers from power through military invasion on August 21, 1968. The 1968 thaw was short-lived and once again Czechoslovakia returned to hard-line Communism.

By this time, young Petr of Prague had worked hard and graduated from university. Thanks to the Prague Spring, he and his brother had applied to do post-graduate work at different universities abroad. Petr was accepted by the University of Alberta. He was supposed to fly to Montreal from Prague in late August.

Petr continues his story: *A few days before our flight could happen, Soviet tanks rolled in. The Prague airport was taken over by Soviet military transports, and what should have been a routine, if exciting, journey turned into a real adventure. My brother and I persuaded a Dutch friend with a car to take us across the border. It was not very far, only about a hundred miles, but these were not normal times. A combination of Russian roadblocks and rumours convinced us to give up the idea of driving west to the border of West Germany. Instead, we were told to turn south and east toward Austria, where the crossing was supposed to be easier and safer.*

It might have been safer, but the border crossing was farther, and more difficult to reach. Some roads were blocked by the Russians, other roads were blocked by Czechs trying to make life difficult for the Russians. There were a few scary moments. The scariest one was the most surreal. The vehicle was moving along a narrow country road, which was not even marked on the map they were using then. Suddenly, a dark shape appeared in front of us! We were sure it must be a tank. It had the shape, and the two headlights. It was getting closer. There was no way of getting off the road safely; there were deep ditches on both sides. Stories about Russian tanks driving over cars in the streets of Prague were fresh in our minds. Would he stop? Would he give way? And if he didn't, what should we do? The car slowed down to a crawl. The tank showed no signs of giving way. You could cut the tension inside the little VW Beetle with a knife. But then, when all seemed lost, there was a bend in the road, and what we as nervous travellers believed was a Soviet tank turned out to be a house, some distance away from the road, with its two windows shining in the gathering darkness.

Our small car with its three occupants eventually made it to the border, only to be told that one of us, my brother Jan, would not be allowed to cross. He apparently needed one more stamp in his passport. The customs people assured us that in Prague he would be able to get that stamp right away, but they could not give it to him, and they were unable to let him go—orders, regulations, you know. . . . We were at a loss. . . . What to do next! Going all the way back to Prague only to race back to the border was not a welcome prospect, besides, what would the Russians do in the meantime? Would they be closing the border? And if they closed it, when would it open again? In a few days? In a year? Ever?

But then we recognized a person travelling in a vehicle that was being processed in the next lane. It was my friend from trade school who was travelling with a family consisting of a father, a mother, and two little boys. Their small car was loaded to the gills with clothing and other useful things. Before leaving Prague, the two men had each taken a swig from a bottle of liquor they had along. Their action was not quite legal; after all, they were driving, but under the circumstances, it was perhaps, understandable. They then passed the bottle to the lady, who was sitting, not very comfortably, in the backseat with the two children. The idea was that she should have a shot of liquor, too—to steady her nerves—and that she would then hide the bottle somewhere amongst the winter coats and all the other odds and ends in the back of the vehicle. But she did not. Nervous as she was, the lady kept the bottle in her lap, and, without thinking, every once in a while, she took small swigs from it all along the way. By the time they reached the border, the small bottle of liquor was empty and the lady was lit up like a Christmas tree!

Every car at the border crossing was being watched over by a soldier, a border guard, submachine gun at the ready. But even gunmen have human emotions, and this one could not help but laugh when the well-dressed, but visibly inebriated, lady waltzed out of the car. Why don't you let him go! Don't you know what's happening, she asked the guard.

"No can do, I have my orders ma'am," was his reply. His orders were to shoot anyone trying to leave the country without proper authorization. However, the guard's logic was no match for this woman's ingenuity.

"Yes, but what if you don't see it?" she asked. She stepped up to the man with the gun, grabbed him by the shoulders, turned him around, and told him: "Do not look!"

The guard laughed and obeyed. In the meantime, the lady took Jan by the hand, pushed him on the back seat of their tiny Fiat 850, covered him with a couple of winter coats, and sat her two sons on top of the new surface. Then she stepped up to the obedient guard, turned him around, and asked him archly, "So, did you see anything?"

He just laughed, and signalled to the other guards that the small blue Fiat 850 was good to go. Two minutes later and a few hundred metres down the road, they were in Austria, and there was a lot of hugging going on.

A few minutes after that, a lone customs official from the other side came to advise the Austrians that the Russians had just arrived on the other side and that the border crossing would henceforth be closed to traffic. What had been Prague Spring turned into a cold, Russian-style winter that lasted over twenty years, until the fall of 1989.

"Petr of Prague" is the same Petr Mirejovsky who soon began a teaching career of forty years at Camrose Lutheran College and Augustana faculty, University of Alberta. He was the lead interpreter and host for all Czechoslovakia hockey teams that participated in the Viking Cup, but was not allowed to return to his native country until the fall of Communism in 1989. Petr was indeed a gift to the Viking Cup from Czechoslovakia.

Rebuilding the Sport

Numerous examples were evident during this time of how the Czechoslovakian people turned to their favourite sport, hockey, to show displeasure in Russian domination. Russian hockey teams took the brunt of the tension.

For example, in the 1967 World Championships in Vienna, which Czechoslovakia lost, 4–2, the game ended in multiple fights. Moreover, the Soviet anthem played during the final ceremony was accompanied by deafening boos and catcalls from the audience. The regime had lifted some of the restrictions on travel to the West, and the 1967 World Championship was the first tournament abroad (and close to the border) at which Czechoslovak spectators could attend and show their emotions. The Communist government response referred to the game as "the scandalous end of the match between the two best friends." The closed system did not allow for open and candid reporting.

Hockey's most important demonstration of Czechoslovak hostility to the USSR came during the 1969 World Championships, the first held after the August 1968 invasion. The IIHF initially scheduled the 1969 championships for Prague, to commemorate the sixtieth anniversary of hockey in Czechoslovakia. But in September 1968, Prague announced that it could not host the tournament because of "technical, economic, and organizational conditions." (The real concern was for crowd behaviour in Czech–USSR games.) When the tournament was held in Stockholm, it had serious political repercussions.

Amazingly, Czechoslovakia defeated the USSR twice during the tournament.

Crowds celebrated the victories in Czechoslovakia with massive street gatherings and chants like "Russians go home!" and "Czechoslovakia: four; Occupation Forces: three!" and "Your tanks can't help you here!"

Other groups demonstrated against the crackdowns and this became a pretext for hard-line Communist leaders to bring an end to any good remnants that remained of the "Prague Spring." Hard-liner Gustáv Husák was appointed to lead the country on Moscow's terms, as now clearly stated in the Moscow Protocol, a document agreed to under duress.

The government once again used hockey as a tool to impose rigid leaders and controls on the Czechoslovakian people.

In the meantime, the mighty Russian hockey machine clearly surpassed and dominated the hockey scene behind the Iron Curtain and, for that matter, in all Europe. From 1963 to 1990, the Russians won twenty World Championships and the Czechs won only four. Clearly, Czechoslovakia had some catching up to do with Russian hockey, which was ready to challenge the bastion of hockey, the NHL.

Hockey Returns to Glory in Czechoslovakia (Polishing the Crown)

In 1994, while on sabbatical leave from Augustana University College to examine pre- and post-revolution (1989) education in the Czech Republic and Slovakia, I included a look at ice hockey as part of the project. My observations and conclusions were based on numerous contacts and visits through the Viking Cup exchange, and many interviews with hockey leaders, including Dr. Vladimír Kostka and Dr. Josef Dovalil, considered Czech hockey system architects; and Miro Šubrt, long-time Czech Ice Hockey Federation representative to the IIHF. Dominik Hašek had been helpful in making arrangements to visit sport-related schools, including his home school in the city of Pardubice. Related to the *new* look at hockey (and other competitive sports) during the '70s and '80s, the following was stated in my concluding remarks, and provides a better understanding of why the Czechoslovakia U18 team participated in the Viking Cup and what they were representing. It was a part of what I refer to as the "polishing of the crown."

> After a rocky beginning, hockey became the poster boy of the Communist government in Czechoslovakia. The peoples' long love affair with hockey and pride in accomplishments in the first half of the century were stronger forces than the punitive measures introduced in the early years of Communism. Under the leadership of Professor Kostka, who also coached the Czechoslovakia national team, from 1962 to 1972, the year they won the World Championship, was a massive education program to train coaches/leaders. From the first class of twenty student coaches in 1951, over a thousand were trained in the sport faculty at Charles University, and by the end of the 1980s, graduates of the program had stepped into leadership positions of the government-supported Czech Ice Hockey Federation. The hockey programs of Canada, Sweden, and Russia were researched thoroughly and worthy concepts and practices incorporated into the 'made-in-Czechoslovakia' development program. Dr. Kostka and others, such as Rudolf Bukac, former coach of the national teams of Czechoslovakia, Austria, and Germany, wrote manuals and published numerous articles giving continuous direction for the numerous young coaches all trained in the Kostka tradition. The program was restoring Czechoslovakian hockey to its former glory days.

In my interviews with Kostka and Dovalil (interpreted by Dr Pavel Soudsky, Czech coach in Viking Cup '86), Dr. Kostka stated, "The good result was good propaganda for the regime," and Dr. Dovalil echoed, "The Communist Party supported the hockey system because of its success—it was to be conveniently considered representative of the success of the Communist system."

In achieving such favour with the Communist regime, the university-led ice hockey program attained an independence and control that few groups ever did in Communist Czechoslovakia. Such favour left little space for free-thinking dissenters to this uniform system. In essence, the national head coach established the system of play, the system of summer training, and the system of winter training, and all coaches accordingly followed the plan.

By the end of the '80s, ice hockey was well established as a dominant force within the Central Sports Committee of the Czechoslovak government. The university visionaries had achieved an enviable position of success and influence and were well rewarded for good results. The sport flourished as its dependence upon rigid government control and finances ever increased. As the poster sport, it helped to open Czechoslovakia to the world.

Czechoslovakia Comes to Canada—Viking Cup '82

The Viking Cup '82 magazine included the following statement: "What do you do with the best seventeen-year-old hockey players in Czechoslovakia? Why, tour Canada, of course."

Here we understand that Czechoslovakian hockey strategy was being launched further into the international sphere, and by 1981, the national U18 team was given government approval to "cross the line" into Canada. They knew they had to play the best to be the best.

Coach Julius Kovac of the first team to participate in the Viking Cup commented, "It is absolutely necessary for a confrontation between Czechoslovakian and Canadian teams. The Europeans play a technical style and the North Americans play a more physical style. The two styles together make a better player."

But why did Czechoslovakia send its national U18 team to Camrose?

It was quite serendipitous. I had heard that a Czechoslovak junior team was about to tour through parts of BC. I contacted their Canadian agent, George Kent, and invited the team to come to Alberta, and play in the week-long Viking Cup. As he was looking for additional games, it was a perfect fit.

There was one problem. The Viking Cup was more than a hockey tournament. It was also a cultural exchange experience, which included billeting of players with Camrose families. We did not have the means to pay for hotel accommodation and meals. Mr. Kent informed me that this arrangement would be contrary to government policy.

"You do realize we are dealing with a Communist government? They do not want to risk defections."

I knew Mr. Kent needed these games to complete their tour, so I impressed upon him our commitment to make this work for the benefit of all. Approval was reluctantly granted, and Mr. Kent informed me that he would not be available when the team arrived. I understood that to mean I would break the news of "family living" to the team.

Upon their arrival at the Camrose arena in mid-December, I introduced myself to the leader, Mr. Dvorsky, and I soon found out he was closely connected to the Communist party. He was conspicuous in the group by his big fur hat, and he left no doubt that he was in charge. As if it was normal procedure, I then introduced him through our interpreter to the billet families who had gathered around in anticipation of meeting "their boys." When Mr. Dvorsky realized what was happening, he responded through the interpreter.

"We know nothing about this family living and our government would never approve of such an arrangement. You must take them to the hotel."

After I produced Mr. Kent's letter of approval, Dvorsky reluctantly acquiesced. But for one night only! He continued to insist that "hotel rooms must be booked by tomorrow!"

I think the boys were all on our side (as well as the billets), for when they came to practise the following day, they pleaded with their coaches to let them stay in their newfound homes—with lots of good food, of course. I informed Mr. Dvorsky that the plans could not change and he tried again. "OK, one more night only." By day three, the experiment was working too well to change, and I think the leaders were enjoying some supervision relief and assistance from newfound Camrose supporters.

Nevertheless, there were fragile moments as the Czechoslovakians felt their way with us and each other. Everyone seemed to want to escape from the watchful eye of Dvorsky. Verlyn Olson recalls one such occasion.

> One night, Mardell and I wanted to take the team doctor and trainer out for pizza after a game. They were very excited, but also nervous about doing so. In fact, before they agreed, they went around the (by-then) empty rink to ensure that no other officials were still around, and then said, "OK, the coast is clear."
>
> There was more excitement when we got them to the pizza place. We were sitting there in a booth when two uniformed city policemen came in for coffee and sat at the booth straight across from us. For a time, the conversation at our booth came to a stop and I remember the look in Jan's and George's eyes. They definitely weren't used to friendly policemen. We became good friends and, one day after practice, they called me into the storage room where all of the equipment and supplies were being kept. They showed me a bunch of beautiful Bohemian crystal and asked if I'd like to buy anything. I pointed to them and said, "You guys are capitalists!" I ended up buying over $200 worth of crystal. They needed cash to buy nylons and jeans for their wives.

As the week continued on fine terms, so did the friendship with Dvorsky and the coaches. I'm sure their winning ways on the ice had something to do with it, but not as much as the Camrose hosts, who cheered loudly for "their boys" at each game. Near the end of the tournament, Dvorsky, on behalf of the Czech Hockey Federation, invited the Augustana Vikings to Czechoslovakia the next season for a series of games with their national U18 team. By now, we had lots of goodwill in common.

But it was outstanding hockey that really won the week for the Czechoslovakian team at Viking Cup '82.

Czechoslovakia Wins Gold in Its First Viking Cup ('82)

The Czechoslovakia U18 national team that participated in Viking Cup '82 was assembled from eleven different cities and teams across Czechoslovakia. Co-coach Vladimír Šustek gave his assessment in advance the tournament: "The talent is downright impressive on this team. One half of the team will graduate to our World Junior (U20) team next year."

It was one of the strongest teams from Czechoslovakia to ever participate in a Viking Cup.

In a summary article in the *Viking Cup '82* magazine on one of the finest games ever played in the Viking Cup (Czech National U18 team: 2, Prince Albert Raiders: 1), the writer commented:

> The fast tempo and intensity of play were sustained for the entire sixty minutes, while both netminders, Dominik Hašek of the Czechs and the NHL draftee, Gil Hudon of the Raiders, held court in their respective ends. Immediately one sensed the two different approaches to hockey—both teams came out to skate, with the Raiders knocking the Czechs into the sides and corners whenever possible, and the Czechs methodically engineering their positional and passing game. The first period was a standoff. The battle continued in the middle frame and neither side yielded. Dominik Hašek, for his part, deftly challenged the Raider forwards, straying, at times, fifteen feet from the net.

> Hašek, by the way, at sixteen, is the youngest goalie ever to play on the Czech Junior team. Remember his name!

> With the Czechs short-handed, Petr Klima broke through on a breakaway, was hauled down by Raiders' Joe West, and a penalty shot was called. Klima made no mistake as he bore in on Hudon and let go a hard blast from ten feet, finding the net high over Hudon's right shoulder. The Czechs carried this 1-0 lead into the third period. The third period was thrilling, featuring great end-to-end rushes with beautiful and precise passing plays from both teams. It was hockey at its finest.

> Finally, it was PA's turn and Louis Lemire broke Hašek's domination with a long, low slapshot. Seven minutes later, two Czechs broke in alone on Hudon and Klima perfectly used his mate as a foil and fired it past Hudon for a 2-1 lead. The Raiders then threw every piece of artillery they had at the young Hašek in the final minutes. He wouldn't break. (The Raiders had outshot the Czechs by a close margin of 27-22.)

Two days later, the same two teams met in front of a sold-out boisterous crowd for the gold-medal game. One could smell the anticipation in the arena.

Prince Albert, with two players already drafted by the NHL, would seek revenge not only for their close loss to Finland in Viking Cup '81 but now for their 2–1 squeaker loss to the Czechoslovakia Selects two nights earlier.

Vladimír Šustek, the Czech coach, explained their game plan in simple terms, "Our aim was to stop Prince Albert between the red and blue lines."

"With the outstanding and bold net-minding of Dominik Hašek, the Czechs built up a 4-2 first-period lead. . . Julius Kovak, the second Czech coach later surmised: 'If Prince Albert had scored with the two-man advantage (early in the second period), it would have been a different game.'

"In spite of many opportunities, the Raiders could not score on the rock-solid Hašek and, at times, left PA goaltender Hudon defenseless to the sharpshooters from Europe. Dave Reierson of the Raiders scored at 6:50 of the second period, but after that it started raining Czech goals for a final incredible score of 11–3. The score belied the type of game as the Raiders outshot the Czechoslovakians, 23–19. Hašek was once again the star of the game."

At this time, a future Augustana Vikings player, Lyle "Steamer" Hamm, was a high school classmate of a Raider player in Prince Albert, Saskatchewan. He had listened intently to the play-by-play broadcast of the games on the PA radio station. He commented on his discussion with a Raider player following the Viking Cup.

> When we returned to school in January and resumed our classes and hockey schedules, I asked my friend who played for the Raiders and was in social studies with me why he thought they had lost to the Czechs. He was very reflective in his response.
>
> "They were really fast and skilled. Like, really, really fast—and skilled."
>
> "You guys are really fast and skilled," I countered. "I watch your practices; I attend your games."
>
> My friend thought about that for a moment. He was one of the Raiders' big recruits that year out of the Notre Dame program. He had played with excellent players who were now strewn about Western Canada on their respective junior hockey teams.
>
> "Steamer, there is good and then there is great. Remember, we are just one team in a province. The Czech team we played are some of their best players in their country."
>
> We went back to our work before he offered his final piece.
>
> "It also didn't help that we couldn't score on their goalie."
>
> "Who was the goalie?" I asked.
>
> "I don't know. Some guy named Dominik. Honestly, he stoned us from every direction. That is, during the short periods of time we had the puck," he chuckled.

Who could forget the name Dominik Hašek—the Dominator?

Dominik was the all-star goaltender in Viking Cup '82, and was drafted shortly after by the Chicago Blackhawks in the tenth round. At the time, NHL teams feared that a player chosen from behind the Iron Curtain would be a wasted pick, in that they would likely never be allowed to play in the free world. Hašek later told me that he didn't even know he was drafted until a friend in Prague said he had read it in a newspaper some months earlier! It was certainly an auspicious start for the Dominator, now known as one of the best goaltenders of all time. He won the Vezina Trophy in the NHL six times as the top goaltender and still holds the highest career save percentage of any goaltender, at .9223.

But perhaps his most outstanding moment in history (and world hockey) was when he put on one of the most dominating individual performances in the game's history. In the 1998 Japan Olympics, in six games, the Dominator allowed only six goals and recorded two shutouts, with a .961 save percentage. He blanked Russia 1–0 in the gold game and, unfortunately for the Canadians, stopped all five Canadian shooters in the semi-final game shootout. (Canadians still wonder why Gretzky was not chosen as one of the five.) Gretzky commented at the time: "He is the best player in the game."

A newspaper reported that, with his gold medal, Hašek flew home to Prague, where the team was greeted by some 140,000 slightly gonzo Czechs. Among the celebrators was President Václav Havel, who said Dominik could have his job and then commented, "In two weeks, the team has done more for the Czech people than the government has done in two years." Teammate Jaromir Jagr commented, "He's a gift to us and can win games by himself."

Hašek has been inducted into the NHL Hall of Fame, the Czech Ice Hockey Hall of Fame, and the IIHF Hall of Fame.

Indeed, *remember the sixteen-year-old kid in Viking Cup '82!*

During Viking Cup 2000, the *Edmonton Journal* published an article, "Stopping Pucks easier than starting Ski-Doos" about Hašek (not long after the '98 Nagano Olympics). It described the introduction of two Czechoslovakian goaltenders to the finest of snowmobiling in the spacious and beautiful Battle River Valley, just a few kilometres from Camrose in 1982. Jim and Marie Brager were billeting the boys and brother Allan lived on the banks of the Battle River with Ski-Doos in his yard.

"They had never seen Ski-Doos, so we thought we would let them try it," Jim said. "It was about dusk when they went out, and we thought they would be fine. But then it got dark and they still weren't home. So, I took my pickup truck and went down by the river and found them walking back to the farm in the dark (moonlight) in the snow. One of the players, unable to speak a word of English, had the first name Dominik, last name, Hašek. Put the two together and you now have the goaltender of the Buffalo Sabres, and the winner of the most valuable player trophy in the NHL for the past several seasons [with a gold medal from the Olympics to boot]!"

Dominik Hašek with Stanley Cup 2002
(Photo courtesy Dominik Hašek)

Jim said, "The boys had pulled the 'kill switch,' and when that happens, the machine stops. They had been trying to start the machine for some time, gave up, and found their way back. Luckily, we had given them good Ski-Doo suits to wear! The boys were OK, but a bit cold."

Recently, I asked the Dominator about his Viking Cup memories. "I remember Ski-Dooing in the valley, and it was cold. I now know what a kill switch is!"

It was as if Hašek had discovered the "kill switch" just before playing the powerful Prince Albert Raider machine in Viking Cup '82! And he'd used it for the rest of his impressive career. His best performance may have come in an overtime playoff game in 1994, when he stopped a record seventy shots in a 1–0 victory for the Sabres.

Hašek returned to Camrose on a couple occasions to visit with friends he made while at Viking Cup '82. One such occasion was to assist in promoting minor hockey in Camrose and, earlier, learning the game of golf. Jim Brager, a well-known artist, had painted a scene of the Battle River Valley as a special gift to the Hašeks from the city of Camrose. Dominik looked for the Ski-Doo on the painting!

Hašek receives Brager painting from city mayor, Norm Mayer
Alena Hasek, Norm Mayer, Dominik Hasek, Jim Brager

Petr Klíma was the MVP of Viking Cup '82, and was drafted by the Detroit Red Wings after participating in the Viking Cup. Klima defected in 1985, to play with the Red Wings; hence, his well-known jersey number, eighty-five, "to signify my freedom," as he would say. "It was hard for me to leave my family at seventeen years old and come over here to play hockey. I knew the Viking Cup was my chance," he told *Viking Cup '90* magazine. "I started to think NHL at that time so I played hard to get out, even harder against the Canadian teams."

When Klíma was traded to the Edmonton Oilers, it was like coming home to Viking Cup country. Petr reacquainted himself with his Viking Cup billets Ray and Esther Olson while commenting that "Esther's home-cooked meals were really good."

As for the Viking Cup, Klima commented, "It's the best tournament I've ever played in. The 1984 Canada Cup and the Viking Cup are my fondest hockey memories."

Klíma played with the Oilers until he was traded in 1993. Known as a "clutch" goal scorer, he scored a career-high forty goals with the Oilers in a Stanley Cup-winning year of 1990—no great surprise to Camrosians, who had witnessed his explosive Viking Cup record of ten points in four games just eight years earlier.

Benefits Mount for the Czechoslovakia Junior Hockey Program

Viking Cup '82 may have paid dividends as the Czechoslovakia National U20 team won three silver and one bronze in the World Junior Championships (U20) in the following four championships.

And how did their U18 teams do in the spring European Championships after playing in the Christmas Viking Cup?

In *Viking Cup '92* magazine, Miloš Broukal commented,

> For the past two years, the teams that have played in the Viking Cup have become European champions. The Viking Cup is good preparation to become European champions. It helps them very much. It is a great opportunity for Czech players to learn something new.

Broukal was general secretary of the Czech and Slovak Ice Federation at the time of the Velvet Revolution.

The Development of an Exchange Program Following Viking Cup '82

To our good fortune, the Czechoslovak Ice Hockey Federation assigned Miro Šubrt to be their representative in all our exchange negotiations and arrangements. Mr. Šubrt was also a long-time vice-president of the IIHF (1969–2004), where he oversaw international junior programs in the U18 and U20 categories during the Viking Cup years.

With my wife, Dianne, our initial meeting with Šubrt and his assistant, Miro Voytechek, in Prague in June of 1982, laid the groundwork for the Vikings first trip behind the Iron Curtain in December, 1982 and Czechoslovakia commitments to Viking Cup '84 with full approval for "family living," as he said.

Šubrt was a great fan of including a cultural component in youth sport exchanges. He understood the objectives of the Viking Cup and was our number-one supporter in Europe. I was his guest at the World Championships in Prague in 1993, and in Vienna in 1995, where we were able to promote the Viking Cup amongst the hockey fraternity of other countries and bring back some ideas in running major international hockey tournaments.

This then was the beginning of an eighteen-year alternating exchange program with the Czechoslovakia and (later) the Czech Republic Hockey Federation with the Augustana Vikings. Czech and Slovak players continued to live with Camrose families, with no expressed concerns from the Communist Czechoslovakian government. On return trips, Augustana Vikings were accommodated in government-sponsored sport-training centres or hotels. The Czech government covered all costs while in Czechoslovakia (save for the few sticks given to gatekeepers of the Iron Curtain to assure safe and smooth passage).

The educational and cultural experience of participating Augustana Viking players was unique and enhanced their education at this very unusual time in history. In later years, many have reflected with enthusiasm on the memories.

Todd Voshell ('92), who is now an Alberta architect, comments:

> The architecture of the buildings in Prague made a huge impression on me. I wanted to learn more of what I saw. . . The Prague castle and the unbelievable cathedral. It was so huge, awesome, majestic. The Charles Bridge, with all the sculptures to help relive history! Old Town Square. We went up the stone

stairs to the famous clock to see history still working. There were three-inch divots in the centre of each step! That had to take many centuries—nothing comparable back home. I saw *real* cobbled streets.

Augustana Vikings' First Trip to Czechoslovakia

When the Finnair jet took off from the smooth Helsinki airstrip bound for Prague on January 5, 1983, we feared a rough landing on the typically less well-maintained strips behind the Iron Curtain. The landing was OK, but when we departed Prague five days later, we were stranded on the tarmac for two hours as a maintenance crew with crude tools replaced a tire before takeoff. We nervously watched the whole ordeal through the small windows of our plane as some of the senior members of our fan entourage recalled "fixing" tires with hand tools in the small service stations of the prairie towns back home.

I was recently reminded that many in our group had purchased the famous Pilsner beer to bring home as a gift to parents. Thirsty hockey players consumed all of it while sitting on the Prague air terminal tarmac!

But what happened between touchdown and takeoff was a different story—one of fine hospitality, excellent hockey, and engaged hockey people. Upon arrival, our host had offered a deal to customs officials: quick passport passage for two genuine Canadian hockey sticks (made in Finland, I think!). That did the trick and our departure was similarly smooth—except for the tire replacement on the tarmac!

The Vikings became regular visitors to Czechoslovakia biannually and each trip had many high points.

Remember Liberec

Eddie, our faithful team bus driver, led the way from our base in Kolin, just east of Prague, to a northern mountain centre called Liberec, a beautiful city close to the East German border. We arrived early to be welcomed by the city mayor at the Vienna-style city hall. This was followed by a very nice afternoon lunch and tour of historical parts of the city. Our leaders and fans shared numerous toasts and all were in a jovial and friendly mood. The reception seemed as if long-lost friends were getting together, although I understood we were the first Canadian hockey team to play in Liberec.

The game was a sellout. The crowd of 4,000 people were madly in love with their home team but, I must say, respectful of the visitors.

As the combatants lined up on the bluelines for the national anthems, I could detect some teary eyes amongst our group, including myself, as we stood for "O Canada." The realization that we were representing our country in a land officially hostile to the West was overwhelming, and we all felt so proud and grateful for Canada.

It was the first of many patriotic moments in Czechoslovakia for our Vikings in the years that followed, and our national anthem never grew old. During the Communist era, it had a special significance, but even later its meaning never waned.

To cap off the well-orchestrated opening ceremonies, small minor hockey players dressed in their team sweaters skated, one to each of our players, to deliver a bag of gifts and souvenirs from the city while reaching up (way up) to extend a friendly handshake. The joining of hands of our tallest player, 6'7" Rob Roflick, and the diminutive, happy Czech youngster was a picture never to be forgotten. (Rob's ancestry was Czechoslovakian.)

Player Yvon de Champlain remembers "the warm apple cider for the players on the bench and two Pepsis—always—for each player after the game."

Following the opening, the minor Czechoslovakian players took their places in the first row behind our bench and shouted, "Go Kaun-ah-dah, go!" throughout the game while waving homemade Canadian flags with a visible red maple leaf at their centre. Of course, our travelling bus of fans joined right in—and we all felt like we, too, were a home team.

I should mention that there was a payoff for our Czech minor hockey supporters—dressing room goodies like candy, gum, and maybe a few Canadian hockey sticks or worn equipment. That day and night, "our cheerleaders" dramatically reinforced a message: we belonged in Liberec that night.

One of the most beautiful outcomes of the Viking Cup are lessons we learn from one another through our exchange experiences. The practice of assigning a Camrose minor hockey team to be the official cheerleaders for each Viking Cup team is a direct "borrow" from Liberec, Czechoslovakia. Every team was a home team in the Viking Cup and the players and spectators loved it. Thank you, Liberec.

Opening Ceremonies at Liberec

"I saw my half-brother: my dad stopped at the border"

Encountering the Iron Curtain for the first time was, to most, a fearful but meaningful experience. For some, like Rob Roflik, it was emotional, as well.

Rob's father, Vince, was travelling with our group and enjoying games in Sweden and Finland. By the time we arrived at the Czechoslovakia border, he had departed in another direction—for Germany, to be exact. Rob tells the Roflik story.

> My dad, Vaclav (Vince) was arrested and put in jail for speaking out against Communism and putting up posters. After spending some time in jail, he escaped. He had thought he made it into Germany, but the police arrested him just before the border and threw him back in jail. Later, he escaped again and, even though he was shot through the leg, made it into Germany, where he lived for a while. He had a job sneaking documents and sometimes people out of Czechoslovakia. He said all he knew was that he was getting cheques from the US government. Eventually, he made his way to Canada.
>
> I met up with my half-brother and two nephews when they came to one of our games. My dad wanted to be there, but couldn't risk another visit to the jail. It wasn't until after the wall fell in '89, that my dad could go back and see his old family and friends.

Miro Šubrt in Mladá Boleslav

The following night, the team travelled to Mladá Boleslav, home of Škoda cars. There, we were hosted by Miro Šubrt of the IIHF and Czech Ice Hockey Federation. A Canadian embassy representative accompanied him.

The game was penalty ridden. Yvon de Champlain recalls, "There were no boos from the crowd, but there sure was a lot of high-pitched whistling. We hadn't heard that before!"

Miro Šubrt (Photographer: Ben Welland / HHOF-IIHF Images)

A Tribute to Miro Šubrt

In his country, he was called the "jeweller of ice hockey." On the international stage, he was called the "ice hockey diplomat." But to Camrose, he was the partner and flag-bearer of the Viking Cup in Czechoslovakia and in the European circles of the IIHF.

Šubrt believed strongly in the power of youth sport to make our world better. As a leader in Czechoslovakian ice hockey, he was quick to invite the Camrose Lutheran College Vikings to Czechoslovakia following the first visit of the Czechoslovakia U18 team to Viking Cup '82 . . . and the exchange arrangements continued for twenty years, back and forth. But he had Canada on his mind as a young boy playing hockey on the frozen waters of his village. He remembered: "We called our fishpond battles 'Canada'. We kept at it until we were half-dead."

No wonder he was a strong advocate for exchanges with Canadian hockey.

After his playing career, he became an organizer and builder of ice hockey in his home country and the member nations of the IIHF. Šubrt served as chairman of the 1959 IIHF World Championship Organizing Committee, and was elected the same year to the IIHF Council.

He was part of fourteen Olympic ice hockey tournaments, beginning in Squaw Valley in 1960. He stepped down from his role with the IIHF in 2003 after fifty-five years of service. The following year, Šubrt was inducted into the IIHF Hall of Fame.

For his contribution to sports in general and to the game of hockey in particular, Miro Šubrt was awarded with the Olympic Order during the 2002 Olympic Games.

"Miro was instrumental in introducing the U20 and the U18 World Championships into the IIHF program, long before people realized what potential those events had," said René Fasel, who worked closely with Šubrt for more than twenty years.

By then he had been a passionate advocate for the Viking Cup and other youth exchanges for some time and liked what he saw.

When Miro Šubrt passed away in 2012, he was the longest-serving high-ranked official in international ice hockey.

Crystal and Toast

It only took one visit to Czechoslovakia to feel the country's great hospitality in multiple toasts (usually strong Becherovka or the like) and gifts of fine crystal. Beyond the gifts, most of our group purchased the fine Czechoslovakian crystal as souvenirs, often adding a lot of weight to our hockey bags on the way back home. One year, our assistant coach Bill Steen distributed his purchases to several of the hockey bags to avoid personal overweight charges!

The Czechoslovakians were known for an overweight problem, too. Camrose bus driver Marvin Despas noted that one bag got progressively lighter on their extended road trips in Canada. Marv commented, "It was the bag filled with rum, vodka, and other spirits. The leaders were always toasting and taking a swig whenever we stopped!"

I can relate the reverse story when visiting Czechoslovakia. The Czech and Slovak people are very hospitable, and their usual gift was a bottle of homemade spirits: high-alcohol plum brandy or wine, for example, or possibly heavy crystal. But there were other gifts, as well. Following a game in the small town of Vimperek, an exuberant fan insisted on giving me a large glass jar of mushrooms. I took them, but left them for the cleaning lady in the next hotel, not because I didn't appreciate the gift, but there is a limit to the contents and weight of luggage, especially during Communist times when luggage was subject to a thorough check. At the same game, Pat Seeley was awarded the star of the game, and given a fresh loaf of Czech bread as a prize. Needless to say, the whole team shared the loaf, communion style, on the bus back to the hotel—just another way to celebrate with friendly people in Czechoslovakia.

The bus trips were always a hoot in Czechoslovakia, but they were in Canada, too, for the Czechoslovakians.

Road Trips through Western Canada

by Dr. Petr Mirejovsky, interpreter and exhibition tour leader

Road trips were an important aspect of the Viking Cup. They were used to pay for the plane tickets for the Czechoslovak and Soviet teams, and they helped to spread the word about the Viking Cup from the interior of BC, across small-town Alberta and Saskatchewan, into deepest Manitoba. They were an experience—on a number of different levels—for the teams, for the officials, as well as for some of us who accompanied them.

One thing about Canada that invariably makes an impression on most over-seas visitors is the sheer size of the country. Czechoslovakia was a relatively small country. Separately, the Czech Republic and Slovakia are smaller still. Prague, the city from which many of our visitors came, sits in a large bowl, but as soon as you drive out of it, you are likely to see hills to the north, the west, or the south, and beyond those hills there are different countries, populated by people who speak different languages, and pay their bills using different money. (After a few months spent in Europe, my daughter Anne, then two and a bit, asked, with just a hint of concern, if we were still in Canada, as the car reached the wide-open spaces of the Superstore parking lot on the west side of Camrose.) On a good road, you could get to the border from Prague in an hour or two, and even more importantly, few Czechs were allowed to travel to most of those places, most of the time throughout much of the Communist period. Hockey players, especially those associated with top-level teams, were an exception. They did get to travel abroad reasonably often. However, like the rest of their compatriots, they were used to living within a rather small world. Contrast that with what they experienced here.

Instead of returning to Camrose, after an afternoon game in Daysland, not far from Camrose, the bus turned east, and it just kept going. Hour after hour. Wainwright, the Battlefords, Prince Albert. In the gathering darkness, open prairie and parkland gave way to forest, and the bus still kept going. So many Christmas trees, so many lakes and rivers, and it was still Canada and we were not there yet. Enough to drive a man to drink! Fortunately, some liquids were available, and they were administered, strictly for medicinal purposes, to select participants, under medical supervision. And all of us enjoyed Don Cherry's Rock'em, Sock'em videos and assorted action movies, generously provided by Daryll Philips, faithful host for the Czechoslovak team.

The game was in the rather starkly industrial Flin Flon, Manitoba, while we stayed overnight in a beautiful lakeside lodge in the nearby—and utterly different—pristine Creighton, Saskatchewan. The Czech Republic is a country full of hills. Towns and villages are spaced rather evenly, one about every two or three kilometres, connected with an endless variety of roads. Some are good, some not, but they all share one thing: they all have many twists and turns. Their layout owes more to medieval horse-drawn carts and less to more recent surveyors. As a result, one source of fascination for our visitors were our wide-open spaces and long, seemingly endless, perfectly straight roads, stretching, at times, from horizon to horizon

Elsewhere, I mentioned the trip to Trail, BC, the home of the Smoke Eaters. On the way back to Alberta, I was chatting with our bus driver, I believe his name was Nick. I asked him where his next trip would take him, and he told me that, right after the Viking Cup, he would be taking a group of Camrose seniors to Manitou Beach, Saskatchewan. I was surprised. Why should anyone want to travel from the fleshpots of Camrose to the frozen wilds of Saskatchewan in the middle of January? And to a beach, at that! Of course, my surprise merely reflected my own ignorance of the wonders of our neighbouring province.

Two years later, the pre-Viking Cup road tour took the Czechoslovak team to a number of places throughout Saskatchewan. We visited Humboldt. The game was great. It was well-attended, and, of course we were blissfully unaware of the tragic event that would bring Humboldt and the Broncos into the headlines many years later. I recall that the team officials were impressed by their rather new hockey arena. They said that, in Czechoslovakia, they paid attention, perhaps too much attention, to the building of large stadiums located in the bigger places with major league teams and not enough, perhaps not nearly enough, to the building of arenas in the smaller and medium-sized centres, which may be producing as many promising hockey talents as their larger counterparts.

And then we got to Manitou Beach. We stayed in the little hotel, and got a tour of the adjoining spa in the morning. We did not get to use the facilities; they were being cleaned and overhauled over the Christmas break. Even the lake—Saskatchewan's Dead Sea—was partly frozen, but we were told about the wonderful properties of its waters, capable of healing paper cuts and smallpox and everything in between.

Well worth a road trip then, even in the middle of winter! The road trips took us to many places throughout Western Canada. The games were played in an endless variety of venues—in large, modern arenas, as well as in the much smaller and older hockey rinks. Most of the people we met were friendly and eager to help.

The experience encouraged quite a few to travel to Camrose—in the middle of winter—and take in the Viking Cup.

Our guests tended to be nice people, too. They told all kinds of stories. Some involved memorable incidents from hockey road trips at home. Some were about their trips to all kinds of faraway places, some of which sounded much more exotic to us here in the 1980s than they perhaps would now, places such as Siberia or North Korea. But of course, especially on these long trips, our guests made fun. Usually of each other. All manner of rivalries associated with their club teams back home came to light. Some involved strange practices and initiation rituals said to be practised by those teams. But I better stop right here. A lot of it was, well, locker room talk, and besides, some former or current members of those clubs graduated to stellar careers in the NHL and elsewhere. But, who knows, some of those stories, perhaps those that involved dining on the flesh of, shall we say, unusual provenance, might have even been true. . . .

As so often happens in large groups, one or two people seemed to attract more of the ribbing than most of the rest. This was no doubt the case on the road trip that took the team from Czechoslovakia to northeastern British Columbia one year. On that occasion, one person, who shall forever remain nameless, was the butt of many of the jokes and comments. Most of the latter were harmless—friendly, even—and the individual in question appeared to take them well enough. However, past a certain point, I could not help but to feel a bit protective. I guess that was just as well, as it was at that point, just after we left beautiful downtown Prince George, that the person in question asked me if I could contact the hotel we had just left as he seemed to have left his dentures there. The story of teeth in a glass left in a room would undoubtedly have made the conversation on the bus a lot livelier that morning, but my lips were sealed. Oh, and the missing dentures were rescued from their predicament and returned to their rightful user quickly and in the strictest confidence.

On a more serious note, our guests appreciated the experience. The officials frequently mentioned that the Viking Cup was different. Special. Unlike other trips and tours, the players and officials did not just get to know the insides of the dressing rooms of arenas and lobbies of the various hotels—they got to meet people. All players and most officials stayed in private homes. That made the experience far more immediate and personal. Some of those memories—and personal contacts —are still with us.

And one last note about the Czechoslovak teams: In the early years, few of the officials and hardly any players had much English. That was to change, quite dramatically, as time went on—as many of you, undoubtedly, would have noticed. Among the last couple of teams that came, a number of the officials spoke English well, and there were quite a few players who were perfectly able not just to carry on a conversation with their hosts, talk to the scouts, but, even more importantly, chat up local girls.

From Corn Flakes to Carp—Lessons in Hospitality

Family Christmas celebrations for billets were always just a little different with two or more players a part of their family. Our Christmas Eve tradition was to gather as a family at my wife's parental home for dinner and an exchange of gifts. There were usually about thirty-five, plus, on occasion, additional guests.

For Viking Cup '86, three of our families, including my mother-in-law, Mrs. Olson, were billeting, to make a total of six Czech young guests plus team doctor, Dr. Nohejl, who had been invited from his room at the Norsemen Hotel. One of the boys, Ivan Matulik, from a typically small family, had taken a great liking to Corn Flakes, which he indicated were not available in Czechoslovakia. According to Mrs. Olson, all he wanted for breakfast was Corn Flakes . . . every day!

As Ivan, later drafted by the Edmonton Oilers, viewed the large table with a generous smorgasbord of Christmas food, he secretly whispered to his new Viking Cup grandmother, "Do you think you could find room for Corn Flakes?"

For that Christmas, amongst all of the array of Christmas dinner food, was a box of Corn Flakes, conspicuous at the table's centre, only for Ivan! Ivan's roommate Juri Jurik recently commented, "We were billeted with Babichka. She was terrific. Great food! Family life was beautiful!"

On the Vikings' return visit to Czechoslovakia the following December, Dr. Nohejl invited Dianne and myself to his home in Prague for a typical Czech Christmas Eve carp dinner. We had visited a central town square in České Budějovice the previous day, where we had observed an abundance of vendors selling live carp from water-filled tubs to Christmas shoppers. We were told that they would be put in tubs of water back home, often the bathtub, until their time on Christmas Eve!

This was our first typical Christmas Eve dinner in a Czechoslovakian home. It was wonderful—the meal and the fellowship of this small family of six to include two young children and two grandparents. What a contrast to large Christmas gatherings back home.

Following the dinner, Dr. Nohejl disappeared briefly to another room. I could see the children becoming anxious, but still polite.

Suddenly, the ringing of a bell by Dr. Nohejl was the signal that the baby Jesus had arrived with gifts put under a real Christmas tree. The children ran to see the tree and gifts for the first time.

How special it was to be a part of the excitement of the children and the enjoyment of the parents and grandparents in such a faraway land.

Yes, our gifts were under the tree, too. But the greater gift was wonderful hospitality—on both sides of the Iron Curtain.

Shining Stars . . . Ice and Homes

In February 2018, jersey number twenty-six was retired to the rafters of the Prudential Coliseum, home of the New Jersey Devils. Patrik Eliáš, a Viking Cup star, had completed an astonishing twenty years with the Devils, retiring with two Stanley Cup rings, and as the team's all-time leader in points, goals, and assists. Eliáš played for the Czech Republic in four World Championships and four Olympics.

Of Eliáš, New Jersey GM Lou Lamorello said: "He was one of the best 'all-situation' players, ever. . . He had true hockey sense." A popular player, the New Jersey fans would say: "He was our guy, he made us just want him to win!"

Viking Cup billets Don and Margaret Falk also said: "He was our guy!"

Patrik and Václav Varaďa lived with the Falks at Viking Cup '94. Later, Don along with sons Thomas and Mackenzie watched Patrik play the Flames in Calgary. New Jersey won in overtime with the goal scored by Eliáš. Patrik presented an autographed game-winning stick to the boys after the game. The Falk's daughters, Leah and Christina, flew to New Jersey in November 2014, and stayed at Patrik's guest condo. They attended two New Jersey home games. "Patrik gave them a tour of the New Jersey dressing room, a highlight for sure!" Margaret remembers. "Like many people, in Leah's mind, Patrik was one of the best hockey players in the world!"

And he was! In 2009, he was awarded the Golden Hockey Stick, signifying the world's best Czech hockey player. Jaromir Jagr had won the award in the previous four years.

As for Camrose and the Viking Cup, Eliáš comments in the *Viking Cup 2002* magazine:

> The Viking Cup opened my eyes and those of my teammates. For young kids
> like we were, it was great to realize what it takes to play in North America.
> We could see the differences. We never played on a small rink like that one in
> Camrose. It was a tougher and stronger game. I liked the style of play from
> the first day! It was my first time in North America. We lived with a family.
> We got to know the people—that was great!

Václav Varaďa had a ten-year career in the NHL with Buffalo and Ottawa after skating in Viking Cup '94. Now, as leaders in sport, Václav Varaďa and Patrik Eliáš were the coaches of the Czech national U20 team in the World Championships of 2019 (Vancouver) and 2020 (Ostrava).

Don Falk, who also served as the official host for several Czechoslovakian teams, said: "We made so many great connections with wonderful people. I enjoyed travelling with them on the exhibition tours. We were like one family. One player that I remember well was Žigmund Pálffy, who stayed in our home the year the Iron Curtain fell. He was from Slovakia and was drafted in the first round by the Islanders. He had a great career, primarily with the Islanders and LA Kings. We would go to Edmonton to see him when he played against the Oilers."

The Czech team of Viking Cup '94 kept the scouts in the stands drooling throughout the tournament. Twelve players were drafted, and the three that had the longest NHL careers were Eliáš, Varaďa, and Hejduk.

Milan Hejduk became a favourite of our family as his Viking Cup billet.

"Milan has not forgotten his Western Canada experience of a decade ago," reads an article in the *Viking Cup 2004* magazine, appropriately entitled, "The Finisher." "We stayed almost a month with families. It was fun!"

To us and throughout his spectacular career, he was "the Duke."

More recently in a phone call, he asked how Jeff, Dale, Lana, and Beth (our kids) were doing and spoke of his twin boys. Then he reminded me that he saw his first NHL game in Edmonton while he was in Camrose . . . and he loved it. "I wanted to play that kind of hockey."

The Duke did play that kind of hockey, and all fourteen years of it with the Colorado Avalanche, with an unbelievable record.

On January 6, 2018, Hejduk's number, twenty-three, was retired into the rafters of the Pepsi Center (now the Ball Arena) in Denver, the Avalanche home stadium. His achievements are enormous, including most career games of any Avalanche at 1,020 and 805 points, only to be outdone by two other Czech players, Jagr and Eliáš. In 2003, he won the Maurice "Rocket" Richard Trophy as the league's top goal scorer, with fifty goals! For eleven of his fourteen years, he played on the top line always, with Joe Sakic, and he served as team captain for two years. The Duke's highest achievements were a Stanley Cup championship in 2000–01, and Olympic gold for his home country in Nagano in 1998.

František (Frank) Kučera and Robert (Bobby) Holík stayed in our home for Viking Cup '86 and '88, respectively. Holík received a silver medal in Viking Cup '88, was drafted tenth by the Hartford Whalers, and had an eighteen-year career in the NHL. He played eleven years for the New Jersey Devils, where he was on two Stanley Cup-winning teams. The Holík name is well known in hockey circles. Robert's father and uncle played on the Czechoslovakia national team and his brother-in-law, Frank Musil had a fifteen-year NHL career, mainly with Minnesota, Calgary, and Edmonton. At present, Robert is coaching the national hockey team of Israel. He comments on the legacy of the Viking Cup in Chapter 12.

Kučera was drafted by Chicago and had a twelve-year career in the NHL. He played for the Czech national team at several World Championships and the Olympics in 1998, when they won gold. Frank comments on his visits to Camrose elsewhere in this book.

Of our first billets in Viking Cup '82, Vlado Kolek is head coach of the Iceland national team and Miroslav (Miro) Marcinko was at one time the captain of the Slovak national team.

His son Tomáš was the first second-generation player to play in the Viking Cup, in 2006. Tomáš was drafted by the New York Islanders.

Miro, through Tomáš in a recent email, commented: "Not speaking your language did put little worries on our shoulders, but people working and living in Camrose were very warm and helpful and nice to us, so it made that transition easier. I still remember the Viking Cup as such a great event and tournament, and me and Tomas speak a lot about it!"

Libor Polášek stayed with us at Viking Cup '92. Libor, who spoke no English at the time, was drafted in the first round by the Vancouver Canucks that spring and recently told Jeff, my son, the story of his first trip to the Canucks training camp.

> I arrived at the Vancouver airport at night, but there was no one to pick me up and I spoke almost no English. I had a phone number for the Canuck office, so I tried it—several times. Finally, a night watchman answered, and eventually the general manager picked me up. That was my introduction to pro hockey in North America! But my introduction to Canada was Camrose. The Viking Cup was so well known. Everyone seemed to know it. Dale Johnson took me to show his set-up for playing music at the games. That was impressive for me. Our team members started buying and selling hockey cards . . . we Czechs were big entrepreneurs by this time!

Michael Frolík and Jiří Tlustý, both first-round draft picks following Viking Cup 2004, were billeted with Lee and Cathy Katcher. Jiří is now retired back in his hometown of Kladno, but he remembers Camrose well.

"We went to the grandparents for Christmas. I got stuck with the snowmobile!" On another occasion, Lee took four Czech players into a cattle corral. Lee commented; "I looked back to see them stalled while the one turned his red jacket inside out, fearing the charge of a bull! I think it was Michal Sivek, drafted by Washington." The Katchers would later meet Tomáš Plekanec of the Montreal Canadiens following their games in Edmonton. As for the Viking Cup, Plekanec looks back and says, "It was a hell of an experience, my first trip abroad, living with a Canadian family and a chance to make the NHL!" And the Katchers' comment? "The Viking Cup was a builder of lifelong friendships!"

Ruth and Darryl Phillips billeted fourteen Czech and Slovak boys over the years and visited twelve of them in Czechoslovakia later, including Martin Straka and his family (mentioned earlier in this chapter) and Milan Kraft, who played for Pittsburgh Penguins.

Ruth commented, "Initially, we did it for the kids. It became a great family experience, so we just kept doing it and loved it. I learned a few Czech phrases to show off, and then I just kept talking louder when they didn't understand! Darryl would say, 'Don't talk so loudly, that doesn't help!' Then I would look into their eyes and do some pantomiming! We went to Czech and Slovakia to visit all of them."

Allan, Eloise, and Wes Gordeyko billeted players from Czechoslovakia and Slovakia six times, from '86 to '96. Can you imagine these boys driving into the Gordeyko yard with fifty to a hundred heavy Clydesdale horses welcoming them? Some had already been sent off for Budweiser beer commercials!

"The boys really fit in well," Eloise said. "We almost adopted them! When we corresponded later, it was always, 'to our Canadian family' or 'from your Canadian family.' We were invited to two of the boys' weddings. Oh, yes, they sure ate a lot of fruit!"

Allan commented, "It was a great opportunity to get to know the other billets. We kind of became like a big family with our new boys. Everybody sure enjoyed our horses and the sleigh rides."

Wes, being of similar age, followed the careers of all their guests, including Pavol Demitra. (See the rest of the story on Pavol Demitra later in this chapter.)

Capturing the Hearts

Bruce Hogel, news and public affairs manager of CFRN-TV, commented on the Czech–Camrose connection in his editorial of January 4, 1984.

> The Czechs, particularily, captured the hearts of all residents of Camrose. Prior to the last appearance two years ago, no hockey or any other team from Czechoslovakia had ever been billeted out. They undoubtdly, were initially suspicious.

> But, then thanks to the good people of Camrose, they really found what Canadians were like. The young Czechs found out that people opened their homes to them not for compensation and not to spy on them. They did so from the goodness of their hearts. And because they cared about young people being thousands of miles from home at Christmas. The open-heartedness of Camrose explains why the Czechs were delighted to come back.

Loose Connections on the Iron Curtain

There are always numerous details to attend to when planning exchange projects, whether at home or away. What would normally be a harmless glitch occurred between Miro Šubrt and myself when preparing for the 1986-87 tour of Austria and the Czech Republic.

Our Atlantic flight landed in snowy conditions in Frankfurt, Germany. Thereafter, a German bus was to take our group to Linz, Austria, the nearest Austrian city to our Czech destination of České Budějovice. Of course, the Iron Curtain lay between.

Normally, the bus trip would take about four hours, which would see us arrive about 9 p.m. But with the very bad driving conditions, we arrived in Linz after midnight, to meet two Czech buses for transfer at the Linz railway station. Upon our very late arrival, the only person on site was a night watchman. He immediately indicated that two Czech buses had been parked for hours awaiting our arrival. They had left after the last train arrived at midnight as we were not on it. Obviously, they had not been informed by the Czech Ice Hockey Federation that our arrival at the train station would be by bus. Had it not been for the weather delay, it would not have mattered.

It was impossible at that hour to contact Mr. Šubrt or the Czech Federation, as we had assumed that the Czech buses had returned to Czechoslovakia empty. The German bus driver wanted to return to Germany, but we had nowhere to go, so he turned the key and waited for the problem to be solved. A few of our players began to walk the surrounding streets in search of Czech buses, in case the drivers had chosen to retire in Linz for the night. Fortunately, two Czech buses were discovered, the drivers were awakened about 3 a.m., and the transfer from German to Czech buses occurred. A distraught German driver became furious when he discovered that with all the lights on, his battery was short of power to start his bus. Feeling that we shouldn't leave him stranded, we made a deal. If he would once again become his calm, friendly self, our strong Canadian hockey boys would all join forces to push his bus far enough to start it. It worked, and the last we saw of him was a happy driver returning to Frankfurt.

This was our first and only experience of crossing the Iron Curtain at 3:30 a.m.

We arrived to barking German Shepherds and a guard opened the big gate, surprised and suspicious to see such a large group at such an unusual hour. After all passports were taken, we were informed that they could not be processed until a new crew arrived at 7 a.m. Two token hockey sticks didn't help; I guess they were not hockey fans. A picture that remains in my mind is the whole team sleeping on cold concrete floors and benches in the border "holding docket" of this Iron Curtain crossing. A memory of the Communist era, for sure.

We arrived in České Budějovice about 9 a.m., after being first in line for border clearance. Luckily, the Hotel Gomel had been informed that we would be late for breakfast and check-in. After a short sleep, the boys played a tough game at 5 p.m.

Lesson learned: if something can go wrong, it probably will. Think ahead and cover all details. Remember Linz.

It was that kind of trip. On our departure from the very comfortable Hotel Gomel, player Lindsay Haag had lost his passport—a serious problem behind the Iron Curtain. As our host was calling the police department, I took a final trip to his room and discovered the passport where he had hidden it, under the tablecloth on the table. Didn't Lindsay also get his necktie caught in the skate sharpener in Vienna while playing in a tournament there?

Stitches in Strakonice: Thumbs Up!

Few people in Czechoslovakia spoke or understood English at the time we were making regular hockey trips there. Fewer still of our groups understood the Czech language. Communication could therefore be a problem, especially if official interpreters were not close at hand. One such misunderstanding occurred involving assistant coach, and former player, Lyle Hamm. Our group had played a game in one of our favourite towns, Mariánské Lázně, and were scheduled to visit Prague the next day. Lyle tells his story:

It was near the end of the trip on Charles Bridge in Prague when my stomach began to feel queasy. I thought I could sleep it off.

The next day, our team doctor walked me down to the hospital in the small city of Strakonice, where, through hand gestures, we informed the attending nurse that I was in some type of trouble. I was led into an examination area and, after a short while, a young doctor came in and put his hands face up to inquire about what my problem was. Like me, he knew there would be some communication difficulty between us. I waved my hand over the infected area and made a grimacing face and he instantly knew my problem and nodded his head. He proceeded to press gently into my stomach and remove his fingers quickly. There was no pain on the press, but there was some pain when he removed his hand. He looked at me, smiled, and gestured with his two thumbs up. Then he walked out.

I felt relief with his thumbs up sign, as I believed the doctor was communicating to me that the pain would somehow pass and I would get to the game that night and then over to Amsterdam with the rest of the team before embarking on our trip back to Canada. Admittedly, my anxiety lessened, but only for a moment. The curtain was pulled back and the nurse who had admitted me was there. She put both thumbs up and said in broken English, "Operation, two o'clock." And she walked out.

My brain didn't process her communication well because I wanted to argue that the doctor said I was OK. Then it dawned on me. Two thumbs meant two o'clock. That was that. The next moment, I was taken down a hallway, helped to a stretcher, and prepared for surgery. Our team doctor came in and said good luck, he'd be back, and left to join the team at the rink for practice.

All the doctors and nurses nearby were speaking the Czech language, which obviously I didn't understand. Upon much reflection, that was probably best, because I would have increased my own anxiety with asking questions. They seemed jovial, which helped a great deal.

I was wheeled into the operating room, the blanket was removed, and just before the mask went on my face to put me out, I gestured to one of the doctors that I wanted to see my appendix after it was removed. I did this by pointing my two fingers to my eyes and then to my lower right side. I don't know why I did this. I don't think I really wanted to see it and I trusted the doctors and nurses. Perhaps I was trying to be funny to lighten how I felt. But the doctor looked at me strangely, nodded OK, and placed the mask on me.

When I woke up, my throat was sore, and I was very thirsty. A gentle hand went under my head and slowly raised me toward a paper cup. I could feel the pressure on my stomach where they had operated. I thought it was water in the cup and I prepared to take a small drink. Instead, it was my appendix. I looked at the doctor and he looked at me as if to say, "We got it; you will be fine." And I went back to sleep.

As a final note, I was treated very well for the week I was in the hospital. After I was released, I stayed for several more days with the Strakonice hockey coach Vladimir, his wife, and their son Jan. They took good care of me and got me safely back to Canada. I had no money left at that point and, thankfully, my great friend Kevin Riemer had slipped $100 in my wallet. The experience was one of the best in my life and, in fact, helped me get my first teaching job in Cessford, Alberta, later in 1991. I had written the experience down on my resume and that was what the superintendent wanted to talk to me about first during the interview!

Unforgettable Welcome to Canada—Montreal Police Department Calling . . .

The Viking Cup was a springboard for many students to advance their education and skills in different countries.

Following a game in Příbram, Czech Republic, in 1992, a player from the Příbram team approached me about pursuing his education and hockey in Canada. Not understanding English, he spoke through a young girl who acted as interpreter. As I had experience in international student exchange procedures, I suggested he upgrade his meagre English language skills and begin the application process.

The youth, Jan "Honza" Stepan, studiously followed through, learning English skills to a basic level, good enough to register in the summer Viking Cup English language program in Camrose. The next I heard of Jan Stepan was in a call from the Montreal police department asking if I was expecting him on a flight that day. Honza tells his story.

It was not the hockey tournament that initially brought me to Canada, but the Viking Cup summer program that I participated in with other hockey players from around the world. I had just turned nineteen. Surprisingly I was not overly nervous until I landed at the airport on Canadian soil.

While some travellers remained seated to continue their journey to Chicago, those connecting Canadian flights were advised to board a hydraulic bus that was docked to the airplane. While entering the bus, I noticed a familiar female my age. I approached her only to learn that we had known each other from elementary school. We walked on the bus together.

Two gentlemen with police badges all of a sudden stood over us and directed us to follow them. The girl and I were taken by two different police cars—the last time

I saw her. At the airport police station, I went through a process I had only seen on TV: providing fingerprints, having pictures of my face taken from all sides, having my luggage, including my hockey equipment, ransacked.

I did not speak any French, but it didn't matter because I did not speak much English either. It was not until the police found a middle-aged pilot of Czech descent with very broken Czech that the situation was clarified. Interpol was looking for a young male from Slovakia who had committed a murder at the time in Europe. He was travelling with a female accomplice.

The police assumed that, after landing in Montreal, the girl and I were connected, and, as I found out later from a photo, I had similar features to the male being sought. The sergeant who arrested me probably thought that he would get a medal for catching the real criminal, who apparently walked free!

Except for the missed connection to Edmonton, it had a happy ending for me.

The police put me in a nice hotel with a minibar full of pop, chips, and chocolates, things that mattered the most to a teenager.

The next day I was on an alternate flight bound for my new home in Camrose, where I got a university degree from Augustana while playing hockey for the Vikings. And there was another bonus.

I got to play against the best U18 Junior players in the world—from Sweden, Russia, Czech Republic, the US, Finland, and Slovakia—in the Viking Cup in Camrose!

One could only imagine the number of interesting stories that could be lifted from the diaries of players and accompanying parents and fans during the Viking Cup international exchange program. Only a few have been mentioned to give a taste of Viking Cup experiences on both sides of the Iron Curtain.

The Velvet Revolution 1989

The Velvet Revolution has been referred to as a second "Prague Spring," but with a very different outcome. In 1968, Czechoslovakia's road to freedom was blocked by the armies sent there by the hard-line communist government in Moscow. By 1989, however, many cracks had formed in the infamous Iron Curtain, and new roads around earlier obstacles and blockades opened up.

In Russia, President Gorbachev had installed a liberalized form of Communism through the doctrines of *glasnost* (openness) and *perestroika* (restructuring). The Berlin Wall, the concrete symbol of the separation of East and West, had fallen on November 9, 1989, and other Eastern Bloc countries were seeking new ways to restore and improve depleted economies from four decades of one-party rule—the Communist way.

In the world of sport—and, in particular, hockey—the growing popularity of inter-nation competition created a new wave of participation, communication, and openness. Doctrines of inclusion were beginning to out-distance those of exclusion.

Czechoslovakia's strong love of hockey and its emphasis on strong leadership development in the '70s and '80s left the sport in an advantageous position to influence government policy. Increasingly, hockey, by now a poster sport, opened Czechoslovakia to the world, where winning in hockey was considered a victory for the Communist state.

The revolution began on November 17—International Students Day, ironically enough—at a government-sponsored rally. Czech students filled Wenceslas Square to peacefully march in remembrance of the students killed by the Nazi occupation fifty years earlier. The rally, however, took a different turn. Soon students began demonstrating in favour of government reform.

That peaceful student protest ended with brutal violence when riot police blocked off escape routes and severely beat students taking part in the demonstration. During the next several days, hundreds of thousands of student demonstrators were joined by dissenters from unions, theatres, etc., in Prague (the Czech capital) and Bratislava (the Slovak capital), "jingling their keys" as a sign that it was time for the current crop of leaders to leave. The masses of close to a million overwhelmed the hostile government who, as they discovered, no longer had the backing of Moscow as in the Prague Spring. President Gorbachev was later asked, "What is the difference between the Prague Spring and the Velvet Revolution?" "*Twenty years!*" he said.

Viking Cup '90 and the Velvet Revolution

The responsibility entrusted to the Viking Cup steering committee by the Czechoslovak Ice Hockey Federation for the security and well-being of their National U18 team was enormous. The spectre of possible defections and subsequent recriminations in Communist Czechoslovakia was always a concern, as the team included the elite players of their national U18 program. North American agents and scouts were always present and anxious to talk to the players as prospective clients. The players were all of draftable age for the NHL. Security and safety were paramount, as there was always the possibility of serious incidents or accident, on or off the ice.

The revolution of '89 overshadowed all life in Czechoslovakia, including hockey plans and schedules.

During those weeks I found it next to impossible to communicate with the Czech Ice Hockey officials as their offices were closed, either because of the demonstrations, or "due to uncertainty." No information was available. For several days in late November we were reduced to following the developments in Czechoslovakia on TV, and watching as the standoff between demonstrators and riot police intensified through into December. The question on everyone's minds was, will the army be brought in to clear the streets, as in the 1968 Prague Spring? And what would the consequences be?

Throughout these tense weeks, we were acutely aware of the Czechoslovakian commitments to the Viking Cup and the many Western Canadian communities scheduled to host exhibition games prior to the Viking Cup.

The team was scheduled to arrive on December 12. The last word we received from Prague was that they were still scheduled to come, but that many of their players were presently committed to the street demonstrations in Prague. The outcome was uncertain.

In Camrose, we continued to watch the standoffs unfold on TV until hard-line president Gustáv Husák swore in the first democratic government in forty-one years, on December 10. That was a huge relief, but we still were not sure if all or part of the team would actually arrive at the Edmonton International Airport. Putting on a positive spin, the Camrose bus drove to the airport as scheduled.

Many years later, I learned that amongst the throngs on the streets were Czechoslovakian hockey players from former Viking Cup teams.

In the summer of 2019, as I was having lunch with František Kučera at his and his brother's arena in Prague when he told me his story.

> I was playing for Dukla Jihlava (army team) at the time along with Dominik Hašek. We were in the army just to play hockey; never the less we were classified as soldier. We heard that police were beating students in Prague. It seemed to continue for a few days. On November 24 or 25, Dominik and I and another friend jumped in Dom's old Škoda car and went to Prague to find out first-hand what was happening. There was a mass demonstration on Wenceslas Square. We saw all these buses bringing people in. We were nervous that someone would see and recognize us. Then we thought that the army might be instructed to clear Wensesles Square. It was risky for us, but it worked out fine. We both had productive careers in the NHL and helped to win gold for our country in the '98 Olympics—but it might not have turned out that way!

There are so many memorable moments in the thirty-year history of the Viking Cup exchange, but this night might top them all.

To be there, at the Edmonton International Airport to welcome the "full" Czechoslovakian national team, the first to come to the Viking Cup from a "free Czechoslovakia". That was not only hockey, that was history. History in which hockey played a role.

As the doors of Canadian customs opened, every team member burst through, all wearing the same red, white, and blue ribbons (flag colours) that were worn by the students and other demonstra-

Freedom Ribbon

tors on the streets of Prague hours or days earlier. They called them their "freedom ribbons." Freedom indeed.

Through those doors had walked the first Czechoslovakian team of the Viking Cup with no more defection fears and a wide-open Iron Curtain to welcome them on their return to their "new" country.

Several players from that team were drafted in the spring, including players Martin Straka, Žigmund Pálffy, and Jozef Stümpel, who went on to have impressive NHL careers. The team won silver in Viking Cup '90 after completing the eleven-game pre-tournament exhibition tour scheduled for them.

On December 29, 1989, Václav Havel was officially installed as the new president of the Democratic Republic of Czechoslovakia. The Czech team of Viking Cup '90 was watching the events on TV screens of Camrose. The Velvet Revolution had won and the Iron Curtain was opening —all the way.

Ice hockey had played a vital role in the forty-year history of life behind the Iron Curtain. From a devastating beginning, strong central government control and financing had given hockey a boost in the later years of Communism and leadership from well-trained coaches prepared many young players for advanced levels of hockey, such as in the NHL. One hundred and thirty-five of these players were drafted or played in the Olympics after playing in a Viking Cup. (see the list at the end of this chapter)

Velvet Revolution Aftershock

The aftershocks of the revolution for all sport were severe.

Gone was the machinery of the central sports committee vital for the unified system. Severely challenged was the continuity and authority of leadership emanating from the university sports faculty. New sources of revenue had to be found in the emerging private sector, as socialism lost its roots.

During this time of rebirth, the federation had to reassess its programs. Not only did the Czechoslovakian Ice Federation send their national U18 team to the following Viking Cup ('92), but they continued the exchange program into the new century.

The Velvet Divorce

It may not be normal to celebrate a divorce, but when both countries agree to separate without rancour, let alone bloodshed, then it is different—and the Vikings were there to participate.

The official date of the separation was January 1, 1993, the same date that the Augustana Vikings had the unique opportunity to celebrate New Year's Eve in a performance theatre just off the famous Wenceslas Square in Prague.

The activities on Wenceslas Square that night will never be forgotten, as fireworks, smoke, flying objects, and noise filled the air. A birth occurred. Twins were born. Czechoslovakia was replaced by two democratic republics—the Czech Republic and Slovakia.

We wondered what this would mean for future Viking Cup participation, and were informed that *both* countries would try to send their national U18 teams. The Czechs continued to participate through Viking Cup 2004 and the Slovaks participated from Viking Cup '98 through the final year, Viking Cup 2006. Unfortunately, the Augustana Vikings did not continue their biannual trips to the Czech Republic after 1997.

As a matter of interest, the World Junior Championships (U20) were occurring in Sweden during the Velvet Divorce. The team was called Czechoslovakia up to January 1, but for the rest of the tournament, it was called "Czecho-Slovakia."

One of the players (from Slovakia) who played at those same World Junior Championships and at Viking Cup '92 was Pavol Demitra.

While at the Viking Cup, Pavol was billeted with the Gordeyko family, on their Clydesdale horse farm near Camrose. Pavol's "Canadian mom" Eloise Gordeyko describes him as thoughtful, well mannered, and talented.

> After enjoying the West Edmonton Mall rides followed by a sleigh ride behind our horses on our farm, he and teammate Petr Jas described that day with our family as the 'best day of their lives.' We kept in contact with Pavol and his family for many years and followed his career with the St. Louis Blues with keen interest.

Although not drafted until the 227th pick in the 1993 draft, Demitra blossomed with the Blues into a feared scorer with great speed and a quick release.

On a breakaway or shootout, he was money in the bank, and he finished his career with 768 points in 847 regular-season games with St. Louis, Minnesota, Los Angeles, Ottawa, and Vancouver. He had an exceptional NHL career and was described as one of the best Slovak players ever.

Pavol Demitra and Peter Jas with Allan, Wes, and Eloise Gordeyko

But then tragedy struck. While playing his last year with Lokomotiv Yaroslavl in Russia, Pavol was killed along with his teammates in a plane crash in 2011.

Josef Vašíček, Viking Cup '98 star who stayed with the Jerome Stetar family, was also killed in the same plane disaster, as was Russian Igor Koralov of Viking Cup '88. After being drafted by the Carolina Hurricanes in the fourth round in 1998, Josef played eight years in the NHL. He then played three years in Russia. The Josef Vašíček Award is given annually by the Carolina chapter of the Professional Hockey Writer's Association to a player for most outstanding cooperation with the media, a tribute to Josef's cooperative spirit.

In Viking Cup '98, Josef played against David Tanabe of Team USA. Little did they know then that they would be teammates and roommates with the Stanley Cup-winning Carolina Hurricanes seven years later. Recently, David had this to say about his friend.

> Josef was really a nice guy—a smart individual. He played hard and knew how to relax off the ice. He was so instrumental when we won the Stanley

Cup together in Carolina, so humble and fun to be with. I used to kid him about putting ketchup on his steaks. He came from a wonderful family.

René Fasel, president of the IIHF, described the tragedy as "the darkest day in the history of sport."

In the End

While many may have predicted a severe setback for hockey when the "props" of Communism were knocked out, the sport has recovered amazingly well. To that I attribute a long, impressive history with hockey, a culture of love for the sport originating from Canadian mentorship, and well-schooled leadership fit to thrive and find a way through the challenges of the political environment. In fact, hockey played a role in determining the political outcomes.

The Czech Ice Hockey Federation wastes no time in giving the Viking Cup credit for contributing to their success in hockey which, through the opening the Iron Curtain, has led to free and progressive competition on a global level.

"The Viking Cup itself and each entire trip with series of games was the golden point in the Junior National team program," says Slavomír Lener, International Affairs Director of the Czech Ice Hockey Federation (2019), reflecting on the Viking Cup days.

> Everybody wanted to make a team, be there, experience it—both players and coaches. The whole environment—the tour across Alberta, wild broad nature, number of games, people around hockey, and fans—this was all very special. For our players and coaches, it was an unbelievable idea that they could stay in Canadian homes, with players and their parents or friends. Nobody would even think it was possible not to stay in the hotel. The family routines, houses, cars, food, fridge ("take and eat everything you want, feel and do like at home"), this all was unforgettable experience about real life in Canada. The Communist regime could talk and badmouth people and regime in the West as much as they could, but the personal experience of every single player or coach was priceless.

The Czechoslovakia Ice Hockey Federation and later the Czech and Slovak Ice Hockey Federations sent their national U18 teams to the Viking Cup twelve consecutive times and played host to the Augustana Vikings a total of eight times during a twenty-year exchange era. A total of approximately 400 Czech and Slovak players played in the Viking Cup. It's no wonder that the Viking Cup became so well known in the Czech Republic and Slovakia.

The *Viking Cup '92* magazine quotes Dom Hašek and František Kučera after they revisited their Viking Cup billets and were introduced to golf in Camrose. Dominik said, "Among young hockey players [back home, the Viking Cup] is very popular. The young Czech hockey players all know this Cup. It's always in the newspapers whether [the Czechs] finish first, second, or third. They have all the results." Frankie, chimed in: "If anyone asks what it was like in the Viking Cup, I say you'll have a very great time in Canada."

"This international tournament has name recognition in Europe," says Jan Hrdina, Viking Cup '94 star and NHL player with Pittsburgh, Phoenix, New Jersey and Columbus. "It's very well known . . . everybody wants to go because the NHL scouts are there. It was a dream come true for the guys to come over and play in the Viking Cup."

Many Augustana Vikings who experienced an unusually high quality of hockey and a very different way of life behind the Iron Curtain—and, later, the aftershocks of a revolution—say the same thing. How better to have a great time in Czechoslovakia than to be a visiting hockey player from Canada?

Beyond the Game

The plan was to spend time with Dr. Richard Pink on his home turf. Richard had lived with us in 2004 while working with surgeon Dr. Franco Leone in the Camrose hospital and improving his English skills. It was an arrangement made by a mutual friend, Josef Straka, a former Viking Cup coach from Czechoslovakia, and myself, while I was a member of the Alberta Legislature.

The Pinks' summer cottage was near the Austrian border close to the town of Nová Bystřice. It was near this town that Richard drove us to a very nice country hotel named Peršlák, for an evening Czech dinner.

Peršlák was not always a hotel. It was a military barrack for soldiers patrolling the Iron Curtain during the Cold War. I looked around and then said to Richard, "Where was the wall?" We walked a few metres into the forest and stopped. Richard said, "You are on the wall—the curtain."

Not long before our visit, Dr. Pink had visited Peršlák with his young son, Lucas, to carefully explain the realities of the Iron Curtain. Soon Lucas said, "Dad, why didn't they just crawl over the fence?" At that point, he knew that he had to tell his young son more.

At that moment, I too was being told more. I realized how effective nature had been in healing the wounds and scars of the Iron Curtain. Young trees had grown into the barren line and were now as tall as the older forest of trees on both sides.

The Viking Cup and other sport exchanges of the Cold War era have also played a role in removing the scars of separation and giving new possibilities to a young generation. Sport is always a means and an opportunity to achieve higher goals in life for the betterment of mankind. And so, the effects of the Viking Cup go far beyond hockey.

Dr. Pink, now a maxillofacial surgeon in his homeland, speaks of his advantage. "I am not a hockey player, but I spent time in general surgery in Canada because of the Viking Cup." Now he is the head of surgery in his hospital. For his part, Jan Stepan from Prague received a BA from Augustana while playing with the Vikings. Jan explains: "I came to Canada because of the Viking Cup. Now I am a Canadian citizen."

The curtain was opened, the forest reclaimed its barren path, the persecuted became the parliamentarian, the prisoner became the president, and a hockey nation found an open door to new opportunity in the little Canadian city of Camrose.

CZECHOSLOVAKIA, CZECH REPUBLIC, SLOVAKIA ROSTER

VIKING CUP PARTICIPANTS WHO PLAYED IN THE WINTER OLYMPICS (AS OF THE CONCLUSION OF 2018 GAMES)

Name	Viking Cup Team	Year(s)	Olympic Team	Year(s)
Jan Alinč	Czechoslovakia	1990	Czech Republic	1994
Martin Cibák	Slovakia	1998	Slovakia	2010
Pavol Demitra	Czechoslovakia	1992	Slovakia	2002, 2006, 2010
Ivan Droppa	Czechoslovakia	1990	Slovakia	1998
Patrik Eliáš	Czech Republic	1994	Czech Republic	2002, 2006, 2010, 2014
Michael Frolík	Czech Republic	2004	Czech Republic	2014
Pavel Geffert	Czechoslovakia	1986	Czech Republic	1994
Jaroslav Halák	Slovakia	2002	Slovakia	2010, 2014
Dominik Hašek	Czechoslovakia	1982	Czechoslovakia	1988
			Czech Republic	1998, 2002, 2006
Jan Hejda	Czech Republic	1996	Czech Republic	2010
Milan Hejduk	Czech Republic	1994	Czech Republic	1998, 2002, 2006
Milan Hnilička	Czechoslovakia	1990	Czech Republic	2002, 2006
Jan Hrdina	Czech Republic	1994	Czech Republic	2002
Tomáš Kapusta	Czechoslovakia	1984	Czech Republic	1994
Ľubomír Kolník	Czechoslovakia	1986	Slovakia	1986
Roman Kontšek	Czechoslovakia	1988	Slovakia	1998
František Kučera	Czechoslovakia	1986	Czech Republic	1998
Ján Lašák	Slovakia	1998	Slovakia	2002, 2006
Miroslav Marcinko	Czechoslovakia	1982	Slovakia	1994
Tomáš Marcinko	Slovakia	2006	Slovakia	2014, 2018
Stanislav Medřík	Czechoslovakia	1984	Slovakia	1994
Andrej Meszároš	Slovakia	2002	Slovakia	2006, 2010, 2014
Jiří Novotný	Czech Republic	2000	Czech Republic	2014
Žigmund Pálffy	Czechoslovakia	1992	Slovakia	1994, 2002, 2010
Róbert Petrovický	Czechoslovakia	1990	Slovakia	1994, 1998, 2002
Tomáš Plekanec	Czech Republic	2000	Czech Republic	2010, 2014
Libor Procházka	Czechoslovakia	1992	Czech Republic	1998
Michal Rozsíval	Czech Republic	1996	Czech Republic	2014
Martin Růžička	Czech Republic	2004	Czech Republic	2018
Alexander Salák	Czech Republic	2004	Czech Republic	2014
Andrej Sekera	Slovakia	2004	Slovakia	2010, 2014
Richard Šmehlík	Czechoslovakia	1988	Czechoslovakia	1992
			Czech Republic	1998, 2002
Peter Smrek	Slovakia	1998	Slovakia	2002
Rastislav Staňa	Slovakia	1998	Slovakia	2002, 2010
Antonín Stavjaňa	Czechoslovakia	1986	Czechoslovakia	1988
			Czech Republic	1994
Martin Straka	Czechoslovakia	1990	Czech Republic	1998, 2006
Jozef Stümpel	Czechoslovakia	1990	Slovakia	2002, 2006, 2010
Marek Svatoš	Slovakia	2000	Slovakia	2006
Radek Ťoupal	Czechoslovakia	1984	Czechoslovakia	1992
			Czech Republic	1994

Roman Turek	Czechoslovakia	1988	Czech Republic	1994
Ján Varholik	Czechoslovakia	1988	Slovakia	1994, 2998
Josef Vašíček	Czech Republic	1998	Czech Republic	2010
Tomáš Vokoun	Czech Republic	1996	Czech Republic	2006, 2010
David Volek	Czechoslovakia	1984	Czechoslovakia	1988
David Výborný	Czechoslovakia	1992	Czech Republic	2006
René Vydarený	Slovakia	1998	Slovakia	2014

VIKING CUP PARTICIPANTS SELECTED IN NHL ENTRY OR SUPPLEMENTAL DRAFTS

Player	Viking Cup Team	Year(s)	Selected By	Draft	Round	Overall Selection
Jan Alinč	Czechoslovakia	1990	Pittsburgh	1992 Entry	7	163
Martin Bakula	Czechoslovakia	1988	Edmonton	1993 Entry	8	189
Karel Bětík	Czech Republic	1996	Tampa Bay	1997 Entry	5	112
Michal Blazek	Czech Republic	2000	Dallas	2001 Entry	6	167
Michal Broš	Czech Republic	1994	San Jose	1995 Entry	5	130
Petr Chvojka	Czech Republic	2000	Montreal	2000 Entry	6	182
Martin Cibák	Slovakia	1998	Tampa Bay	1998 Entry	9	252
Jozef Čierny	Czechoslovakia	1992	Buffalo	1992 Entry	2	35
Martin Čížek	Czech Republic	2002	Buffalo	2002 Entry	9	271
Pavol Demitra	Czechoslovakia	1992	Ottawa	1993 Entry	9	227
Ivan Droppa	Czechoslovakia	1990	Chicago	1990 Entry	2	37
Marek Dubec	Slovakia	2000	Buffalo	2001 Entry	8	247
Patrik Eliáš	Czech Republic	1994	New Jersey	1994 Entry	2	51
Peter Fabuš	Slovakia	1998	Phoenix	2000 Entry	9	281
Jan Fadrný	Czech Republic	1998	Pittsburgh	1998 Entry	6	169
Ondřej Fiala	Czech Republic	2004	Minnesota	2006 Entry	2	40
Michael Frolík	Czech Republic	2004	Florida	2006 Entry	1	10
Juraj Gráčik	Slovakia	2004	Atlanta	2004 Entry	5	142
Miloslav Gureň	Czech Republic	1994	Montreal	1995 Entry	3	60
David Hájek	Czech Republic	1998	Calgary	2000 Entry	8	239
Jaroslav Halák	Slovakia	2002	Montreal	2003 Entry	9	271
Peter Hamerlík	Slovakia	2000	Pittsburgh	2000 Entry	3	84
			Boston	2002 Entry	5	153
Radek Hamr	Czechoslovakia	1992	Ottawa	1992 Entry	4	73
Dominik Hašek	Czechoslovakia	1982	Chicago	1983 Entry	10	199
Jan Hejda	Czech Republic	1996	Buffalo	2003 Entry	4	106
Milan Hejduk	Czech Republic	1994	Quebec	1994 Entry	4	87
Milan Hnilička	Czechoslovakia	1990	New York Islanders	1991 Entry	4	70
Robert Holík	Czechoslovakia	1988	Hartford	1989 Entry	1	10
Robert Horyna	Czechoslovakia	1988	Toronto	1990 Entry	9	178
Jan Hrdina	Czech Republic	1994	Pittsburgh	1995 Entry	5	128
Martin Hrstka	Czechoslovakia	1986	Vancouver	1985 Entry	6	109
Zbyněk Irgl	Czech Republic	1998	Nashville	2000 Entry	6	197
Marek Ivan	Czech Republic	1996	St. Louis	1997 Entry	9	244
Jiří Jakeš	Czech Republic	2000	Boston	2001 Entry	5	147
Lubomír Jandera	Czech Republic	1994	Chicago	1994 Entry	9	222

Robert Jindrich	Czech Republic	1994	San Jose	1995 Entry	7	168
Petr Kalus	Czech Republic	2004	Boston	2005 Entry	2	39
Vladimír Kameš	Czechoslovakia	1982	New Jersey	1984 Entry	8	149
Tomáš Káňa	Czech Republic	2004	St. Louis	2006 Entry	2	31
Tomáš Kapusta	Czechoslovakia	1984	Edmonton	1985 Entry	5	104
Ladislav Karabin	Czechoslovakia	1988	Pittsburgh	1990 Entry	9	173
Petr Klíma	Czechoslovakia	1982	Detroit	1983 Entry	5	86
Juraj Kolník	Slovakia	1998	New York Islanders	1999 Entry	4	101
Ľubomír Kolník	Czechoslovakia	1986	New Jersey	1990 Entry	6	116
Roman Kontšek	Czechoslovakia	1988	Washington	1990 Entry	7	135
Jakub Koreis	Czech Republic	2002	Phoenix	2002 Entry	1	19
Milan Kraft	Czech Republic	1998	Pittsburgh	1998 Entry	1	23
Jan Kubista	Czech Republic	2002	Boston	2002 Entry	4	130
František Kučera	Czechoslovakia	1986	Chicago	1986 Entry	4	77
David Kuchejda	Czech Republic	2004	Chicago	2005 Entry	7	202
Tomáš Kudělka	Czech Republic	2004	Ottawa	2005 Entry	5	136
Vladimír Kútny	Slovakia	2002	Detroit	2003 Entry	8	258
David Květoň	Czech Republic	2004	New York Rangers	2006 Entry	4	104
Ján Lašák	Slovakia	1998	Nashville	1999 Entry	2	65
Tomáš Linhart	Czech Republic	2002	Montreal	2002 Entry	2	45
František Lukeš	Czech Republic	2000	Phoenix	2001 Entry	8	243
Tomáš Malec	Slovakia	2000	Florida	2001 Entry	3	64
Tomáš Marcinko	Slovakia	2006	New York Islanders	2006 Entry	4	115
Ivan Matulik	Czechoslovakia	1986	Edmonton	1986 Entry	7	147
Roman Meluzín	Czechoslovakia	1990	Winnipeg	1990 Entry	4	74
Marian Meňhart	Czech Republic	1994	Buffalo	1995 Entry	5	111
Lukáš Mensator	Czech Republic	2002	Vancouver	2002 Entry	3	83
Andrej Meszároš	Slovakia	2002	Ottawa	2004 Entry	1	23
Jaroslav Miklenda	Czechoslovakia	1992	Ottawa	1992 Entry	7	146
Tomáš Mojžíš	Czech Republic	2000	Toronto	2001 Entry	8	246
Milan Nedoma	Czechoslovakia	1990	Buffalo	1990 Entry	8	166
Jan Němeček	Czech Republic	1994	Los Angeles	1994 Entry	9	215
Jiří Novotný	Czech Republic	2000	Buffalo	2001 Entry	1	22
Žigmund Pálffy	Czechoslovakia	1992	New York Islanders	1991 Entry	2	26
Petr Pavlas	Czechoslovakia	1986	Washington	1988 Entry	9	189
Róbert Petrovický	Czechoslovakia	1990	Hartford	1992 Entry	1	9
Ľubomír Pištek	Slovakia	1998	Philadelphia	1998 Entry	8	222
Libor Pivko	Czech Republic	1998	Nashville	2000 Entry	3	89
Jan Platil	Czech Republic	2000	Ottawa	2001 Entry	7	218
Tomáš Plekanec	Czech Republic	2000	Montreal	2001 Entry	3	71
Martin Podlešák	Czech Republic	2000	Phoenix	2001 Entry	2	45
Libor Polášek	Czechoslovakia	1992	Vancouver	1992 Entry	1	21
Jiří Poner	Czechoslovakia	1982	Minnesota	1984 Entry	5	89
Marek Posmyk	Czech Republic	1996	Toronto	1996 Entry	2	36
Tomáš Pospíšil	Czech Republic	2004	Atlanta	2005 Entry	5	135
Libor Procházka	Czechoslovakia	1992	St. Louis	1993 Entry	10	245
Petr Punčochář	Czech Republic	2000	Chicago	2001 Entry	6	186
Roman Pylner	Czech Republic	1996	Colorado	1996 Entry	8	188
Pavel Rajnoha	Czechoslovakia	1992	Calgary	1992 Entry	7	150

Luboš Rob	Czechoslovakia	1988	New York Rangers	1990 Entry	5	105
Antonin Routa	Czechoslovakia	1986	Montreal	1986 Entry	9	183
Michal Rozsíval	Czech Republic	1996	Pittsburgh	1996 Entry	5	105
Petr Rucka	Czechoslovakia	1984	Calgary	1984 Entry	10	200
Martin Šagát	Slovakia	2002	Toronto	2003 Entry	3	91
Ladislav Ščurko	Slovakia	2004	Philadelphia	2004 Entry	6	170
Andrej Sekera	Slovakia	2004	Buffalo	2004 Entry	3	71
Michal Sivek	Czech Republic	1998	Washington	1999 Entry	2	29
František Skladaný	Slovakia	2000	Colorado	2001 Entry	5	143
Zdeněk Skořepa	Czech Republic	1994	New Jersey	1994 Entry	4	103
Pavel Skrbek	Czech Republic	1996	Pittsburgh	1996 Entry	2	28
Richard Šmehlík	Czechoslovakia	1988	Buffalo	1990 Entry	5	97
Zdeněk Šmíd	Czech Republic	1998	Atlanta	2000 Entry	6	168
Peter Smrek	Slovakia	1998	St. Louis	1999 Entry	3	85
Rastislav Staňa	Slovakia	1998	Washington	1998 Entry	7	193
Antonín Stavjaňa	Czechoslovakia	1986	Calgary	1986 Entry	12	247
Ondřej Steiner	Czechoslovakia	1992	Buffalo	1992 Entry	3	59
Martin Straka	Czechoslovakia	1990	Pittsburgh	1992 Entry	1	19
Jozef Stümpel	Czechoslovakia	1990	Boston	1991 Entry	2	40
David Švagrovský	Czech Republic	2002	Colorado	2003 Entry	4	131
Marek Svatoš	Slovakia	2000	Colorado	2001 Entry	7	227
Jaroslav Svejkovský	Czech Republic	1994	Washington	1996 Entry	1	17
Petr Svoboda	Czech Republic	1984	Montreal	1984 Entry	1	5
Petr Svoboda	Czech Republic	1998	Toronto	1998 Entry	2	35
Martin Sychra	Czechoslovakia	1992	Montreal	1992 Entry	6	140
Jiří Tlustý	Czech Republic	2004	Toronto	2006 Entry	1	13
Roman Tománek	Slovakia	2004	Phoenix	2004 Entry	4	103
Radek Ťoupal	Czechoslovakia	1984	Edmonton	1987 Entry	6	126
Michal Trávníček	Czech Republic	1998	Toronto	1998 Entry	8	228
Tomáš Troliga	Slovakia	2002	St. Louis	2002 Entry	3	89
Roman Turek	Czechoslovakia	1988	Minnesota	1990 Entry	6	113
Michal Valant	Slovakia	2004	Buffalo	2004 Entry	5	145
Lukáš Vantuch	Czech Republic	2004	Boston	2005 Entry	6	172
Václav Varaďa	Czech Republic	1994	San Jose	1994 Entry	4	89
Josef Vašíček	Czech Republic	1998	Carolina	1998 Entry	4	91
Josef Vávra	Czech Republic	2002	Ottawa	2002 Entry	8	246
Ľuboš Velebný	Slovakia	2000	Toronto	2000 Entry	7	223
Jakub Vojta	Czech Republic	2004	Carolina	2005 Entry	4	94
Tomáš Vokoun	Czech Republic	1996	Montreal	1994 Entry	9	226
David Volek	Czechoslovakia	1984	New York Islanders	1984 Entry	10	208
Roman Vopat	Czech Republic	1994	St. Louis	1994 Entry	7	172
David Výborný	Czechoslovakia	1992	Edmonton	1993 Entry	2	33
René Vydarený	Slovakia	1998	Vancouver	1999 Entry	3	69
Jiří Vykoukal	Czechoslovakia	1988	Washington	1989 Entry	10	208
Miroslav Zálešák	Slovakia	1998	San Jose	1998 Entry	4	104
Lukáš Zeliska	Slovakia	2006	New York Rangers	2006 Entry	7	204

VIKING CUP PARTICIPANTS WHO PLAYED IN NHL AND WERE NOT SELECTED IN NHL ENTRY OR SUPPLEMENTAL DRAFTS

Name	Viking Cup Team	Year(s)
Peter Sejna	Slovakia	1998

Scrimmage, by Jim Brager (Viking Cup '94)

CHAPTER 7

Missing Link . . . USA Connections

"Canada has a tradition of small communities getting involved that rivals no other place in the world. We want to expose our Junior players to that, and there's no better tournament than the Viking Cup to do that. We've built so many great friendships over the years with the people of Camrose, and that's another big reason we keep coming back."

—David Tyler, "Hockey and Hospitality – The Rose," *American Hockey Magazine*, March 2004.

David Tyler didn't send his teams to the Viking Cup; he brought them. He wasn't a bystander; he was a participant.

David, an Iowa attorney, served USA hockey interests well. He acted as vice-president and Junior Council chairman of USA Hockey for twenty-five years and, prior to entry into Viking Cup '96, he had worked as president of the USA Junior Hockey League for twelve years.

As David was no stranger to international hockey, the Viking Cup caught his interest. It brought back memories of the numerous international events where he'd represented USA Hockey, including the famous Miracle on Ice at Lake Placid, where the Americans won gold.

It had been difficult to attract a USA representative team to the Viking Cup until USA Hockey proposed an all-star team from the USA junior hockey leagues. They would wear the official USA hockey jersey. That is when David Tyler entered the picture, along with his good friend Joe Benedetto, staff liaison for USA Hockey Junior Council. Joe served as the team leader.

At the time, USA junior hockey was somewhat of an enigma. There was much said about USA college and university hockey, and high school hockey, but junior teams seemed more suited to the Canadian system of hockey, less related to educational institutions. Our previous invitations to American colleges had only attracted two teams—Augsburg College, a sister Lutheran school from Minneapolis, and a team from the University of Arizona. Neither team did particularly well. It seemed that the college teams were very restricted by the NCAA or other governing bodies in the number of non-league games permitted, and there was ample opportunity to play exhibition games in home states with less expense.

Players from the USA junior teams were more suited in age to the European and Canadian junior teams, which soon became a better draw at the Viking Cup. The St. Paul Vulcans, a junior team from Minnesota, had played in Viking Cup '84, reciprocating an earlier exchange visit of the Camrose Vikings team to Minnesota. Although not in the medals, the Vulcans were competitive.

For Viking Cup '96, Dave and Joe did a great job assembling an all-star team from the three American junior leagues: US Hockey League, North American Hockey League, and American West Hockey League. All were preparing youth for career advancement in collegiate programs or professional hockey. At the time, there were thirty-two league teams from which to choose the all-star team—not an easy task, I'm sure!

The team, under Coach Mike Hastings, was a great credit to the tournament, winning the silver medal. In a letter of response following the experience, David Tyler commented, "It is the interaction between the participants and the community that is the genius of this tournament."

In his weekly column, *Camrose Canadian* sports editor Tim Chamberlain quoted Tyler: "We hope that we'll be invited back and I suspect that we will be because I think that we belong here." Chamberlain goes on to say, "It is in fact a huge compliment to the tournament coming from one of the USA's most influential and respected hockey men."

Coach Hastings commented on the experience:

> It is something really that I can't put into words. The people of Camrose, and the way that this first-class tournament is operated, I think, are second to none. The people of this community are phenomenal. They open their doors to people they've never met before, they let them eat out of their fridge and sleep in their beds, and they break bread with them at the table. In today's society, to meet a community like Camrose is out of the ordinary. I couldn't imagine coming up there and seeing the way this tournament is run.

Responding to strong recommendations to participate in Viking Cup '98, the USA U18 national team under the leadership of well-known coaches Steve Pleau, Lou Vairo, and Neil Broten, was sent by USA Hockey. Broten had been a member of the famous Miracle on Ice US Olympic gold team of 1980. In the *Viking Cup '98* magazine, USA Hockey president Walter Busch commented, "We are proud to be a participant in this prestigious international tournament."

Although the team did not place in the Viking Cup '98 medals, the NHL drafted a total of fourteen of their players, including well-known players like Minnesota's Jordan Leopold and David Tanabe. For Camrose, it was like an extension of the long sporting and Scandinavian connection with Minnesota, beginning with the famous Hansen brothers, who moved from Camrose to Minneapolis for college and professional hockey careers in the early part of the twentieth century (see Chapter 1).

Tanabe was drafted by the Carolina Hurricanes in the first round and had a nine-year NHL career, mostly with Carolina but also with Phoenix and Boston. He later played in

Switzerland. He was a product of Minnesota high school hockey, which we in Canada know little about but probably should look at more closely.

About his high school hockey experience, David had this to say:

> I had the opportunity to play in front of 18,000 fans at the state high school championship last year. That was awesome. Hockey is such a big thing in Minnesota. There is no other level of hockey like that where you play in front of all your friends and peers from school.

Following high school, David was chosen for the US National Team Development Program at Ann Arbor, Michigan, where he joined his teammates to make the trip to Camrose for Viking Cup '98. The following year he played in the NCAA with the Wisconsin Badgers, where he made the all-conference rookie team. In David's first year in the NHL, he was surprised that his appointed roommate was Czech Josef Vašíček, whom he had played against in the Viking Cup.

There was also an Edmonton Oiler connection.

Hall-of-Famer Paul Coffey, who helped the Oilers win three of their five Stanley Cups, was playing for the Carolina Hurricanes at the time. In the *Viking Cup 2004* magazine, David commented, "I had the opportunity to start my career on defense with Paul Coffey. It was invaluable to watch him skate and receive some of his tips. He taught me a lot!" Ironically, David's first NHL goal came against Oiler Grant Fuhr!

David's time in Camrose was special. "The hockey was great," he said, in a 2019 interview.

> I thought Minnesota was the hockey hotbed until I got to the Viking Cup. Now I was playing against the best from the world. I was playing against players like Mike Comrie and Henrik Zetterberg and Ossi Väänänen. My mom and dad were there and they talked about it later. Wow, I learned things there that I hadn't picked up on at the time. So, in the context of the time, the Viking Cup was an important step in that it brought me to a new level of competition. It became a new measuring stick for me personally and I gained a new level of confidence from it. I learned that I could play with the best and really enjoy it.
>
> When I first heard that we were going to be living with families for a two-week period, I didn't know how to react. It ended up being a blessing just to get a chance to meet some people. The people were great and the Viking Cup is a great tournament. It was one of my first experiences internationally. I had a lot of fun.

And there is also the Calgary connection. Jordan Leopold is a graduate of the University of Minnesota, where he won a Hobey Baker Award in 2002 as the top US collegiate player. He played four seasons for the Calgary Flames as a key defenseman, and a total of seventeen seasons in the NHL. He also played for the USA national team and, in 2006, while with the Flames, he achieved his goal of playing for Team USA in the Turin Olympics.

"The atmosphere is awesome," Jordan told the *Viking Cup 2006 Magazine* while in Calgary. "I never played in a city that is so devoted to their hockey. They have been through the rough times and the good times. It's the best place to play by far in my books. Hockey is number one in Calgary and always will be. The players really appreciate the fans. They are the ones we go out and battle for. We like to win for them."

Like David Tanabe, his teammate at the Viking Cup, Leopold was a graduate of Minnesota high school hockey, after which he joined the US National Team Development Program in Michigan. The talented blue-liner played in sixty games that year, including four at the Viking Cup. "It was my second or third time up to Canada. I ended up billeting with a family in Camrose. It was neat and interesting."

Relative to the many mentors who had helped him develop his hockey skills along the way, he told *Viking Cup 2004* magazine, "Ultimately, you have to remember where you come from and always donate your time and presence to benefit the hockey community. It is one big fraternity. Hockey is very important to all of us, and we want it to succeed."

NHL and American university scouts filled the upper bleachers with a special interest in the five European and American U18 teams that dominated the eight-team tournament. In fact, fifty-two players were drafted by the NHL from Viking Cup '98, an all-time high.

With growing strength in the USA junior hockey program and a keen thirst for more of Camrose, Dave Tyler and Joe Benedetto returned to Viking Cup 2000 with a well-balanced and well-disciplined team of league All-Stars. Dave commented, "No matter the result, the experience of participating in this tournament is a lasting, positive memory for all participants." A positive memory for sure. Team USA won gold at Viking Cup 2000.

Dave and Joe continued to bring excellent Junior All-Star teams to each Viking Cup and, in the end, sixty-three of their players were drafted and/or played in the NHL or Olympics. In *American Hockey Magazine*'s March 2004 issue, Mike Antonovich, a Minnesota-based scout for the St. Louis Blues commented, "It is always interesting to see all the different styles of hockey [at the Viking Cup]. I think it says a lot about the US kids to be playing as well as they have been here. It shows that American kids are getting good coaching, and they're getting better and better all the time."

"This is a great tournament," agreed Coach Joe Shawhan of Team USA. "It's a great way to gauge how our country is doing as far as developing players on the world stage, and it gives our players memories I'm sure they will never forget."

Joe Pavelski, who had a thirteen-year stint (four as captain) with the San Jose Sharks before playing with Dallas, is one of the stars who has great memories of the Viking Cup. I contacted him in his Wisconsin home during the COVID-19 suspension of play.

"We had a lot of success with our offensive game at the Viking Cup until we ran into the Finnish style of strong defensive hockey in the gold-medal game," he told me. "Now, it didn't help that Tuukka Rask, tournament MVP, was the Finnish goaltender! We fired about forty shots but could only score twice. Not enough to beat the flying Finns."

At the time, of course, Joe didn't realize he would be shooting pucks at Rask in the Boston Bruins' net for many years to come.

"Going into the Viking Cup, I didn't realize it would be so much fun, staying with a family and all that." The fun continued when Joe returned to his junior team in Iowa, the Waterloo Blackhawks, to complete the season. The Blackhawks won the USA Junior championship and Joe was given the Dave Tyler Junior Player of the Year Award as the most outstanding American-born player in USA Junior Hockey. Coincidentally, this same Dave Tyler, of Viking Cup fame, was also from Waterloo, Iowa!

"Joe was Captain and Paul was the leading scorer... they stayed with us"

Joe Pavelski and Paul Stastny stayed with Paul and Lianne Samoisette, who were regular billets for American teams at the Viking Cup. The Samoisettes remembered with enthusiasm, "Joe was captain of the team and a real gentleman. Later, when he was playing for the San Jose Sharks, he would meet us after they played the Oilers in Edmonton…. We had a good time with Paul and his parents as they came to Camrose for the whole tournament."

The Stastny name is well known in international hockey circles. In the same year as the first Viking Cup (1980-81), three brothers from Czechoslovakia defected to play with the Quebec Nordiques. Their names were Peter, Anton, and Marián Šťastný (Marián actually arrived one year later). It rocked the hockey world at the time and was a precursor for an influx of Iron Curtain players entering the NHL in years to follow. Many had their first contact with North American Hockey, at a young age, through the Viking Cup.

"My fondest memory was sitting with Peter Šťastný"

So it was, in 2004, twenty-four years later, Paul Stastny, son of Peter, came to Camrose to play with USA in the Viking Cup. Paul was the leading scorer in Viking Cup 2004, but that may not be a surprise. Peter, sometimes known as "Peter the Great," was the first European player to achieve 1,000 points in the NHL. Peter, father and St. Louis Blue scout, was in the Camrose crowd, watching.

Rick Forster, American team co-host, enjoyed the Šťastnýs. "My fondest memory of the Viking Cup was sitting with Peter Šťastný, talking about hockey and family and watching Paul play."

Following Viking Cup 2004, Paul was drafted in the second round by Nashville and since has had a fifteen-year NHL career with Colorado (eight), St. Louis (four), Winnipeg (two), and Las Vegas. He played in the 2010 and 2014 Olympics for the USA.

Forster served as co-host of Team USA for Viking Cups '94, '96, and '98 and he and wife Gail billeted in '96 and '98. Rick comments, "Had we known it would be so much fun, we would surely have billeted in '94, as well."

"I practised with the team . . . and sat in their roped-off section"

Rick continued, "The USA players really inspired our young son, Brett, and other Camrose kids, such as Brendan Evans, Ryley Redell, and Tyler Bouck—all on Brett's Bantam team and all of whom advanced to have professional hockey careers. One day, at Viking Cup '98, Joe (Benedetto) asked Brett if he wanted to practise with the US team. There was no hesitation."

Now looking back, Brett says, "I was lucky enough to face off against Adam Hall and run drills with John-Michael Liles, Jordan Leopold, and Dave Tanabe. It was fun to be in their dressing room—like brotherhood."

> Then they invited me to sit with them in the players' roped-off section as we watched other Viking Cup games. I especially remember sitting with Leopold and Henning. One day, Olli Jokinen was trying to teach everyone Finnish there. I needed more time to catch on, but I could not wait to learn the language and find out more about where many of these players were from. You know what? I skipped school to watch my Team USA play in the final game!

Adam Hall played in Viking Cup '98, and was drafted in the second round by Nashville. After graduating from Michigan State University, he had a fourteen-year NHL career with seven teams including three years with Nashville and three years with Tampa Bay. He played with the USA national team in five World Championships.

Following Viking Cup 2004, the Colorado Avalanche drafted John-Michael Liles. After he graduated from Michigan State University, he became a regular high scoring defenseman with the Avalanche for seven years before being traded to Toronto. Three years later, he was traded to Carolina, after which he completed his fifteen-year NHL career in Boston. Liles played for the USA in the 2006 Olympics.

"We found ourselves cheering for the Americans . . . they became our boys"

Joan and Doug Petruk billeted American boys at five Viking Cups. "It was a family event and especially good for our kids, Shawn and Cara," remembers Joan. Shawn did the stats for three US teams, and the Americans took turns cooking with the Petruk kids. "They talked a lot about their families. They were very mature kids. One was going to med school. One night, I loaned my car to one of the boys to go to the show. He made a special effort to thank me for trusting him."

"What a legacy for the Viking Cup," Joan continued. "It made us more open minded and tolerant. It was amazing how connections were built with each country. We got away from the political stuff, and we understand the game better!"

"The American team put on a big dinner for all their families at the Norsemen Hotel one night," remembers Doug, who chaired a committee at the Viking Cup. "Each player sat with his newfound family. What a great idea."

One of the players who stayed with the Petruk family was Johann Kroll, an Ohio State University recruit on Team USA 2004. He comments in the March 2004 issue of *USA Hockey Magazine*: "They just go out of their way to make sure that this is as good an experience as it can be. It's really unbelievable that a small town like this can turn a tournament like this into such a big deal."

The Viking Cup Is More Than Just A Junior Hockey Tournament

By W. David Tyler

Camrose is not a place — it is an experience. To be more precise, it's an experience of a lifetime for most, if not all, of the participants at the Viking Cup.

Every two years for the past quarter century, this small community on the plains of Alberta, Canada, has opened its hearts and homes to visitors from foreign lands, who speak different languages and come from different cultures, with different diets and personal habits.

The common denominator for everyone involved is a love for the game and the pursuit of the Viking Cup championship.

Over the years, the local small, church-related college has hosted this event, and the whole town has participated in one way or another to help make the tournament a success. From commercial sponsors, to billet families, to tournament committees — it takes almost the town's entire population to pull it off.

This year's tournament featured six European teams. Over the years, virtually every hockey-playing nation in Europe has sent a representative team to Camrose.

Participation from USA Hockey began early on when the St. Paul Vulcans Junior team from the United States Hockey League entered the tournament in the '80s. After an extended absence, USA Hockey started sending a representative team in 1996 and has continued to participate ever since.

As every player who has ever played there can attest, the hockey is of the highest caliber and the fans are most appreciative and knowledgeable. Because of the presence of the Europeans, the tournament is heavily scouted by both professional and college teams. Many players have improved their draft status and have gone on to compete successfully in professional and/or college hockey.

But the Viking Cup is much more than a hockey tournament — it is a life experience, with an international flavor, giving all participants the opportunity to test their skills against systems and philosophies from other countries, while wearing the uniform of his country.

Recently, the opportunity to share in the experience was made available to All-Star players selected from USA Hockey's domestic Junior program. In eight appearances, the USA Selects have captured one gold and two silver medals as they have successfully competed in the tournament.

This issue of *American Hockey Magazine* chronicles the steps taken by this year's silver-medal winning U.S. Team, and more importantly looks at what makes the Viking Cup such a unique hockey tournament and cultural experience.

W. David Tyler
USA Hockey Vice President
Junior Council Chairman

American Hockey Magazine - March, 2004

"They were an engaging bunch"

Former RCMP officer Merv Griffin enjoyed the American kids who stayed with his family (and other players that congregated in their rumpus room to play ping pong). "It was an engaging time. They were awesome, the American kids and their leaders. They were an all-star team, coming from many states. The Viking Cup made the community known worldwide."

"They were running up and down the ice"

No, this is not hockey, but curling!

"Two of our billets were from the village of New Norway," says Lindsay Aker, co-host of the American team. "They put on a potluck for the team and all the families at the local curling rink. Most players had never curled before. We all had a blast, running up and down the ice. They caught on fast, these kids from Michigan, Minnesota, Dakota, Iowa, New York, Florida, and California."

Dave Tyler could see a growing rivalry in hockey between the USA and Canada that would be beneficial to the Viking Cup. At Viking Cup 2000, he commented: "I think it is true that both sides, Canadian and American, measure themselves against the other team and their program, so there is that rivalry, that intensity that today is probably greater across our common border than it would be with any other international teams."

Beyond team quality, the USA's place in the Viking Cup became more like a partner than a guest. They believed in the goals of the Viking Cup and their participation, feedback, and friendship became high points for all in the Viking Cup family of workers.

But there is an explanation for this supportive relationship. While other international hockey federations generally sent a new group of leaders to each Viking Cup, the USA was consistently represented with the same leaders: Dave and Joe. It was more like a homecoming each year.

Of course, the quality of competition was foremost for the Americans. But player billeting and cultural exchange were also attractive Viking Cup features. For the Americans, the Viking Cup was "a lifetime experience," as Dave Tyler described in the *American Hockey Magazine* in 2006.

David Tyler loved the Viking Cup, but he also saw the great potential for it to be even better. In visualizing its growth, he correctly identified the need to involve referees from participating countries. He saw the need to address teams' age differences to better accommodate the young national teams from Europe. He understood the unique benefits of having young national teams from Europe, because that was a magnet that drew the US to the tournament. He understood the importance of putting a top-notch product on the ice to draw the crowds needed to sustain the Viking Cup. And he was in tune with the American way of marketing sport.

Dave Tyler was forward-thinking, but he was also quick to reflect on his experiences with past Viking Cups. He once commented, "I believe that the Camrose experience has had a major impact on the lives of a lot of young people over the years, and I certainly know that it has had a major impact on the USA Hockey program and our teams and management."

The Missing Link

From his retirement home in Florida, Dave Tyler today (2020) looks back on his many years with USA Hockey.

> At the time that USA Hockey was first invited to participate in the Viking Cup (1995) on a bi-annual basis, it was an answer to prayer for those of us involved in the development of the Junior-aged hockey player within the USAH organization. In the mid-'90s, USAH had a strong youth program for sixteen-and-under players, both men and women, but our program for the sixteen-to-twenty-year-old player, both men and women, was struggling to find an opportunity for international competition for those players.

> Because the USAH program in Ann Arbor was non-existent, we were relying upon the USHL in the Midwest, the NAHL in the Michigan and central states area, and other programs at the Junior-B level in New England for the development of these players. After our participation in the Viking Cup, we were then able to enjoy improved recruitment of our Junior players at the collegiate level and

an improved level of interest in our Junior players by the NHL when it came time for the draft. The program then became a recognized part of the USAH Junior hockey-development program.

*The opportunity provided by the Viking Cup and the successful participation of our athletes during the competition, provided by Canadian as well as international programs, brought instant recognition in the US, to the value of the development being provided within our Junior program. The invitation to international competition of the quality provided by the Viking Cup was most certainly **the missing link** in the further development of our program on the US side of the border.*

Many graduates from the USAH Junior program who had the opportunity over the years that we did to participate in the Viking Cup, went on to receive collegiate scholarships and were invited by the NHL draft to continue participation at that level. These young people related most of their opportunities achieved to the USAH Junior program, and their appreciation of the memories they enjoyed while participating in the Viking Cup.

From the USAH perspective, the quality of the opportunity provided by the Viking Cup cannot be underestimated and must be recognized and appreciated. The investment by the community and the college in the development of the competition at the level of the Viking Cup needs to be recognized and complimented. The method used to billet the players allowed our participants to enjoy an unbelievably valuable life and international experience within the Canadian community, in addition to the competition on the ice.

Those memories remain clear and strong, even today, as friendships that developed during those years remain a positive memory today. I shall never forget the anticipation as we all waited for the hour of midnight during the changeover from 1999 to 2000, wondering whether or not the computers would continue to function, following our entry into the new year!

There was no missing link from the old to the new century, and now the missing link in USA junior hockey had been found. The computers remained faithful into the new century, and so did Dave Tyler and USA Hockey.

In the end, one of the greatest contributions of the Americans to the Viking Cup was to tell us "just what we had going for us." As Joan Petruk, a regular billet for the American boys, said so aptly, "The really rewarding part is listening to people who are new to the community describe it back to you. They're so excited about it, and that reminds you how special it is."

Their message of affirmation was motivating and reassuring that the stars were aligned in the Viking Cup, and USA Hockey was shining as one of them—the voice of visitors, partners, and trusted neighbour.

USA

VIKING CUP PARTICIPANTS WHO PLAYED IN THE WINTER OLYMPICS (AS OF THE CONCLUSION OF 2018 GAMES)

Name	Viking Cup Team	Year(s)	Olympic Team	Year(s)
Jordan Leopold	USA	1998	USA	2006
John-Michael Liles	USA	1998	USA	2006
Joe Pavelski	USA	2004	USA	2010, 2014
Paul Stastny	USA	2004	USA	2010, 2014

VIKING CUP PARTICIPANTS SELECTED IN NHL ENTRY OR SUPPLEMENTAL DRAFTS

Player	Viking Cup Team	Year(s)	Selected By	Draft	Round	Overall Selection
PJ Atherton	USA	2002	Tampa Bay	2002 Entry	6	170
Patrick Aufiero	USA	1998	New York Rangers	1999 Entry	3	90
Zach Bearson	USA	2006	Florida	2005 Entry	7	224
Kyle Clark	USA	1998	Washington	1999 Entry	6	175
Joshua Dewolf	USA	1996	New Jersey	1996 Entry	2	41
Matt Doman	USA	1998	Calgary	1999 Entry	5	135
Joseph Fallon	USA	2004	Chicago	2005 Entry	6	167
Troy Ferguson	USA	1998	Carolina	2000 Entry	9	276
Justin Forrest	USA	2000	Carolina	2000 Entry	6	181
Brian Foster	USA	2006	Florida	2005 Entry	5	161
Tom Gilbert	USA	2002	Colorado	2002 Entry	4	129
Robert Goepfert	USA	2002	Pittsburgh	2002 Entry	6	171
Matt Greene	USA	2002	Edmonton	2002 Entry	2	44
Nathan Guenin	USA	2002	New York Rangers	2002 Entry	4	127
David Hale	USA	2000	New Jersey	2000 Entry	1	22
Adam Hall	USA	1998	Nashville	1999 Entry	2	52
Mike Hanson	USA	1996	New Jersey	1994 Entry	11	269
Adam Hauser	USA	1998	Edmonton	1999 Entry	3	81
Barrett Heisten	USA	1998	Buffalo	1999 Entry	1	20
Brett Henning	USA	1998	New York Islanders	1999 Entry	9	251
Andrew Hutchinson	USA	1998	Nashville	1999 Entry	2	54
Todd Jackson	USA	2000	Detroit	2000 Entry	8	251
Doug Janik	USA	1998	Buffalo	1999 Entry	2	55
Joe Jensen	USA	2002	Pittsburgh	2003 Entry	8	232
Steven Kampfer	USA	2006	Anaheim	2007 Entry	4	93
Kyle Klubertanz	USA	2004	Anaheim	2004 Entry	3	74
Craig Kowalski	USA	2000	Carolina	2000 Entry	8	235
Jordan Leopold	USA	1998	Anaheim	1999 Entry	2	44
William Levesque	USA	1998	San Jose	1999 Entry	4	111
Trevor Lewis	USA	2006	Los Angeles	2006 Entry	1	17
John-Michael Liles	USA	1998	Colorado	2000 Entry	5	159
Tony Lucia	USA	2006	San Jose	2005 Entry	6	193

Trevor Ludwig	USA	2004	Dallas	2004 Entry	6	183
Marty Magers	USA	2002	Buffalo	2002 Entry	4	121
William Magnuson	USA	1998	Colorado	1999 Entry	5	142
Doug Meyer	USA	1998	Pittsburgh	1999 Entry	6	176
Brian Nelson	U of Arizona	1988	New York Rangers	1984 Entry	8	161
Kyle Okposo	USA	2006	New York Islanders	2006 Entry	1	7
Joe Pavelski	USA	2004	San Jose	2003 Entry	7	205
Derek Peltier	USA	2004	Colorado	2004 Entry	6	184
Nick Petrecki	USA	2006	San Jose	2007 Entry	1	28
Jason Platt	USA	2000	Edmonton	2000 Entry	8	247
Grant Potulny	USA	2000	Ottawa	2000 Entry	5	157
Danny Richmond	USA	2002	Carolina	2003 Entry	2	31
Troy Riddle	USA	2000	St. Louis	2000 Entry	4	129
Tony Romano	USA	2006	New Jersey	2006 Entry	6	178
Shaun Sabol	St. Paul	1984	Philadelphia	1986 Entry	10	209
Ben Simon	USA	1996	Chicago	1997 Entry	5	110
Jim Slater	USA	2000	Atlanta	2002 Entry	1	30
Alex Stalock	USA	2006	San Jose	2005 Entry	4	112
Paul Stastny	USA	2004	Colorado	2005 Entry	2	44
David Tanabe	USA	1998	Carolina	1999 Entry	1	16
Ryan Turek	USA	2006	St. Louis	2006 Entry	4	94
Chris VandeVelde	USA	2006	Edmonton	2005 Entry	4	97
Mike Walsh	USA	2002	New York Rangers	2002 Entry	5	143

VIKING CUP PARTICIPANTS WHO PLAYED IN NHL AND WERE NOT SELECTED IN NHL ENTRY OR SUPPLEMENTAL DRAFTS

Name	Viking Cup Team	Year(s)
Alex Brooks	USA	1996
Chris Conner	USA	2002
Alex Foster	USA	2004
Andy Greene	USA	2002
Peter Harrold	USA	2002
Jack Hillen	USA	2004
Chad LaRose	USA	2000
Greg Rallo	USA	2002

Rosehaven, by Audrey Pfanmuller (Viking Cup '98)

CHAPTER 8

We Can, Too . . . Russian Connections

"You know I had never seen such attention by the fans. As a young kid coming over here, I soon learned that hockey was such a big thing, seeing so many people paying to see the Viking Cup. And they cheered for us, too! It was something special and I think this was the biggest memory of Camrose and the Viking Cup!"

—Sergei Gonchar, Viking Cup '92, first-round draft pick,
Washington Capitals

It only seemed right that the Soviets should compete in the Viking Cup.

The Cup's genesis dates back to the Vikings' first visit behind the Iron Curtain, in January 1980. At that time, in the historic city of Leningrad (St. Petersburg), the Vikings played their best hockey but still lost both games to a highly skilled Russian team. Their pass-oriented style of play was as elegant as it seemed unbeatable and it brought out the best in our team.

Star defenseman Kerry Preete of the Vikings remembers it well. "The Soviet hockey experience was as fascinating as was the cultural experience," he's said.

> I recall the first game getting trounced pretty good by the Leningrad Junior team. Their speed, constant motion, regrouping, and attacking as a five-man unit were overwhelming! It was much different than the up-and-down game we were used to playing. We were able to adjust some in the second game to be more competitive. My own game took a new turn that day…much for the better. I'm sure the European experience helped me to make the University of Saskatchewan Huskies coached by Dave King the following year. (Kerry went on to be an all-star in Canadian University hockey)

After our first hockey game, few if any in our Canadian group realized that we had only seen half of what hockey was all about in Russia. We had to go to the ballet to get an understanding of the other half—the part that takes place away from the ice.

With the fall of Communism, this cultural capital of Russia reclaimed its original name, St. Petersburg, as a tribute to its founder, Tsar Peter the Great, who was a lover of art. Between the two games in this magnificent city, the Vikings entourage got a taste of Russian art and culture at the famous UNESCO-designated Hermitage and the St. Petersburg Ballet. It seemed that the style of hockey played in this city had a lot to do with its cultural character.

The father of hockey in Russia, Anatoli Tarasov, viewed hockey as an art with the coach as choreographer and the players as performers, perfecting the principles of dance and artistry. A 2002 ESPN article entitled "Russians Regroup on Other Side of the Red Line" describes how he integrated elements from ballet, chess, and bandy into a rigorous training program and emphasized creativity in team play. "Play beautiful; play as one," he would say. Tarasov had been a watchmaker, so he thought in terms of parts working together in clockwork precision to produce the desired effect. In hockey, that clarified his concept of building the team.

Following WW11, Stalin appointed Tarasov to introduce ice hockey into the Soviet Union. In the movie *Of Miracles and Men*, journalist Vsevolod Kukushkin gives the reason: "After the Russians defeated the Nazis in World War II, they had to continue to prove their strength. It was done through sport. Hockey was chosen by Stalin because it was a high-profile Olympic sport. They would use it as propaganda on the world stage."

Separated by the Iron Curtain, there was little help or influence from Canada. So, the Soviets developed their own unique hockey system, merging elements of the arts with sport.

While the cultural life in St. Petersburg was indeed advanced, the Russian train was shaky on our return to the border city of Viborg. From there, we would speed on the perfectly smooth Finnish rails into Helsinki.

On that aged train, our trip debriefings on European hockey now included the Soviets; we had earlier played the Swedes and the Finns.

We wondered. Would these European teams be interested in paying a visit to Canada to play hockey? How about organizing inter-country hockey games in Camrose, like we had just experienced in Europe?

There was no doubt that the Russian stars would belong, if our tournament musings on those rails of Russia should find wheels.

As we reached the Soviet border at the city of Viborg, I reflected on memories of the origins of the Spengler Cup of Switzerland. Had it not been founded to break down the barriers of a Europe divided by the First World War? I mentioned this to Coach Voytechek and Camrose travel agent Carman Mason as our belongings were searched a second time on that imposing border. It was then we knew that Russia belonged in the Viking Cup. Sport has a way of removing barriers.

By this time, Soviet ice hockey was the talk of the sports world. The Russian stars had been shining in their own galaxy and now were beaming for all the world to see.

From their first World Championship in 1954, followed by their first Olympics in 1956, the Soviets became stronger each year. Leading into the first showdown with North American professional hockey in the famous '72 series, the Soviets had won nine successive IIHF World Championships.

While the NHL All-Stars won the '72 series on Paul Henderson's most famous goal in the final seconds of the deciding game, the Soviets outscored the NHL and won the '74 series against the best from the rival World Hockey Association, which included Gordie Howe and Bobby Hull.

The NHL began to take notice.

Team Canada coach, Harry Sinden, noticed new possibilities immediately. As quoted in that 2002 ESPN article, "The '72 series did wake us up to two new things: People on the planet other than Canadians can play the game very well and we had something to learn about the physical condition of our players."

The next instalment of "our best versus their best" came in 1979. This time, our best included more than just Canadians. The NHL put together an all-star team of the "greats," including Swedish stars Börje Salming, Anders Hedberg, and Ulf Nilsson. Staged in Madison Square Garden and billed as the "series of the century," Challenge Cup '79 was a best-of-three affair. The first two games were split and then the Russians crushed the NHL stars in the deciding game, 6-0. Even NHL insiders attested to Soviet brilliance. As quoted in Derek Drager's book *Clare Drake, The Coaches' Coach,* the great Hall-of-Famer Jean Beliveau said: "They have shown us that hockey is a game of speed and we have never had a team as fast as theirs. We must regroup and examine what we have lost."

From 1973 to 1987, the Soviets continued to dominate the IIHF World Championships, winning nine times. Unexpectedly, they lost to the Americans in the Miracle on Ice. Yes, it seemed that most nations needed a miracle to beat the Russians.

The Russians also dominated in junior (U20) hockey. Up to 1978, they had won gold in ten of the fourteen years of World IIHF tournaments. Soviet hockey was strong at all levels. This was the golden era of ice hockey in Russia, and their high standards were affirmed in their challenges to Canadian teams.

On another important level, sport competition with Western teams was viewed as an extension of the Cold War. Victory in sport was an important tool of the Communist government to demonstrate superiority over Western democracies, led by the United States. (The converse may have also been true.) From the Miracle on Ice Olympics through the Cold War, a second great rivalry in hockey was spawned: Russia vs USA.

Meanwhile, another important development was occurring on the international hockey scene. In response to demands for a true World Championship involving the best of all professional and amateur players from all the hockey nations, the Canada Cup was established in 1976. It occurred on five occasions up to 1991. (It was thereafter replaced by the World Cup of Hockey in 1996.)

The Canada Cup was sanctioned by all three of the major hockey bodies—the IIHF, Hockey Canada, and the NHL—and this joint initiative left no doubt about ice hockey supremacy in the world. Of the five Canada Cups, Canada won four and the Russians won one, that one being in 1981, as the Viking Cup was starting. The interest in international ice hockey was truly at a pcak, and everyone wanted to see the mighty Russians play at any level, especially against the Canadians.

It is no wonder then that, in the advent of the Viking Cup tournament of 1980, we enlisted the CAHA (now Hockey Canada) for assistance in obtaining a strong Russian team. While we negotiated directly with hockey federations of the other hockey nations, President Murray Costello indicated that the CAHA would make the contacts with the Russians, now seen to be in a category of their own. All efforts by the CAHA to obtain a Soviet team remained fruitless up to the planning of Viking Cup '88. Then something interesting happened on the horizon. . . The stars were aligning.

Of all the Canada Cup series, 1987 is likely remembered as the most outstanding. After splitting the first two games in a best-of-three final, both 6–5 in overtime, Canada's Mario Lemieux scored from Wayne Gretzky with seconds remaining, by a third identical 6–5 score. Following the series, Wayne Gretzky commented that this was the best hockey he was ever a part of. "There is no question at the time they were the best team in the world—they were that good," he said, as quoted in *Clare Drake, The Coaches' Coach.*

If you ever wondered whether sport could inspire a nation, and energize its finer qualities of unity, pride and joy, just think of Canada Cup '87. The interest and benefits of international hockey were surely now at a peak in Canada . . . and the Russians had largely made it so!

Two of the early games of this marvellous series were held at the Calgary '88 Olympics' new Saddledome, with Czechoslovakia tying Canada and Sweden defeating the Soviet Union. I attended the Czechoslovakia-Canada game, having previously made arrangements to meet with Miro Šubrt from Prague to make final arrangements for the Czechoslovakia national "U18" team to participate in Viking Cup '88, which was then less than four months away.

I knew Mr. Šubrt well, having made arrangements with him for all the Viking Cup exchanges, which by then included three hockey tours by the Augustana Vikings to Czechoslovakia, as well as regular Czechoslovak participation in the Viking Cup. Šubrt at the time was the vice-president of the IIHF and its longest-serving member.

Šubrt was very well connected in the hockey world. He was a great supporter of the Viking Cup, and indeed a good friend. His English was seemingly perfect, so no interpreter was needed whenever we met. (See the article on Mr. Šubrt in Chapter 6.)

During our meeting in the Calgary Westin Hotel lobby, it occurred to me that Šubrt would have good contacts with the Russians. "Miro," I said, "for six years, we have tried to attract the Russians to the Viking Cup, without success. We need your help."

Šubrt thought for a moment, and then responded, with some tongue in cheek, I think: "Well, LeRoy, we Czechs don't always get along that well with the Russians, but there is a leader in their federation that is quite good to deal with. He is here with their team and his name is Yuri Korolev. I'll go over to reception and call him. He may be in his room."

As it turned out, Korolev had entered the hotel with the Russian team following their game at the Saddledome. Šubrt brought him over to meet me and my son, Jeff, who was accompanying me. Korolev could only speak Russian and I only English. Šubrt spoke both languages fluently, so he was obviously a key to our communication.

After their five-to-ten-minute discussion about the Viking Cup and Czech participation, all in Russian, Šubrt turned to me and, in his excellent English said, "Mr. Korolev has never heard of the Viking Cup, but he is very interested. He will meet you at nine o'clock tomorrow morning with his interpreter to talk more about it."

Jeff and I had been planning to drive back to Camrose that night, but we quickly adjusted our plans to meet with Korolev.

Upon meeting Korolev promptly at 9:00 a.m. the following morning, we immediately recognized the Russian interpreter as the translator for Russian coach Viktor Tikhonov's comments on the CFCN late sports news the night before. He proved to be very capable and seemed especially interested and engaged in the discussions.

Mr. Korolev was direct with his questions and soon asked why I was inviting their National U18 team to Viking Cup '90 (two years hence). "Why not Viking Cup '88?" he asked, referencing the tournament that was a mere three months and a bit from our conversation.

I had assumed an abundance of red tape in Russia, and figured the best we could expect would be participation in the biannual tournament in 1990. All the teams had already been secured for Viking Cup '88. Furthermore, how could all the usual pre-tournament exhibition games be arranged for the Soviets in little more than three months with Canadian team schedules already set?

I was shocked at their immediate interest and felt an urgent need to somehow make it happen. Mr. Šubrt had indeed done a good job for us the previous evening! I responded to the interpreter: "We have already confirmed all six teams, but, you know, well, we could probably add another team! Do you really want to come to Viking Cup '88?"

Korolev said, "Yes, we are interested."

He then indicated that I should work out the details, including all arrangements for a pre-tournament exhibition tour of centres in Western Canada, with the Russian Ice Hockey Federation office in Moscow in the coming weeks.

I was indeed surprised by Korolev's openness and readiness to launch into this new territory. I later wondered if this was concrete evidence of what we were hearing of a new political era in Russia through the policies of *glasnost* (openness) and *perestroika* (restructuring) to revive a stagnant economy and shake off the burdens of Stalinism. Mikhail Gorbachev had become the new Communist general secretary to lead into a new era of Russian politics. Gorbachev soon became the Soviet head of state and, in 1991, president. This new sense of openness caught on very quickly, and soon ended the Cold War. I'm sure Korolev was in tune with the new political winds that were then beginning to blow in Soviet politics. Sport and politics were inseparable, especially in the Communist world.

I knew that I would be pushing my good fortune if I told Korolev at this time that our policy was to billet the players in private homes while they were in Camrose. But it had to be said. I gambled that now was the proper time to broach the subject, as it was clear that I was talking to someone with the authority to make immediate and important decisions. I could not risk delays in working out details of an agreement with federation personnel in the short time available.

So, through the interpreter, I said, "Mr. Korolev must know that all players will be billeted in private homes while they are in Camrose."

The response was quick and certain.

"That would be impossible! Our players do not speak English, we must keep close reins on our players, we have never done this before, and our government would certainly not allow it. They must stay in hotels!"

It seemed that this was enough to derail our good progress. While the interpreter looked to me for my response, I thought to myself: *I have gone through this before.*

To the interpreter, I said, "Mr. Korolev has said exactly what the Czechs said when they came to their first Viking Cup. But do you know what? They tried it! [Billeting, that is.] And now they wouldn't have it any other way. In fact, some of their coaches even want to be billeted now."

The interpreter and Mr. Korolev now had a fairly lengthy discussion, and it was obvious that more was being said by the interpreter than I had said to him. Soon, the interpreter turned his attention back to me and Jeff and, with a wink and twinkle in his eye, said, "Mr. Korolev said if the Czechs can do it, we can, too."

Somehow, I felt the interpreter was on our side—and the Czechs, too!

I knew in my mind even then that I would have to find another team to complete an eight-team format. And with the Russians coming with their National U18 team, we needed a *good* team. The national teams from Europe always expected to meet tough competition in Canada.

On our way back to Camrose that day, I thought of my friend Clare Drake, the legendary coach of the University of Alberta Golden Bears. No one knew more about Russian hockey than Clare, I thought, and Clare was always helpful. Didn't he once say to our coach Mike Johnston that he would like to be in the Viking Cup some day?

Clare Drake and Russian Hockey

As I thought of Drake, my thoughts wandered back to my childhood. When the Soviets won their first World Championship in 1954, by crushing Canada, 7–2, the world of hockey was shocked at their quick rise to gold behind the Iron Curtain. Canada had won fifteen of the previous twenty championships. This was Canada's most resounding defeat ever to that point in history.

So, it was that, in 1955, Canada pulled out all the stops to regain gold and the Penticton Vees, the Allan Cup winners, were chosen to do the job. Off they went to host Germany, now central to the developing Cold War. Even Foster Hewitt, legendary voice of the Toronto Maple Leafs, was sent by CBC Radio to broadcast to an avidly listening Canadian audience.

Yes, I remember Hewitt's famous broadcast of the final game, which Canada won, 5–0, very well. My ear had been glued to the old living room cabinet radio and I cheered with every goal. I remember how proud I was to be Canadian that day.

What I didn't know until later was that Clare Drake, then coaching in Dusseldorf, had been assigned to scout the Russians in all their games. Canada had never been better prepared! This was, as detailed in Drager's *Clare Drake, The Coaches' Coach,* Clare Drake's first introduction to Russian hockey. He was the first Canadian to scout the Russians and this was only the beginning of his numerous contacts with Russian hockey over the years.

For example:

1) He held discussions on Russian strategy with coach Anatoly Tarasov, the founder of Russian hockey.

2) In 1964, while actively playing with the Lacombe Rockets, he played against the Russians in the Ahearne Cup in Stockholm, where the two teams celebrated Christmas together.

3) As head coach of the 1980 Canadian Olympic team, Drake lost a close game to the Russians before the Miracle on Ice game at Lake Placid. After that game, Drake incredibly predicted a US victory over the Russians.

Clare Drake was a student of the Russian hockey system, always ready and willing to learn more.

And he is, of course, considered the dean of coaching in Canadian university hockey, with winning records never to be broken. His U of A Golden Bears have won the Canadian Championships more than any other team in history. It seemed like a wild thought, but would Drake like another encounter with the Russians? There was no doubt the Bears would be a guaranteed challenge for the Russian National U18 team, and a sure credit to the Viking Cup.

Clare Drake was no stranger to Camrose. His linemate from their UBC playing days, Stu Bailey, was living in Camrose and had been Clare's best man at his wedding. Clare had a special interest in the hometown Augustana Vikings hockey team, as several of its players over the years had moved on to play with the Bears, including Jim Ofrim, Randy Lemay, Bill Andreassen, Curtis Jans, Rob Daum, and John Lamb. But even more important, Drake was always there to raise the standards of hockey and help players and leaders achieve their goals.

I wasted no time in calling Drake upon our return to Camrose.

Whether it was another opportunity to play the Russians, reengage in international hockey, advance the Bears program, or to just help a friend . . . it didn't matter. Clare Drake and the Bears were the eighth team in Viking Cup '88. They also were the champions—in more ways than one.

Once more the stars lined up for the Viking Cup. Interest in Russian hockey was at an all-time high in Canada. Miro Šubrt of the IIHF was there for us at this opportune time. Yuri Korolev of the Russian Federation was booked in the same hotel. Russian *glasnost* and *peristroika* under General Secretary Michal Gorbachev were finding legs. And Clare Drake was ready to lend a hand. A new constellation was about to appear in Viking Cup '88.

My next order of business was to call Murray Costello, president of the CAHA, to obtain their approval and sanction for Russian participation in Viking Cup '88. While I feared that I might have overstepped my authority in speaking with the Russians, the circumstances and Šubrt's involvement seemed to be no problem for Costello. In fact, he was cooperative and helpful, as he had been through previous Viking Cups.

Logistics and Language

The next three months, however, were not without problems, as details were hammered out by telephone (ten-hour time zone difference) and telex from the local Pedersen's Florist. This was a time long before the onset of instant global communications. Many were the times and hours that I tried to make contact with a (rare) English-speaking Russian Ice Hockey official in the wee hours of the morning, meeting with success—occasionally.

The contract was modelled largely on what had been developed for the Czechoslovakians. The Russians would arrive in mid-December, leaving time for twelve exhibition games in Western Canada prior to or after the Viking Cup. I would be given full authority to sell and market all exhibition games in exchange for air tickets from Frankfurt to Edmonton return. The Russians would be responsible for the Moscow-to-Frankfurt flight. In Camrose, the team would be billeted in private homes. On the exhibition game tours, they would be accommodated in hotels provided by the host teams.

Needless to say, it was not difficult to "sell" the games to junior or college teams. Who wouldn't want to see the Russians play against the hometown boys?

The exhibition tour became a big success. The Russians fulfilled all their commitments and the games served to promote the Viking Cup in every community visited. From some of the longer trips, the Russian boys were happy to get "home" to their Camrose "moms" and "dads."

And how did they find their Camrose moms and dads?

Chris Reynolds, a University of Calgary student of Russian language and friend of former Augustana Vikings coach Mike Johnston, had been contacted to be the official Viking Cup host and interpreter for the Russian team and was already on duty to meet the Russian team at the Edmonton International Airport on its arrival. He recalls the fifty-minute bus trip to Camrose and the Soviets first glimpse of northern Alberta.

> We were on the bus driving to Camrose and, through their interpreter, Alexander Semionov, we communicated with the team leaders about the agreed upon billet lodging arrangement. We said the host/billet families would be at the arena when we arrived, so it would be good to assign the boys to the billet families now so that once we arrived at the arena the boys could get "home" quickly after their long journey.
>
> You could have heard a pin drop in the bus as we described the host/billet families; however, this had been in the written agreement. The management's understanding of billets was military-style lodging, and not with Canadian families, as this

type of lodging had never been done before. There was considerable discussion in Russian amongst the management, back and forth with LeRoy, and then it was settled that the top management would stay in a hotel, and the players and coaching staff would stay with billet families. I saw the sweat on LeRoy's brow throughout the discussion, and then heard the sigh of relief when the negotiation was finished. So began an unexpected cultural tour for the Soviet 18 selects with their "new families" in Canada.

They held their practice the next day and there were many curious fans and NHL scouts in the building to see the skilled Soviet select team. The practice was crisp and executed at a high tempo for a group of young athletes that had congregated in Moscow from eleven time zones, and then had a long international flight to Edmonton.

Soon, we were on the bus to Beaverlodge and Grande Prairie to begin our pre-Viking Cup exhibition tour.

The first game was with the Beaverlodge 77s. The game was fast paced and spirited. The Soviet players countered the older and more strategically based home squad with their young exuberance and high skill. Noticing their well-worn equipment, the hosting committee rallied the local folks and presented the visitors with numerous pieces of new equipment following the game. The giving spirit of Christmas had already begun and the Soviets were feeling it in northern Alberta. They were overwhelmed and I was proud because High Prairie in northern Alberta was my home.

The following day, in front of a full house, the Grande Prairie Junior North Stars hosted the Soviets in a real crowd-pleaser. Once again, following the game, the northern spirit of fellowship and friendship prevailed. . . more gifts of new equipment and a wonderful community meal for both teams.

Along their route to Camrose the next day the team enjoyed their first NHL game as guests of the Edmonton Oilers. On our evening return to Camrose, the boys were met by their "Canadian" families at the rink and taken home to finally have some time to relax. The next day at practice I could hear the boys talking about their host families and how much fun they were having in their new environs. There was talk of outings on snowmobiles, which was a new experience, and tobogganing down the hills, riding on horse-drawn sleighs, and of course whispers of how pretty the local girls were.

The Camrose vision of the Viking Cup continued for me as I accompanied the team on the rest of their tour in western Canada and then served as their host in

Viking Cup '88. But I was more than a host. I was a believer. I saw and I lived the Viking Cup with the Russians, Canadians, and others from around the world, and it led to a new career in international sport in the years to follow." (See the Chris Reynolds story later in this chapter.)

Dr. Petr Mirejovsky was the host of Team Czechoslovakia for most Viking Cups, but in consideration of his fluency in the Russian language, he was also helpful in hosting the Russian team.

My first impression of the first Soviet team as it arrived in Camrose was a bit strange. All dressed the same, they even seemed to look the same. They were unusually quiet for kids their age. They seemed rather stiff, only looked straight ahead, appeared to move at right angles. And all their officials seemed rather stern and rigid, as well. I was sure some of it was jet lag, but strict discipline enforced by the team leaders in what for them were unfamiliar and perhaps hostile surroundings appeared to be a part of it, as well. A lot of it wore off as time went on, but, in my experience, the next Soviet team I saw arriving in Camrose appeared to be a lot more relaxed. By that time, the Cold War was ending and perestroika was in full swing in the Soviet Union.

It was becoming possible to have reasonably open conversations, even with Soviet citizens. I recall a highly stimulating conversation I had with one of the Soviet officials. He was quite open, well spoken, well informed, and, well, interesting. At the time, I taught a Soviet history course at the college. We just happened to be talking about some of the recent developments in the USSR. Not thinking much about it, I asked my Soviet conversational partner if he would consider coming to my class—his English was excellent—to talk to the students and answer some of their questions, if need be. The horror in his eyes made me drop the subject in a hurry. There obviously were definite limits to openness still in place.

And one last humorous incident at the end: The Viking Cup was finished; the visiting teams had left when a colleague called me with some concern. It turned out that the people in charge of cleaning one of the rooms that had been used by the Soviets discovered several packages containing strange white powder.

What could it be? Surely it was not? But then again, could you be sure? Fortunately, enough, the packages in question were clearly marked—in Russian—as containing aluminum acetate, the traditional remedy for sprained ankles and such ailments and they could be safely disposed of as a result.

By the time the exhibition game swing was completed, the team was well acclimatized for the Viking Cup tournament. The Soviets were a new, powerful draw for the curious fan, lovers of skilful hockey, and the many hockey scouts from the NHL and North American junior and college teams.

A New Year and a New Day

January 1, 1988, was not a normal New Year's Day in Camrose., With Russian Bears on one blue line and the U of A Golden Bears on the other, and a packed crowd, the Soviet national anthem was officially sung for the first time at the Viking Cup (and perhaps ever in Camrose). The famed Viking Cup Trio harmoniously sang every word in Russian to that beautiful tune that most Canadians by then associated with a Russian–Canadian hockey game. Equally beautiful, the Trio continued with the Canadian national anthem.

That day, there was pride and newness in the air. The anthems, in all their beauty, were symbolic of a new era for the Viking Cup and the successful culmination of a will on both sides of the "red line" to make new things happen. There were some tears that day, mine included, and the words of Yuri Korolev kept ringing in my mind: *We can, too.*

The game was a crowd-pleaser in so many respects. From those who still had politics on their minds to the players' newfound families (billets) to cheering minor hockey teams (behind team benches), it was a test of a Canadian university system against the Soviet way. Not least, there was the sheer excitement of what was clearly a superior and appealing brand of hockey.

The Soviets scored quickly, jumping into a 2–0 lead midway through the first period. But remember, the old master coach Clare Drake was in control of the Golden Bears. Their superior size and strength over the younger national U18 boys began to show through as the game progressed. The final score was Golden Bears 7, Russian Bears 4.

The Soviets won their remaining three games and the bronze medal. Drake's U of A Golden Bears won gold, defeating a powerful Czechoslovakia national U18 team loaded with stars in the sold-out stadium. It was a Happy New Year in Camrose.

Coach of the Russian team Gennady Tsygurov went on to coach the Russian national team for several years, and assistant coach Vladimir Bogomolov returned as coach to Viking Cup '92. He later became general secretary of the Russian Ice Hockey Federation for a time. Several Viking Cup Russian players went on to have impressive careers in professional hockey, including the following.

"They tried to learn Russian and we tried to learn some English"

Andrey Kovalenko, known as "The Tank" for his tough play in front of the net, was drafted by the Quebec Nordiques and had a twelve-year career in the NHL before playing in the Russian Kontinental Hockey League (KHL). Today, he is the chair of the KHL Players Association. The Tank played for the Edmonton Oilers for nearly three seasons, coming from the Montreal Canadiens. He has the distinction of scoring the final goal in the history of the Montreal Forum in a 4–1 victory over the Dallas Stars in 1996. Andrey played for the Russian national team, where he won a gold medal in the '92 Olympics and a silver medal in the '98 Olympics.

He commented on his Viking Cup '88 experience in the *Viking Cup '98* magazine:

> The Viking Cup was my first international experience and my first opportunity to play outside the Soviet Union. I needed to show my talents so I could

stay with the national team. I was fortunate, I scored three goals in a Viking Cup game and was named the best player. I received a new pair of Canadian skates. When I got them, I was very happy…. I remember the friendliness of the community. We had a nice family—Helen and Rob. I cannot say enough about them. They tried to learn some Russian and we tried to learn some English. They had a young son who celebrated his thirteenth birthday while I was there. That was my fondest off-ice memory of Camrose. It was better than staying in a hotel.

"For you I have a big heart"

Sergei Zubov knows all about all-star teams, medals, and trophies. He was chosen to the Viking Cup '88 All-Star team (defense) and, through his long career in the NHL, he has been chosen to the NHL All-Star team as a defenseman four times. He was on Stanley Cup-winning teams twice—once with the Rangers, who drafted him in 1990, and once with Dallas, where he starred for twelve years. In 2019, he was inducted into the NHL Hall of Fame. Zubov won an Olympic gold medal for Russia in '92, and today he is head coach for KHL Sochi, which was the home of the 2014 Winter Olympics.

Of his first visit to Canada in the Viking Cup, Zubov had this to say: "It was a great experience. I learned a lot." His billets, Joyce and Frank Wilcox, would later meet Sergei at Edmonton Oiler games when the Rangers or Stars were the visitors. "He hadn't changed a bit," Joyce commented on these meetups. "He still called me 'Baushka.' He was an outgoing and happy guy. He and roommate Oleg Kobzev loved to talk even though there was a language barrier. Kobzev said 'I school English, Zubov school Deutsch, fool!' We formed a close friend-ship. Before they left, Sergei said to our daughter Mary, 'For you, I have a big heart!'"

According to Joyce, Mark Messier and Kevin Lowe were Zubov's two favourite Ranger team-mates (at the time). "He had praise for everyone, but thought Lowe and Messier were the best!"

"It was different, new, fun to see, and fun to learn something new"

Igor Korolev was drafted by St. Louis in the second round after playing in Viking Cup '88. He played for twelve years with various teams in the NHL before ending his playing and coaching career in the KHL in Russia. He was assistant coach of Lokomotiv Yaroslavl, and was on the flight that crashed on September 7, 2011, killing the whole team, including two additional Viking Cup players from Slovakia and the Czech Republic. Igor had become a naturalized Canadian. His family live in Toronto, where he is buried.

"At the time a tight rein was often placed on players from behind the Iron Curtain," Igor remembered of his Viking Cup experiences in an interview for the *Viking Cup 2002* magazine. "The billeting experience was a welcome change, it was great. The Stetar family was unbeliev-able to me. We felt a part of the family, even though it was a nine-hour flight from home. The

Viking Cup was the first tournament I played at in North America. It was different, new, fun to see, and fun to learn something new!"

"We felt like we were at home"

Sergei Brylin impressed everyone at Viking Cup '92, so much that he was chosen MVP. Small wonder then that he was drafted forty-second overall by the New Jersey Devils. And they liked what they got. Sergei played all of his thirteen NHL seasons with the Devils, winning three Stanley Cup rings. He vividly remembers the Viking Cup in his journey to the Stanley Cup.

> It was the most exciting Junior tournament for us in North America. There were a lot of scouts there. We played pretty good but lost in the finals. It was a great experience for me to spend a month with a Canadian family. We celebrated Christmas with them. We felt like we were at home.

"In Canada, it was a more physical style of game—perfect for me!"

Darius Kasparaitis moved from Lithuania, his home country, to Moscow, to play hockey when he was just fourteen years old. He ended his hockey career by being inducted into the Russian and Soviet Hockey Hall of Fame in 2016. Darius holds the record for most Olympic games played by any player of Soviet/Russian teams, at twenty-eight. But most of his amazing career was spent in North America. It all began at Viking Cup '90, where he was noticed and then drafted fifth overall by the New York Islanders after his first Olympic games (Albertville). He believed the Viking Cup piqued the interest of NHL teams. "We received quite a bit of attention from the scouts at that time. I remember that they awarded the jerseys to the best players of the game."

Darius played sixteen years in the NHL, mostly with the Islanders, Penguins, and Rangers, and was known for his aggressive, physical style of play.

"I really liked the style of hockey in the Viking Cup," Darius said, in an October 2019 interview.

> I was able to play a more physical style of game. It was what I needed at the time, the perfect style for me. The game has changed a lot since the Viking Cup. I think it is very hard to hit now . . . everything is reviewed and they can always find something that doesn't look good, like they call the instigator penalty. . . So, the game is much faster because there is less contact.

The blue-liner has not forgotten his Camrose experience. "Those are great memories," he recalled. "It was cool to stay with the Wicentowich family and live the Canadian style. We spent a month with them. I remember the girl from the Pastuck family, and some of the kids on the block. I was heartbroken when we left her—teenagers, you know."

"In Canada, you are always closer to the puck"

Sergei Gonchar was a natural fit for North American Hockey, and Viking Cup '92 was his introduction. When they saw him play, the Washington Capitals wasted no time choosing Sergei as their first-round draft pick in 1992. He became one of the top offensive defensemen in the NHL and played for an incredible twenty-two years, that being a record for Russian players. From the 2000–01 season to the 2009–10 season, Sergei tallied exactly 500 points, second among NHL defensemen only to Detroit's Nicklas Lidström. He led the league in goals by a defenseman during that span, with 128. Sergei played in five NHL All-Star games and claimed three Stanley Cup rings. He played in four Olympic Games for Team Russia.

I caught up with Sergei prior to a Penguins–Oilers game in Edmonton in 2019, to reminisce about his Viking Cup memories. At that time, he was coaching with the Penguins.

It was my first time I played in Canada—you know, with the smaller ice surface. For me personally, I always liked smaller ice surfaces better, I always played better on them, everything is quicker, you are always closer to the puck.

There was a big difference in hockey styles from the various countries back then. Now everybody learns from each other and we incorporate the best from all systems. Hockey is the same all over. The styles were quite different when I played in the Viking Cup.

We stayed with the family in Camrose. All of us were welcomed with open arms. We were happy. It was a learning curve, too. Like, from Russia we never saw how other people were living. . . Right? For the first time, I had a chance to see how Canadian people were living—from inside, like what the house looked like, what people were eating, what they were drinking and all that stuff—so it was a very cool experience.

I didn't speak English back then. Usually, I was trying to use my arms and tell them this way or that way. We all understood a smile. It is the same in all languages. I learned my first English at the Viking Cup!

I played my entire hockey career in the NHL—Washington for ten years, Pittsburgh for five years, and Boston, Ottawa, Dallas, and Montreal. I was on Stanley Cup-winning teams in Pittsburgh, once as a player and twice as a coach. This last time, I took the Cup to Russia—my home city of Chelybinsk—for all my relatives, friends, and neighbours to see! I was proud of it!

Yes, it was a great day for the young son from Chelyabinsk who came to Canada to play in the Viking Cup!

It is always interesting to trace friendship networks that have originated at the Viking Cup, especially through the unique "family living" component.

The following examples illustrate why the ripples of the Viking Cup have extended far beyond the hockey rink into the hearts and minds and laps of people.

"We drove to Saskatoon"

Pete (an old-timer hockey player himself) and Mary Anne Pastuck opened their doors and swung right into the spirit of the Viking Cup. Pete recalls:

> Boris Mironov and Darius Kasparaitis often came over to our place to hang out with our two Russian boys, Maris Dreling and Sergei Zholtok. It has been fun to follow their careers. We drove to Saskatoon to see Sergei, Boris, and Darius play in the World Junior Championships the following season . . . brought them more fruit . . . stayed in the same hotel. And then we followed their careers in the NHL. Boris played six seasons with the Oilers after his first season with the Winnipeg Jets. Then he was on to Chicago and the Rangers. We kept in touch. He was really outgoing and fun to talk with.

Of the Russian players that stayed with the Pastucks, Pete especially remembered Sergejs Žoltoks. "He was a good kid, a real good family person. Whenever we met him later, like when his team played the Oilers, he wanted our kids (Melanie, Jamie, Lane) to come down to their dressing room . . . even later, he was anxious to hear what they were doing. He called us often. He once said, 'I see a lot of names of players in the NHL that played in the Viking Cup.'" Eleven-year-old Melanie wrote a poem (see below).

Sergejs Žoltoks was drafted by the Boston Bruins in '92, and played ten years in the NHL with Boston, Ottawa, Montreal, Edmonton, Minnesota, and Nashville. On November 3, 2004, while playing in his home city of Riga, Latvia, he tragically suffered a fatal heart attack on the ice and died at the age of thirty-one, leaving a wife and two sons. His secondary school in Riga is now named the Sergejs Žoltoks school in his memory.

"He made us feel like celebrities"

Cheryl and Gordon Leonhardt take pleasure in talking of their guests, Maxim Afinogenov and Andrei Vasilyev, at Viking Cup '96.

"They showed our boys how to hold the hockey stick" said Cheryl. "Whether it was on a dug out or in back-alley shinny,

THE SOVIETS ARE COMING

"The Soviets are coming!" the brochure said
Reading those words I started to dread
The coming of these people was freaking me out!
They told me I'd like them, but I had my doubts
They came to my house at a quarter after seven
When I saw them I thought I'd died and gone to Heaven
They weren't anything like I'd pictured them to be,
Seventeen year old guys, normal like me!
They gave us lots of post cards, a stick, flag and pins
They won the bronze medal, cause you know the best wins
They didn't speak English, so we had some fun
Playing number games and you know what? They Won!
Maris was centre and Sergei left wing
They listened to tapes and said, "Hear Madonna Sing!"
We talked about Gretzky and the Beastie Boys
Lucky for us, they hardly made any noise
They left us this morning with a hug and a kiss
And now you know who I'm going to miss
So Sergei and Maris this goes out to you
We love you, we miss you and please come back soon!

Your Canadian Sister,
Melanie Pastuck
*daughter of Pete and Mary Pastuck
billeting family for Sergei Boldoveshko
and Maris Dreliny of the Soviet Jr. Selects*

"The Soviets Are Coming," by Melanie Pastuck

it was always Russia vs. Canada with the Leonhardt boys. . . We gave each of our Russian boys a pillow for long bus rides on exhibition game trips. They were so popular that they 'rented' them to their teammates. . . Russian entrepreneurs, I guess!"

Cheryl said that their whole family was glued to the TV watching the NHL draft in June. "We were so excited to see Max being drafted in the 3rd round by Buffalo. . . Later Max invited us to come to Buffalo to watch a game and stay with him for a few days. We went to a practice and he invited us into the dressing room where he introduced us to teammates. A teammate said, 'Oh, so you are the ones.' Then he took us out for supper. I held his Olympic bronze medal from the 2002 Salt Lake Olympics."

Afinogenov had a ten-year NHL career, nine years of it with Buffalo, before completing his long professional career in the Russian KHL league.

"Imagine, an international experience in the comfort of your own home"

Jack and Renea Helm didn't know what to expect when asked to billet Russian players. Renea later said,

> Jack walked in the front door with these two big boys. At seventeen, Andrei (Nazarov) was 6'4" and Sergei (Klimovich) was 6'3". I had hamburgers ready. They said 'sleep' after thirty-six hours of travel. Three hamburgers, two apples, and five glasses of milk later, and Jack and I looked at one another and grinned. The next day they were playing street hockey with our kids, John and Mike . . . We put the boys on the mindbender at West Edmonton Mall. They had seen the Moscow circus, but not this ride! . . . We bought them their first blue jeans.

Jack then said, "Andrei was drafted in the first round (tenth) by San Jose and the soft-spoken Sergei was drafted forty-first by Chicago. . . We were always at Andrei's games in Edmonton and often in Calgary when he played with the Flames. When he skated out for warm ups I think he was looking for us."

Sometime later Sergei commented, "I stayed with a great family. That tournament was probably the turning point in my life. The Viking Cup is the reason I'm in the NHL."

Jack concluded, "The Viking Cup was an adventure for us. Once we took our holidays in Quebec, to watch them play in a tournament there."

"We cheered madly for our boys at all their games"

Don Hutchinson loves to recall his billeting story. "As we drove to our home our new guests, Dmitri Mekeshkin and Ramil Saifulin, saw a Viking Cup sign along the highway. Demitri said 'VEEking Cup.' Our kids said, 'no, VIIking Cup.' So began the friendship and fun.

"'Do you speak English?' I asked. Their response was the same toothy grin they had already shown me. Demitri knew a little English, Ramil didn't speak a word of English when he arrived. But he didn't let the language barrier interfere with his determination to flirt with the pretty girls he met, and even share jokes! They were typical teenagers. They loved loud music and hated vegetables! They wanted ketchup on everything, including pizza. But they got their sleep—disciplined kids. . . We celebrated Christmas together. They were very happy with their gifts—jerseys of their favourite NHL teams. Then I skated with them on Mirror Lake. Their passes were absolutely pinpoint. I couldn't keep up!"

"Everyone chuckled when the announcer mispronounced their names. When the Russian team won the gold medal, it was hard to tell who was happier—the players or their Canadian families."

A Letter from Erlan of Mongolia

Erlan Sagymbaev was from Mongolia and Sergei (Sasha) Poliakov from Kiev, Ukraine, six time zones apart, but they shared their dinners at the Cox family farm near Camrose at the Viking Cup.

Verny said, "Ken and I run a cattle operation, so it was quite a new experience for these city boys. Our son, Rusty took them out on the three-wheeler . . . then they always wanted to go. They sure liked the farm! Lorraine, our daughter, drove them to practices and games. When we saw them on the ice, we thought they needed new skates."

Later the Coxes received a note from them, "Thank you very much for your presents, especially for the skates. Everybody envies us because they have the autograph of the best player in the world, Gretzky . . . and we just fly on them!"

Verny then showed me a letter that they received later from Erlan. It read:

> I shall never forget you and those fifteen days spent in Canada with you will remain in my memory forever as one of the most happy and bright moments in my life. I remember how I and Sasha saw you for the first time in your big house resembling our house of culture. I remember distinctly what a cordial welcome you gave us. Your house became a second native home for us. . . My parents are grateful to you for all you have done for us and wish you long and happy life. I told them everything about you and they loved you as I do.

"They played the whole game to protect me"

Verlyn and Mardell Olson know what billeting at the Viking Cup is all about. Verlyn was billeting chair for the first ten years of the Viking Cup, and the Olson family has regularly hosted players from different countries. One player that stood out in particular was Ukrainian goaltender Kostiantyn Simchuk, of the '92 Soviet U18 national team, and the Olsons are still in contact with him.

It all started with a dilemma and a question for Konstiantyn (Kostia).

What do you do when your goaltending equipment and luggage fails to arrive until the last day of the tournament . . . the day before you are about to return to Moscow?

"No problem," said Verlyn. "Duff Layton's Men's Wear, Camrose quickly provided a wardrobe of clothes and Glenn Vinet and others managed to find some good goal equipment."

But that wasn't the only problem Kostia had to face.

Kostia and teammate Alex Alexeyev (Winnipeg Jets draft '92) had a minor snowmobile accident just as the Viking Cup was about to begin. Kostia said, "We had agreed that we would both turn left when we came to the end of the trail, but Alex turned right! When we returned to our family, I was limping. I had injured my leg. But we convinced ourselves that it was not serious and so agreed not to let our coaches know. However, the word spread amongst my teammates.

"I played in goal the next day and, with very few shots, recorded a victory. My teammates played the whole game to protect me." Kostia played again in the championship game, where his team won silver (4–2).

Kostia and Alex had been assigned split billets, living with the Olsons for the latter half of the Viking Cup. Verlyn says, "We have continued to follow Kostia's impressive career and remain in contact."

Following the Viking Cup, Simchuk went on to play with the Ukraine national team in seven World Championships (group A) and one Olympics (Salt Lake), while playing in Russia and in the US. In 2005, he was declared Hockey Player of the Year in Ukraine. Today, he is coaching and works as the director of a large hockey school in Kiev. Kostia recalls his stay in Camrose:

> In all my travels in hockey—Russia, Ukraine, Europe, USA, Canada— the Viking Cup was unique. There was nothing like it anywhere. The culture, the family living—everyone in those homes—the outstanding quality of the hockey. It ranks with my greatest memories.

Right at home with the Ross family

Sergei Tertyshny, Rod Ross, Shtefan Levnid

Katelyn Ross, Shtefan Levnid (Russian guest)

Responsibility and Opportunity

I have often reflected on the great responsibility that the Viking Cup took on as the Soviet/ Russian government and ice hockey federation placed their elite players in our care over a period of close to a month in each of those Viking Cup years. Our Viking Cup committee, Augustana, and the Camrose community can be grateful for the faith the Russians placed in us. There were risks in the venture for sure and safety and security were always the highest priority. But like the waters of our rivers, it led to new opportunities and careers for so many, and made our little college and city proud.

Above the Fog

The Viking Cup welcoming hosts waited for the Soviet team to arrive at the Edmonton International Airport on the evening of December 10, 1992, but no team appeared. An empty bus returned to Camrose, where Verlyn Olson, Terry Ofrim, and I sifted through all documents to verify their schedule.

Canadian Airlines confirmed that the team had failed to appear for their Frankfurt-to-Edmonton flight which I had booked as Viking Cup coordinator. The Soviet Ice Hockey Association was responsible for the connection, but separately booked an Aeroflot flight from Moscow to Frankfurt.

There were no cellphones in those days, and the only possibility for a connection to Moscow in what for them were the wee hours of the morning (a ten-hour difference) was through the home number of the Russian coach, Vladimir Bogomolov. In spite of the hour, I called.

Mrs. Bogomolov, who luckily understood English, answered the phone. She confirmed that the team had left Moscow and became rather worried to hear that they had not arrived either in Frankfurt or Edmonton. And so, of course, were we.

Later we learned that, due to heavy fog over Frankfurt, the Soviet plane had been directed to Berlin after circling above Frankfurt for some time. By the time the fog lifted, their diverted flight to Berlin landed in Frankfurt, but much too late to make the connection on Canadian Airlines to Edmonton. The whole Russian team was stranded, and spent a night sleeping in the massive airport, awaiting instructions from someone—anyone. Eventually, they were located, with the help of the airport public address system, in the transit area, to which they had been confined with no German visas. We immediately contacted a relieved Mrs. Bogomolov in Moscow.

Canadian Airlines came to the rescue, and managed to find seats on later flights through Toronto and Vancouver to Calgary.

A Tim Hortons community bus was available to pick up the team at the Calgary International Airport close to thirty hours later than scheduled, but just in time to drop off their luggage in Camrose homes before rushing to Fort Saskatchewan for their first scheduled exhibition game that evening. Luckily, there was no fog or snowstorm in Calgary or Edmonton at that time.

Despite the many possibilities for schedule disruptions due to changing weather patterns, this was the closest any Viking Cup team came to a game cancellation.

A Medical Emergency in Red Deer

In a game with Red Deer College in Red Deer one night, the Russian goalkeeper was slashed in the throat by an errant skate in a goal crease pile-up. Blood flowed immediately and profusely. Luckily, the Russian team doctor and Red Deer College medical staff were close by and on the ice within seconds to stabilize the situation, while an ambulance rushed to the scene to transport the player to the hospital. Fortunately, the outcome was good.

Two Black Cars

We were wary whenever strangers, other than the hockey scouts, appeared to talk to any of the team members; especially agents whom we did not know, looking for clients.

One day at Viking Cup '94, two large black cars with men in black suits parked in front of the arena. They had a meeting with some of the Russian team leaders, and left soon after. We never knew why they were there. Perhaps they were just visiting old acquaintances or friends.

What we did note was that the team, thereafter, had a newfound means to purchase Canadian goods, including hockey equipment.

The earlier teams from Russia were much more in need and their host families enjoyed the opportunity to share gifts, especially over the Christmas season. From that first Russian team to the last at Viking Cup '96, it was clear that team economics had changed. But it was also evident that there were aftershocks from the fall of the Soviet Union and the advent of the new Russia of 1992.

Masseur Defection

The awareness that we may have to deal with a possible defection during the Communist era was always in the back of our minds. That never happened for any player, but it did for a team masseur following Viking Cup '92. Goaltender Kostiantyn Simchuk recently recalled what happened and relayed it to me.

> While our leaders were loading the bus, our masseur quietly said goodbye to us players, who were already in our seats. He said he was going to stay in Canada, as he thought there would soon no longer be a Soviet Union. Soon after he left, our leaders, sensing that something was wrong, started asking us questions. The police came to the bus but they said nothing could be done about it. We then waited a long time in the bus and missed our shopping trip to West Edmonton Mall before we drove directly to the airport.

The team actually spent close to six hours on the bus in Camrose while Canadian External Affairs officials dealt with the issue. The team leaders were noticeably upset over the defection, but the Russian team returned to play in the next Viking Cup.

Vladimir Shadrin and Yuri Karandin

When Viking Cup steering committee members were hosting a welcoming reception with the Russian leaders prior to Viking Cup '96, we reviewed the bios of each leader. Of course, the one that drew that greatest attention was that for the head coach, Vladimir Shadrin. It read:

> One of the best players in the history of the Soviet/Russian hockey . . . Soviet Union champion in 1967, 1969, and 1976 while with Spartak Moscow . . . scored 213 goals in 445 games in the national championships . . . member of the Soviet national team from 1970 to 1977 . . . played in two Olympics (gold in 1972 and 1976) and eight World Championships (gold in 1970, 1971, 1973, 1975, and 1978). . . After finishing his playing career, worked as a coach in Japan and later, in Spartak. . . Now he is in his third year as a coach of the Russian Junior team (players born 1978).

Vladimir appeared pleased until the head of delegation piped up and said, "Yeah, but they didn't say that Shadrin was the player assigned to check Paul Henderson when he scored the most famous goal in hockey history, in the '72 series!"

Of course, there were roars. Vladimir responded, amid the laughter, "That is one that has been hard to live down. All I know is Henderson said he prayed and God did it. The puck had powers of its own, it was like a gift from heaven. He was just hanging around the goal and the puck went by itself and he happened to be there. How could I change this? I had no control. It was like supernatural!" (*Edmonton Journal*, December 29, 1995). Today, Vladimir thinks more on the lifelong bonds and relationships that were developed between the two teams in that series and, later, showdowns between our countries.

There are good times and humour in all situations, if we make it so. In this situation it was a real "icebreaker."

It is interesting that the head of delegation was Yuri Karandin, who was the referee for one of the games of the famous '72 series. He went on to referee in World and Olympic Championships, and in showdowns between Russia and Canada. He recalled the skepticism of Russian people going into the '72 showdown and related a memory.

As reported in the *Edmonton Journal,* "One guy said if the Russians win a game, he'd eat the paper that they wrote that on. Well, there was a pot on a tripod in the foyer of one of the hotels and they put borscht in it and one guy was ripping the paper into little shreds and the other guy was eating it out of the borscht!"

International Hockey Career

Chris Reynolds came from the University of Calgary to gain experience as a Russian translator in the Viking Cup. He returned with a passion for global hockey.

> My connection with the international hockey community can be traced back to the Viking Cup. The Viking Cup spawned my passion for international sport and foreign languages and it helped me to merge the two in my career abroad.

Following Chris's Viking Cup experience, he volunteered to be the host of the Russian national team in the Calgary '88 Olympics, where he became friends with coach Igor Dmitriev, assistant to Viktor Tikhonov. This friendship then grew into a coaching position with the Soviet Wings in Moscow, where Igor was the head coach. This later led to coaching experience in Switzerland, Germany, and Austria followed by a career in sport management and development with the IIHF in Zurich. From 2001 to 2005, he entered the private world of business as director of European hockey operations for the Anschutz Entertainment Group (AEG), overseeing six hockey clubs in five different European countries.

Before he left Europe, Chris was hired by the IIHF as sport director of the 2006 World Ice Hockey Championships, in Riga, Latvia.

Moscow Symphony

I was fortunate to be part of a government delegation to Russia in 2001 while I served as an MLA in the Alberta government. Considering our mutual interests in the arts, Vladimir Bogomolov, a Viking Cup Russian coach, on two occasions made arrangements to attend the Moscow Symphony Orchestra concert with guest José Carreras in the Kremlin concert hall. It was an outstanding experience and an illustration to me of the numerous networking benefits that have come to so many who have been involved in the Viking Cup.

Why Not Viking Cup '98?

I am often asked, "Why didn't the Russians come to Viking Cup '98 . . . and later?" There are several possibilities:

1) There was fallout in a struggle for control of the ice hockey federation. In a letter of greeting from the president, Valentin Sych, for the *Viking Cup '96* magazine, he states,

> We are always glad to be invited to take part in this top-level tournament, which is being rich sport and life experience for young hockey players from different countries. [The] Viking Cup tournament is a wonderful opportunity to observe skills of young players, to compare different hockey schools, to share ice hockey methods in educating and training young hockey players. I wish success and high results to all participants and sincerely appreciate [the] intensive and fruitful work of the tournament organizing committee and, personally, Mr. LeRoy Johnson, for his great efforts in coordinating organizational arrangements.

In 1997, Valentin Sych began speaking out about how organized crime had infiltrated the sport. It may have been a costly gesture. Sych was shot dead in Moscow in April 1997, in what the *Toronto Star* called a "gangland execution." Sych and other top Russian sports officials who complained about the Russian Mafia's deep involvement in sports simultaneously stood accused (often by each other) of being part of the corruption. "Russian amateur hockey, once the envy of the world, has come to this: hit men and slush funds," wrote Kevin Sherrington in the *Dallas Morning News* as recorded in the article "Russians Regroup on Other Side of the Red Line."

Whatever the real story of the '90s, it was clear that the Russian hockey giant was wounded (and hurting for money).

By now there had been a mass exodus of their Russian stars to the NHL. Canadian coach Tom Renney, CEO of Hockey Canada (2014–2021) commented in 1994, "It looks like a terrible mess over there . . . but their depth is always underestimated."

Through a void in leadership, the federation struggled to find itself. Consequently, there was a pull-back on activities and the Viking Cup felt the effect.

2) The novelty of hosting exhibition games began to recede while the position of Russian hockey normalized worldwide. The Russian hockey Bear was bleeding and it was showing up in its medal counts in world tournaments. In the thirty years preceding 1990, the Soviet national team won twenty gold medals and its junior team won eight gold in the twelve tournaments from 1977 to 1990. From 1990 to the present, the Russian national team has won six gold and its national junior team has won five gold medals. Of course, the Soviet Union represented more countries than Russia and, after 1992, representation was from Russia alone, still a very large country. It was clear that a fog had rolled in and Russian hockey had lost some former glory and glitter. Canadian crowds for exhibition games began to wane.

Meanwhile, Russian authorities maintained their financial expectations to participate in the Viking Cup. It became increasingly difficult to sell exhibition games at the prices necessary to purchase air tickets and cover other expenses.

The Russians always stayed true to their commitments to the Viking Cup. They did, however, look after their federation interests well and were firm negotiators, in my experience. They continued to play excellent hockey, but more and more their very best players were already playing in front of Canada's hockey fans as Canadian junior teams began to entice their fine products following the downfall of Communism.

It is noteworthy that the attitude of the Russian (and Czechoslovakian) coaches and other leaders toward North American agents and scouts at the Viking Cup seemed ambivalent. On the one hand, they were happy for any of their players that might have the opportunity to play in Canada or the US (and eventually the NHL), but they were also aware that these opportunities might weaken hockey programs back home.

3) There were enticements for the U18 national teams to compete in other developing tournaments, particularly those sanctioned or sponsored by hockey federations such as Hockey Canada. The Russian U18 team has participated in the Canadian World Junior Challenge tournament since the demise of the Viking Cup in 2006.

The Russian national U18 team played in Viking Cup '88, '90, '92, '94, '96, winning gold ('94), silver ('92), and bronze ('90). The NHL drafted a total of forty Soviet/Russian players from the Viking Cup, and many played in the Olympics.

During their five visits to the Viking Cup, a total of fifty-two pre-tournament exhibition games were held in numerous places throughout Western Canada. Suffice it to say that many thousands of Canadian hockey fans saw the mighty Soviets/Russians of ice hockey compete in their own communities with their home team. Each game has its stories of outstanding hockey and well-received Canadian hospitality. For the Viking Cup, the Russian Bear was like a mascot with a torch, upholding the quality and reputation of the Viking Cup of which the Soviets/Russians were such an important part.

Final Thoughts

When the CLC Vikings entered the Soviet Union by train in 1980, the ride was very rough. In fact, some wondered if the train would stay on the track. In the '90s the mighty Russian hockey locomotive was derailed and the route to Camrose was terminated following Viking Cup '96.

The era of Soviet and Russian team participation in the Viking Cup coincided with the end of the Cold War and the end of the Soviet Union as it was known. The Communist socialist state had built up a powerful sport empire that ran on the rails of a well-established top-down structure. When the system collapsed, it left a bureaucratic and economic vacuum while a new track was being built on the grades of *peristroika, glasnost*, and other ideology that followed. The reconstruction was slow and uncertain. It was hampered by competing forces wrestling for control amid the massive change.

Meanwhile, Russian stars shone brightly in the Viking Cup, and many joined their countrymen in the NHL, altering the face of hockey and the role of European players in North America and, perhaps, throughout the rest of the world.

When the clouds closed in on Russian participation in the Viking Cup, a new experiment was being initiated by Scotty Bowman, coach of the Detroit Red Wings, to benefit from the unit mentality and puck possession of play in the Russian system.

The Red Wings acquired and assembled the famous Russian Five—Sergei Fedorov, Slava Fetisov, Slava Kozlov, Igor Larionov, and Vladimir Konstantinov—to play as a unit under Bowman. The Wings won two Stanley Cups during that three-year period, breaking a forty-two-year Stanley Cup drought for Detroit.

The final piece to that Russian unit was Russia's finest defenseman, Slava Fetisov. In 1983, Fetisov had been drafted by the New Jersey Devils under the leadership of Lou Lamoriello. After several false promises to Fetisov by Russian Coach Viktor Tikhonov, Slava was finally freed to play for New Jersey at age thirty-two, in 1989. He was the first player from the Soviet national team to play in the NHL. Slava starred with the Devils for five years, until traded to Detroit to reunite the Russian Five.

When Detroit captain Steve Yzerman received the Stanley Cup in 1997, he immediately handed it to Fetisov, who skated a victory lap with the Cup around the famous Joe Louis stadium jointly with Igor Larionov. Slava then turned to Commissioner Gary Bettman and said, "Will you allow me to take it to Moscow?" Bettman was reluctant because of the crime there. Slava then said, "But it's my town" (*Of Miracles and Men*).

On August 18, 1997, Slava Fetisov with teammates proudly hoisted the Stanley Cup in Moscow's Red Square to throngs of admirers.

Today, he looks back with the words, "That's a miracle. That's hockey. It can sometimes change the world" (*Of Miracles and Men*).

Raising the Stanley Cup in Moscow Square for the first time was indeed a watershed moment for hockey and a signal that the Russian Five had a major impact on the way hockey is coached and played today.

But the game was changing long before the Russian Five reached Detroit. From the time master teacher and coach Clare Drake met Anatoli Tarasov and, with his vast network of fellow coaches and protégés, began to incorporate Russian thinking into the game, Canadian hockey slowly metamorphosed into something better. The grassroots process was spurred on by international events like the Summit Series, Canada Cup, Viking Cup, World Junior, and all the high-interest events where Russian players participated. The Russian Five experiment was a final revelation that the Russian system of hockey, while good enough to win world championships and Olympics, was also the major link in winning the Stanley Cup for Detroit.

"These guys brought a completely new style of hockey to the NHL," said Bowman, who attended the first Viking Cup. "When the Russian Five were on the ice, you had to have your popcorn ready because you knew that you were in for a treat. They didn't just play hockey, they created masterpieces on the ice" ("'Russian Five' Changed Hockey's Fabric Forever," Vassili Ossipov).

Coach Scotty Bowman
(photo provided by Bowman)

Jim Devellano, general manager of the Wings at the time, believed that the impact of the Russian Five went beyond hockey. "I grew up with all this propaganda about how the Russians were our enemy. Now here we were, bringing the enemy over here. Then they were so good—the last missing piece for us to win. And they became our friends." Sergei Fedorov agreed, saying, "We need to build more bridges than weapons. That's my deep feeling about what should happen between our countries. Like we did in Detroit, you know?" (Gave, *The Russian Five*).

And like was done in Camrose, too—with the younger Russian rising stars of our galaxy; the Viking Cup . . . Afinogenov, Kovalenko, Zubov, Korolev, Brylin, Kasparitus, Mironov, Žoltoks, Nazarov, Gonchar, and all the rest.

When Sergei Gonchar came to Canada to play in the Viking Cup, he admired the fast pace of hockey and the supporting atmosphere. And he expressed it so aptly in the words, "You are always closer to the puck in Canada."

We are closer to the puck because hockey is our game. Its earliest history lies with us in Canada. Our player passion is not surpassed and, in our smaller, more numerous rinks, Canadians really are close to the puck. But in more recent times the Russians, and other Europeans, have shown us how to possess that puck and today we have a better game for the world to see. And we lived it at the Viking Cup in Camrose.

SOVIET UNION, CIS, RUSSIA

VIKING CUP PARTICIPANTS WHO PLAYED IN THE WINTER OLYMPICS (AS OF THE CONCLUSION OF 2018 GAMES)

Name	Viking Cup Team	Year(s)	Olympic Team	Year(s)
Maxim Afinogenov	Russia	1996	Russia	2002, 2006, 2010
Sergei Gonchar	CIS	1992	Russia	1998, 2002, 2006, 2010
Yuriy Gunko	USSR	1990	Ukraine	2002
Igor Ivanov	USSR	1988	Russia	1994
Darius Kasparaitis	USSR	1990	Unified Team	1992
			Russia	1998, 2002, 2006
Andrei Kovalenko	USSR	1988	Unified Team	1992
			Russia	1998
Oleg Kvasha	Russia	1996	Russia	2002
Vitaliy Lytvynenko	USSR	1988	Ukraine	2002
Andrei Markov	Russia	1996	Russia	2006, 2010, 2014
Boris Mironov	USSR	1990	Russia	1998, 2002
Yerlan Sagymbayev	USSR	1988	Kazakhstan	1998
Bogdan Savenko	CIS	1992	Ukraine	2002
Sergei Tertyshny	USSR	1988	Russia	1994
Vyacheslav Zavalnyuk	CIS	1992	Ukraine	1992
Alexei Zhamnov	USSR	1988	Unified Team	1992
			Russia	1998, 2002
Sergei Zubov	USSR	1988	Unified Team	1992

VIKING CUP PARTICIPANTS SELECTED IN NHL ENTRY OR SUPPLEMENTAL DRAFTS

Player	Viking Cup Team	Year(s)	Selected By	Draft	Round	Overall Selection
Maxim Afinogenov	Russia	1996	Buffalo	1997 Entry	3	69
Alexander Alexeyev	CIS	1992	Winnipeg	1992 Entry	6	132
Artem Anisimov	Russia	1994	Philadelphia	1994 Entry	3	62
Yuri Babenko	Russia	1996	Colorado	1996 Entry	2	51
Alexei Baranov	Russia	1994	Tampa Bay	1994 Entry	8	190
Maxim Bets	CIS	1992	St. Louis	1993 Entry	2	37
Sergei Brylin	CIS	1992	New Jersey	1992 Entry	2	42
Yuri Butsayev	Russia	1996	Detroit	1997 Entry	2	49
Alexander Godynyuk	USSR	1988	Toronto	1990 Entry	6	115
Yan Golubovsky	Russia	1994	Detroit	1994 Entry	1	23
Sergei Gomolyako	USSR	1988	Calgary	1989 Entry	9	189
Sergei Gonchar	CIS	1992	Washington	1992 Entry	1	14
Viktor Gordiouk	USSR	1988	Buffalo	1990 Entry	6	142
Yuriy Gunko	USSR	1990	St. Louis	1992 Entry	10	230
Nikolai Ignatov	Russia	1996	Tampa Bay	1996 Entry	6	152
Darius Kasparaitis	USSR	1990	New York Islanders	1992 Entry	1	5
Mikhail Kazakevich	Russia	1994	Pittsburgh	1994 Entry	10	258
Sergei Klimovich	CIS	1992	Chicago	1992 Entry	2	41
Alexander Korobolin	Russia	1994	New York Rangers	1994 Entry	4	100
Igor Korolev	USSR	1988	St. Louis	1992 Entry	2	38
Konstantin Korotkov	USSR	1990	Hartford	1992 Entry	8	177
Andrei Kovalenko	USSR	1988	Quebec	1990 Entry	8	148
Oleg Kvasha	Russia	1996	Florida	1996 Entry	3	65
Sergei Luchinkin	Russia	1994	Dallas	1995 Entry	8	202
Andrei Markov	Russia	1996	Montreal	1998 Entry	6	162
Dmitri Mekeshkin	Russia	1994	Washington	1994 Entry	6	145
Igor Melyakov	Russia	1994	Los Angeles	1995 Entry	6	137
Boris Mironov	USSR	1990	Winnipeg	1992 Entry	2	27
Andrei Nazarov	CIS	1992	San Jose	1992 Entry	1	10
Askhat Rakhmatullin	Russia	1996	Hartford	1996 Entry	9	231
Dmitri Ryabykin	Russia	1994	Calgary	1994 Entry	2	45
Ramil Saifullin	Russia	1994	Winnipeg	1994 Entry	8	186
Bogdan Savenko	CIS	1992	Chicago	1993 Entry	3	54
Sergei Simonov	CIS	1992	Toronto	1992 Entry	10	221
Yuri Smirnov	Russia	1994	Tampa Bay	1994 Entry	9	216
Sergei Tertyshny	USSR	1988	Washington	1994 Entry	11	275
Alexei Tezikov	Russia	1996	Buffalo	1996 Entry	5	115
Vitali Tomilin	CIS	1992	New Jersey	1992 Entry	4	90
Ivan Vologzhaninov	CIS	1992	Winnipeg	1992 Entry	11	254
Alexei Zhamnov	USSR	1988	Winnipeg	1990 Entry	4	77
Sergejs Žoltoks	USSR	1990	Boston	1992 Entry	3	55
Roman Zolotov	CIS	1992	Philadelphia	1992 Entry	6	127
Sergei Zubov	USSR	1988	New York Rangers	1990 Entry	5	85

Augustana Campus – Established by Norwegian Pioneers

CHAPTER 9

Other European Connections—
Germany. . . Switzerland . . . Norway

Germany:

Jim Setters, coach of the German U18 national team from 1993–2015, was aware of the calibre of hockey in the Viking Cup. A Canadian and a graduate of the University of Calgary's physical education program, Jim journeyed to Europe to coach and direct hockey programs. He wasn't the only Canadian of the highest levels of leadership in German hockey at the time. Long-time coach of the University of Calgary Dinosaurs and friend of the Viking Cup, George Kingston, coached the German national team from 1994 to 1998.

It was not until Viking Cup 2004 and 2006 that Setters brought his U18 national German team to participate and experience what he had heard for years about the Viking Cup. To nobody's surprise, the team found the competition stiff but of great benefit to the young German players. Two players in particular from those two teams have done very well. Thomas Greiss was drafted by the San Jose Sharks and Korbinian Holzer was drafted by the Toronto Maple Leafs. Thomas, currently playing for the Detroit Red Wings, has had an eleven-year NHL career and has consistently played for German national teams in world championships and Olympics. Korbinian has played for eight seasons in the NHL with Toronto, Anaheim, and Nashville and he, too, has been a regular player on German national teams.

As a coach and leader of hockey in Germany, Jim was a good guy for us to know. He was a sounding board on the European style of play for North American coaches and scouts, and so enhanced the finer educational aspects of the Viking Cup. Officially, Jim was a "mentor coach" of the IIHF from 2003 to 2013.

The Augustana Vikings played German teams in different parts of Germany on European tours, including: Füssen, the national ice hockey training centre of Germany (1985); Salzgitter (1997); and Hamburg (1997). Other games with German teams were played in a tournament in Bern, Switzerland (1990).

Germany benefited from coaches of other hockey countries, as well. Juhani Wahlsten, legendary Finnish coach of the gold-winning TPS Turku Juniors in Viking Cup '81, was coaching in Füssen, the national training centre for hockey in Germany, at the time the Vikings played there (1985).

But it wasn't only Finnish and Canadian coaches who helped us find our way in Germany. A former Augustana Viking player, Pat Ryan, played for German teams for several years and helped us find games in northern Germany, with an interesting excursion to historical Berlin. Other Viking graduates, including Trevor Erhardt, Kent Todd, and others, also found employment playing hockey in Germany.

The city of Germany best known to the Augustana Vikings was Frankfurt, the first touchdown destination for most of the Viking Cup trips to Europe. From Frankfurt, the Vikings made their way by bus or other flights to the main hockey countries of Europe. On one trip to Prague, the team stopped at Nuremberg to visit the courtroom of the Nuremberg trials of Nazi leaders of WWII. Playing hockey in Europe was only a part of the much broader educational experiences team members and accompanying fans encountered and valued. To many, Europe was the fatherland of their ancestors, and several were able to touch base with relatives and roots.

GERMANY

VIKING CUP PARTICIPANTS WHO PLAYED IN THE WINTER OLYMPICS (AS OF THE CONCLUSION OF 2018 GAMES)

Name	Viking Cup Team	Year(s)	Olympic Team	Year(s)
Thomas Greiss	Germany	2004	Germany	2006, 2010
Patrick Hager	Germany	2006	Germany	2018
Korbinian Holzer	Germany	2006	Germany	2010
Marcel Müller	Germany	2006	Germany	2010
Moritz Müller	Germany	2004	Germany	2018

VIKING CUP PARTICIPANTS SELECTED IN NHL ENTRY OR SUPPLEMENTAL DRAFTS

Player	Viking Cup Team	Year(s)	Selected By	Draft	Round	Overall Selection
Constantin Braun	Germany	2006	Los Angeles	2006 Entry	6	164
Robert Dietrich	Germany	2004	Nashville	2007 Entry	6	174
Thomas Greiss	Germany	2004	San Jose	2004 Entry	3	94
Korbinian Holzer	Germany	2006	Toronto	2006 Entry	4	111
Justin Krueger	Germany	2004	Carolina	2006 Entry	7	213

VIKING CUP PARTICIPANTS WHO PLAYED IN NHL AND WERE NOT SELECTED IN NHL ENTRY OR SUPPLEMENTAL DRAFTS

Name	Viking Cup Team	Year(s)
Marcel Müller	Germany	2006

Switzerland:

Ice hockey may not be as old as skiing in the Swiss Alps, but Swiss hockey teams have done well in climbing the IIHF placement ladder to eighth amongst hockey nations—usually good enough to play in the A pool of the World Championships.

Along the way, Switzerland has been an inspiration to the Viking Cup through its famous Spengler Cup, which is played each year in Davos during the Christmas break. Extensive TV coverage brings this tournament to the hockey world throughout Europe and North America.

Team Canada has played an important role in the Spengler Cup, winning the tournament a record fifteen times (tied with the home team, HC Davos) in its ninety-five-year history.

Canadian coach Andy Murray (Brandon University, Los Angeles Kings, and St. Louis Blues) has a record six gold medals as a coach for Canada at the Spengler Cup, earning the title "Mister Spengler Cup."

Murray was also a coach of Swiss teams, including Kloten, Zug, and Lugano. In the 2010 World Championships, he acted as a consultant to the Swiss team. In 2012, Murray was named to the IIHF Hall of Fame as a builder.

For the Augustana Vikings, Andy Murray was a valuable link to Swiss hockey. First, he recommended that Mike Johnston, his former Brandon University student, be hired as Augustana coach/general manager when applications were being received. (Mike had been playing and coaching in Australia before coming to Camrose in 1982.)

Second, Andy was helpful in making contacts in Switzerland for the Augustana Vikings to play in a tournament in Adelboden (1987), followed by games in Kloten and Zurich.

So why was the world's oldest invitational ice hockey tournament, the Spengler Cup of Switzerland, an inspiration and model for the Viking Cup of Canada?

I was only vaguely familiar with the Spengler Cup until I met Rudy Killias, a former Swiss national coach, while attending an international hockey symposium in Finland in 1982. Rudy was at the time coaching the Austrian national team and maintained close connections to the Spengler Cup in his home country. He invited me to visit Davos, home of the Spengler Cup, which I did at a later time. I was impressed that such a small town (about the size of Camrose) could build such a large and impressive stadium. Of course, it was primarily because of the Spengler Cup. Of greater interest to me, though, was the origin and purpose of the tournament.

The *Spengler Cup Davos* website describes its beginning:

> The Davos doctor Carl Spengler – son of the physician Dr. Alexander Spengler, who laid the foundation stone for Davos as a health resort – was an enthusiastic supporter of the ice hockey club HC Davos, founded in1921. In an effort to support his club, but also to promote contact between nations that had been on opposing sides during the First World War, he donated a challenge cup at Christmas in 1923. According to the foundation charter, he wanted to offer nations that had previously been enemies the opportunity

to test their strength in peaceful battles and to take one another's hand in friendship.

At its most profound level, the origin of the Spengler Cup speaks to the power of sport to ease tension and unify a continent torn apart by competing ideologies and war. I thought at the time: *Could sport unite people separated by an Iron Curtain?*

Rudy and his wife Reja were great hosts for the Vikings, arranging for participation in a tournament in Vienna, Austria in 1984 and Bern, Switzerland in 1990.

Being horse-loving people, the Killiases followed the Vikings back to Camrose to visit the Dennis and Allan Gordeyko Clydesdale horse farms. (The Allan Gordeykos were regular billets of the Viking Cup.)

Rick Graumann, who was a billet for Swiss players at the Viking Cup, commented, "Our Swiss boys were surprised at the number of trucks in Camrose. . . When we drove by Mirror Lake and saw skaters, they wanted to get out and try it. They said there are lots of lakes in Switzerland, but not frozen like that! Not in Zurich, their home city."

The Swiss national U18 team participated in Viking Cup 2004 and 2006, under coach Roger Bader. Goaltender Reto Berra (6'5") was drafted by the St. Louis Blues after playing in Viking Cup 2004, and began his NHL career with the Calgary Flames in 2013. He played six years with various teams in the NHL, and was a regular player in world championships and Olympics for Switzerland. Although undrafted, Viking Cup 2006 player Raphael Díaz tried out for the Montreal Canadiens in 2011, and made the team. He played there for three years before moving on to Vancouver, Calgary, and the New York Rangers. He, too, played in World Championships and the Olympics for his country.

The original Spengler Cup trophy is on display at the Hockey Hall of Fame in Toronto.

SWITZERLAND

VIKING CUP PARTICIPANTS WHO PLAYED IN THE WINTER OLYMPICS (AS OF THE CONCLUSION OF 2018 GAMES)

Name	Viking Cup Team	Year(s)	Olympic Team	Year(s)
Reto Berra	Switzerland	2004	Switzerland	2014
Matthias Bieber	Switzerland	2004	Switzerland	2014
Eric Blum	Switzerland	2004	Switzerland	2018
Simon Bodenmann	Switzerland	2006	Switzerland	2014, 2018
Luca Cunti	Switzerland	2006	Switzerland	2014
Raphael Díaz	Switzerland	2004	Switzerland	2010, 2014, 2018
Leonardo Genoni	Switzerland	2004	Switzerland	2018
Julien Sprunger	Switzerland	2004	Switzerland	2010

VIKING CUP PARTICIPANTS SELECTED IN NHL ENTRY OR SUPPLEMENTAL DRAFTS

Player	Viking Cup Team	Year(s)	Selected By	Draft	Round	Overall Selection
Reto Berra	Switzerland	2004	St. Louis	2006 Entry	4	106
Luca Cunti	Switzerland	2006	Tampa Bay	2007 Entry	3	75
Julien Sprunger	Switzerland	2004	Minnesota	2004 Entry	4	117
Julian Walker	Switzerland	2006	Minnesota	2006 Entry	6	162

VIKING CUP PARTICIPANTS WHO PLAYED IN NHL AND WERE NOT SELECTED IN NHL ENTRY OR SUPPLEMENTAL DRAFTS

Name	Viking Cup Team	Year(s)
Raphael Díaz	Switzerland	2004

Norway:

Norway participated only once in the Viking Cup (2004) and the Vikings played games in Norway on only two tours, yet the historical connection to Camrose and the Viking Cup runs deep.

Norwegians joined the immigration wave (some from Norway and some rebounding from Minnesota, Iowa, and the Dakotas) to Western Canada around 1900, many settling in Camrose and surrounding areas like Bardo and New Norway. The Norwegians' penchant for education meant a first order of business was to build a school, and so, in 1910, Camrose Lutheran College was built. Camrose and its college later became the birthplace of the Viking Cup.

Names like Servold, Gotaas, and Hansen soon dominated the winter sport circles, even at the Olympic level. Some advanced their training at Camrose Lutheran College, and some went to American colleges, such as the famed Hansen brothers who journeyed to Minnesota. The pipeline continued both ways. Bob Osness and Brian Berg, CLC hockey players of Norwegian descent, journey to play at Scandinavian-based Augsburg College in Minneapolis in 1970, and Augsburg participated in Viking Cup '94.

The first Norwegian hockey player to participate in the Viking Cup was Anders Myrvold, who played for Färjestad Juniors of Sweden at the time. Anders was drafted by the Quebec Nordiques and played for Colorado, Boston, the NY Islanders, and Detroit. He played regularly for the Norwegian national team in World Championships and the Olympics. Jonas Holøs played for Norway at Viking Cup 2004, and was drafted by Colorado. He was the sixth Norwegian player to play in the NHL.

Norway gave the Viking Cup its name, its college, its traditions, and, yes, its very being.

NORWAY

VIKING CUP PARTICIPANTS WHO PLAYED IN THE WINTER OLYMPICS (AS OF THE CONCLUSION OF 2018 GAMES)

Name	Viking Cup Team	Year(s)	Olympic Team	Year(s)
Kristian Forsberg	Norway	2004	Norway	2010, 2014, 2018
Jonas Holøs	Norway	2004	Norway	2010, 2014, 2018
Mathis Olimb	Norway	2004	Norway	2010, 2014, 2018
Martin Røymark	Norway	2004	Norway	2010, 2014, 2018

VIKING CUP PARTICIPANTS SELECTED IN NHL ENTRY OR SUPPLEMENTAL DRAFTS

Player	Viking Cup Team	Year(s)	Selected By	Draft	Round	Overall Selection
Jonas Holøs	Norway	2004	Colorado	2008 Entry	6	170

Practising For The Game by Allen Sapp (Order of Canada Indigenous Artist)
Permission by Aboriginal Heritage Foundation
(Gift from North Battleford North Stars hockey club - Viking Cup '96)

CHAPTER 10

Canadian Junior Connections

The Prince Albert Raiders were not just an ordinary Canadian junior hockey team in 1980. As Canada's best, they rolled into Camrose, setting a gold standard with silver results in the first two Viking Cups, 1981 and 1982.

After their inaugural season in 1971, it did not take long for the Raiders to become one of the most successful franchises in Canadian junior hockey history. From 1977 to 1982, under Coach Terry Simpson, the team, won the Centennial Cup emblematic of Canadian supremacy four times, the last two after competing in Viking Cup '81 and Viking Cup '82. The Raiders won the Saskatchewan/Manitoba championship for seven straight years, up to 1982. In the fall of 1982 the Raiders moved to the highest level of junior hockey, joining the major junior Western Hockey League. Continuing under the leadership of Simpson and assistant coach Rick Wilson, the team won the Memorial Cup in 1985.

So why did the Prince Albert Raiders enter the very first Viking Cup? Simply, they had earned the right to be there.

They were the best Canadian Junior Hockey League team at the time and the Viking Cup was to be a tournament of champions from the hockey-playing nations of the world.

Having become well acquainted with Raiders' super scout Bob Robson, I broached the idea with him and Terry Simpson and extended an invitation. My sense was that they were ready for a new challenge, and that was something we could offer . . . to play European junior teams from Sweden and Finland.

With eyes already on major junior hockey, the Raiders may have seen the opportunity to "up their stakes," as they would be the first to taste European competition.

Robson had already established a recruitment base in the Camrose area as Dave and Steve Reierson of Bashaw were then playing with the Raiders. For the Reierson boys, Viking Cup '81 was a triumphant homecoming, and no doubt brought carloads of fans to the games from the Bashaw area south of Camrose.

In the *Viking Cup 2004* magazine, Dave, who played part of his career in Europe, was asked about his memories of playing in the Viking Cup. "Viking Cup '81 set the stage for success as Canadian champions in the Centennial Cup at Halifax later that year," he said. "The competition in the Viking Cup was really strong. The teams we played against were at least on par or better than we were. It really forced you to play at a top level."

Of Viking Cup '82, the Raiders second kick at the can, Dave remembers playing the Czechoslovakian team, where Petr Klíma was a player. "He got a penalty shot against our goaltender. He came in and took a slapshot that went top shelf. Our goalie didn't even make a move. It was unbelievable." Petr scored both goals in a 2–1 Czech victory.

The Raiders' participation in the Viking Cup paid other dividends for the team. Young players from the Camrose area—including John Lamb, Steve Gotaas, Wally Niewchas, Darren Perkins, and Parker Kelly—all became Raiders in following years. Additionally, three Viking Cup players from Czechoslovakia—Roman Vopot, Milan Kraft, and Marion Meňhart—joined the Raiders following later Viking Cups.

Terry Simpson (right) with Juhani Wahlsten (Finland)

In their two appearances at the Viking Cup, the Raiders featured an impressive crop of players for the Camrose fans to enjoy. From those two teams, eleven players were either drafted or played in the NHL: Robin Bartel, Todd Bergen, Warren Harper, Gil Hudon, Bob Lowes, Greg Paslawski, James Patrick, Dave Reierson, Alan Stewart, Bill Watson, and Dave Tippett. Both coaches, Simpson and Wilson, went on to have distinguished coaching careers in the NHL, as did players James Patrick and Dave Tippett. Dave currently coaches the Edmonton Oilers.

It was no surprise to Simpson that Dave became a great coach. As he said in an article in *The Athletic*, "Hockey was his love. You could see that was a road he could take if he chose to."

Dave's road trip to the Viking Cup is still a strong memory.

> I played my first international game at the Viking Cup. We played AIK Sweden and then lost a close game to a great Finnish team in the final. What I remember most was the *atmosphere* at the Viking Cup. It was so lively and so much fun, so enjoyable! It was a highlight of great memories in my young days of playing hockey.

The New York Rangers drafted James Patrick in the first round after he played in Viking Cup '81 and was declared the top junior player in Canada. He had a stellar twenty-three-year career in the NHL (Rangers, Flames, Sabres, and Stars) and finished his playing career in Germany. In recalling his Viking Cup experience, James recently commented from his Winnipeg Ice coach's office.

We didn't know anyone was interested in us until then! I didn't even know it was my draft year until I saw Scotty Bowman watching us at the Viking Cup! The Viking Cup was my first big stage in international hockey! From there, I played in the World Juniors the next year. But what a great experience at the Viking Cup! Steve and Dave Reiersen, my teammates from Bashaw, invited our whole team to their place one day for dinner. We all watched Wayne Gretzky and the Oilers play on their living room TV. . . But my most vivid memory was the gold-medal game against Finland. Hannu Virta on defense was so smooth and I had never seen such great passes. He had four assists in the final game. When I got to the NHL, I faced him again when the Rangers played the Buffalo Sabres.

In Viking Cup '82, the Raiders faced the invincible Dominator, Dominik Hašek, in goal and sniper Petr Klíma for the Czechoslovakian national U18 team and settled for silver once again. Many rate these games as the best that were played in the history of the Viking Cup. There were sellout crowds and Camrose was abuzz with Viking Cup fever for years to come.

There could not have been a better beginning to the Viking Cup, and the PA Raiders, and their many loyal fans, were in the thick of it all—including a young player named Lyle Hamm, who was from Flin Flon but living and playing B-level hockey in Prince Albert. Lyle reflects on those days:

> Now, in early December, I learned from one of my friends who played defense for the Raiders that they were going to a hockey tournament at Christmastime in Alberta. The tournament was in a city I had never heard of and the tournament was called the 1982 Viking Cup. I remember thinking that [the Raiders] would make short work of their competitors because at that point in their season, they had only lost one game in the Saskatchewan Junior Hockey League (SJHL). More definitively, they were beating their opponents by lop-sided scores all the time.

> That mindset of mine all changed when my grandparents and I were listening to the final game in early January that was broadcast over CKBI radio in Prince Albert and the Czechoslovakian national team ran up the score on our powerful—did I mention the eventual 1982 Centennial Cup champions? —Raiders. I remember my grandma knitting furiously in her chair, cheering on her team, but to no avail. The Raiders were simply trounced. When we turned off the radio, my grandpa said, "Sonny, it would be great if you got a chance to play in that tournament."

Two years later, Lyle "Steamer" Hamm was playing for the Vikings in the Viking Cup.

Years later, in the *Viking Cup 2006* magazine, Coach Terry Simpson commented that the Viking Cup brought credibility to the Raiders:

When we were going there, we had tier-two teams that were as good as there was. The Viking Cup became an important event in the hockey calendar and it still is. For the first couple of years, the college teams played the Europeans and us. It was a real good tournament for bringing recognition to our team and a good measuring stick for our team vis-à-vis the European and the colleges.

I was recently in contact with assistant coach Rick Wilson, who just retired from thirty years of coaching (mostly Dallas) in the NHL. I asked him what he remembered about the Viking Cup. He said: "It was my first experience with European hockey. I admired them and their play. It was an eye-opener." Captain of those famous Raiders, Peter Anholt, now general manager of the Lethbridge Hurricanes in major junior hockey, agreed. "That was a great learning experience and it did our team a lot of good."

From Prince Albert to Saint Albert

The 1983–84 Saint Albert Saints of the Alberta Junior Hockey League were invited to participate in Viking Cup '84, based on an impressive record and a strong emphasis on education. Among their graduates were NHLers Mark Messier (Oilers), Troy Murray (Blackhawks), Mickey Volcan (Flames), Brian Ford (Nordiques), and Ken Solheim (Red Wings).

In 1981–82, six of the Saints' graduating players received scholarships at universities and colleges and two were drafted by the NHL. In 1982–83, eleven players received scholarships, and five players were drafted in the first six rounds of the NHL draft. This represented the highest number of players drafted from any tier-two junior hockey team in Canada.

Under Coach Doug Hicks, a former NHL defenseman, the team did not qualify for the medal round in Viking Cup '84. Dave Kendall (second-leading scorer in the tournament) and Brad Hammett attended Augustana and played for the Vikings the following season, which included a series of games in Austria and Czechoslovakia on the biennial Christmas European tour. Dave played with the Vikings in Viking Cup '86, after which he and CLC Vikings teammate Ken Lovsin played for and graduated from the University of Saskatchewan. Looking back, Dave comments: "I was very fortunate to be able to play high-level international hockey for three years in a row while studying at Camrose. Attending CLC was the highlight of my career."

Few schools have turned out as many hockey players as Notre Dame, in Wilcox, Saskatchewan. In 1983–84, the high school's Notre Dame Hounds played in the Midwest Intercollegiate Hockey League with teams from the US, as there was little competition for the club in southern Saskatchewan. Like Augustana, they were a college team with a strong emphasis on academics and sport, especially hockey. The Viking Cup seemed a good fit for their program. The Hounds, under well-known coach Barry Mackenzie, finished sixth and did not qualify for the Viking Cup '86 playoffs. In 1987, they joined the SJHL where they still play.

No Canadian Junior teams were entered in Viking Cups from 1988 to 1992.

Manitoba Junior Hockey League

Following Viking Cup '92, Augustana Vikings player Jeff Weist, who had played in the Manitoba Junior League—the oldest junior league in Canada — brought to our attention that the Dauphin Kings had just won the Anavet Cup in the Manitoba–Saskatchewan playoff. I agreed that it would be timely to have a Manitoba junior team in the Viking Cup. As an introduction to the Viking Cup '94 competition, the participating Russian national U18 team was sent to Manitoba for an exhibition swing with teams in the MJHL, including Dauphin. The Czech National U18 team had visited Dauphin earlier.

The Dauphin Kings, under general manager Cam Alf and coach Lyle Stokotelny, did not disappoint, as they reached the championship game of Viking Cup '94, but could not match the powerful national U18 Russian team for gold. Kings' forward Lars Mølgaard made the All-Star team and Manitoba was part of Viking Cup history.

The MJHL was represented with a league all-star team in Viking Cup 2000 and Viking Cup 2002. In each year, the Manitoba representatives placed fourth amongst the ten participating teams.

Alberta Junior Hockey and the Viking Cup

Marty Knack knew the Viking Cup—he knew its objectives, its history, and its success. And he liked what he saw. Marty was a sportswriter with the *Edmonton Journal* and was assigned to cover seven of the first eight tournaments. You could always find Marty in the media room between games, talking to scouts and coaches and writing his stories.

At Viking Cup '86, he reported, "It's no exaggeration that the Viking Cup is the finest hockey tournament in Alberta—a classy event."

At Viking Cup '96, he referred to the Viking Cup as the "finest of its kind in North America." And at Viking Cup '98, he wrote, "It has been one of the finest international tournaments of its kind (anywhere) since its inception."

It is no surprise then, that when he was elected president of the Alberta Junior League in 1993, he sought to have junior hockey in Alberta experience the Viking Cup. The Viking Cup steering committee was on side.

It was Marty's proposal that an Alberta Junior All-Star team would be good for the league and the tournament and, of course, he wanted the best for both the AJHL and the Viking Cup.

Our Viking Cup steering committee concurred, and Marty sold the concept to his board. It was a marketing dream for all, and even NHL scouts liked the idea of the best Alberta junior players in the competitive Viking Cup.

The Alberta Junior All-Stars, under coaches Bruno Baseotto of Calgary and Fran Gow of Fort McMurray, proved that they belonged, as they placed fourth in the eight-team tournament. Jeramie Heistad and Dale Donaldson placed on the tournament all-star team and forward Fernando Pisani was the tournament's leading scorer.

It was a great year for Pisani as he continued his torrid pace of scoring with the St. Albert Saints in the AJHL. He won the league scoring race with forty goals and sixty-three assists for 103 points in fifty-eight games. He was chosen by the Edmonton Oilers in the eighth round of the spring draft.

"I had so much fun," Fernando says of the Viking Cup. "I'd never played in front of that many people before. It was just a great feeling to come into the packed rink and be the local team. The people were excited to see us play."

Playing with the Saints, Fernando saw the doors open to combine hockey and university. He received a full scholarship to Providence College, which gave him more time to develop his hockey skills. He played his first game in a seven-year stint with the Oilers when he was twenty-seven, and never lost the scoring touch he had in the Viking Cup. His best playoff was in 2006, when he scored a league-leading fourteen goals, of which five were game winners.

When plans for Viking Cup '98 began, the Alberta Junior All-Stars were inked in early. All knew that Marty and his team, having tasted the Viking Cup menu, would have a strong appetite for gold. Gord Thibodeau (Lloydminster), Brett Cox (Bonnyville), and Jeff Truitt (Camrose) were chosen to coach the team.

Saskatchewan Junior Hockey League

Meanwhile, top teams from the Saskatchewan Junior Hockey League kept their eye on the Viking Cup, ever since the Prince Albert challenge in the founding years.

The North Battleford North Stars were the likely applicants for Viking Cup '96. First, they were a strong team. They had won the North Division of their league and were league playoff finalists the previous year. Second, their coaches, Blaine Gusdal and Jeff Johnson, were Augustana graduates and had experienced the Viking Cup. Third, one of their players, Dmitri Tarabin, had starred on the Russian national U18 team that won gold at Viking Cup '94. He was anxious to lead his teammates back to Camrose.

The *Viking Cup '96* magazine quotes Blaine and Jeff:

> Because of our close ties to the Cup, we have a lot of pride and obviously we want to do well in front of our old hometown and our alma mater and old teammates, who are still around. I think we all want to do the tournament and the Vikings proud. We don't just want to be in because we have a past there. We want to be in on our own merits, which I think we are.

The North Stars were competitive in Viking Cup '96, but failed to summon the necessary depth to win a medal. It was tough going, with several national teams to beat. "My first call when I returned to North Battleford was to our league president, Wayne Kartusch," said Gusdal. "I want to take an SJHL All-Star team to the Viking Cup."

He got his wish when, as head coach, he brought the SJHL All-Star Selects to Camrose two years later for Viking Cup '98. His assistant coaches were Doug Hedley (Labrete) and Larry Wintoneak (Flin Flon), and his former assistant coach and close friend Jeff Johnson had become project coordinator of the Viking Cup. "It was an incredible event, on so many levels," Blaine said. "The team had a great run and ultimately ended up winning the championship game, defeating the AJHL All-Star Selects in the final."

With enthusiasm, Blaine continues,

> The rink was absolutely packed and I've always joked it was the only time I had a good seat for the final game. Mike Comrie was a top forward and the most exciting player with the AJHL team. Henrik Zetterberg played with the Swedish team that we defeated in the semi-finals. Chris Kunitz was an eighteen-year-old rookie forward with our SJHL All-Star team. Viking Cup '98 was a springboard for these great NHLers.

Chris Kunitz was playing for the Melville Millionaires at the time, but soon received a scholarship to play at Ferris State, where he excelled. As a late bloomer, he never was drafted, but he got his start as a free agent with the Anaheim Ducks the year they won the Stanley Cup. After four years, he was traded to the Pittsburgh Penguins, where he played for nine years, winning three more Stanley Cups and playing, for the most part, on a line with Sidney Crosby. He played the final two years of his fifteen-year NHL career in Tampa and Chicago.

As for Kunitz' Viking Cup encounter, Gusdal had this to say, "Chris had a great tournament. He was a hard-working, two-way player, and he just kept pushing. The Viking Cup exposed him to European play, different opposition, and new ideas and strategies in hockey. Chris needed that and he responded very well. . . He took the ball and ran with it—and the scouts noticed. The Viking Cup was exactly what Chris needed at the time."

BC Junior Hockey League

The BCJHL participated as an all-star team in Viking Cup 2000 and Viking Cup 2002. The team won the silver medal in Viking Cup 2002, when the host Augustana Vikings won gold. Six of the BC players were drafted, including Jeff Tambellini, who was named the MVP of the 2002 event.

Winning the MVP award and a place on the all-star team of Viking Cup 2002 was only a part of Jeff's great accomplishments in junior hockey. As a player with the Chilliwack Chiefs, he received the BCJHL MVP award and CJHL (Canadian) player of the year honours. Jeff received a scholarship to play at the University of Michigan and was drafted by the LA Kings in the first round (twenty-seventh) in 2003. He played for the LA Kings, NY Islanders, and Vancouver Canucks before continuing his career in Europe.

Tambellini returned to his family roots in Trail, BC as general manager and coach of the Trail Smoke Eaters, when he retired from playing hockey. His grandfather had played with the Trail Smoke Eaters when they won the World Championships in 1961. His father, Steve, had a ten-year career in the NHL and was general manager of the Edmonton Oilers from 2008–13.

Alberta Junior Hockey League

Mike Comrie, a third-round draft of the Edmonton Oilers, played with several teams in his thirteen-year NHL career. But first he was chosen to the Viking Cup '98 all-star team and later was honoured as the Canadian Junior A hockey player of the year. That same year, the Edmonton native led the AJHL in scoring while his club, the St. Albert Saints, won the league title.

In a feature in the *Viking Cup 2000 Magazine* with the title "A Family Affair," Mike commented: "The Viking Cup helped me to compete against better players."

I spoke to Mike from his LA home about his memories of the Viking Cup twenty-two years later. Most of all, he wanted to thank the people of Camrose for the great experience he had in Viking Cup '98.

> We as players enjoyed it so much… to play with some of the best players of world at that age level. It left a big impression with me, but everyone reaped rewards—the players, the fans, the workers, the community. You can only put on an event like that with dedicated people that live in the community. It was in the category of 'elite tournaments'. I attended the University of Michigan, so I heard about the tournament there as well, because the USA national U18 team was training there—to come to the Viking Cup. It was a big tournament. It was good for hockey.

Gord Thibodeau, dean of coaching in the AJHL, was the head coach of that team and again in Viking Cup 2002. He was also a member of the U of A Golden Bears as a player at Viking Cup '88.

> There was immense buy-in from the whole town. Everywhere we went, people would talk about it. We didn't realize how important it was until we saw how involved the people were. It was incredible. It was magical.

> In Viking Cup 2002, we lost out in the semis, so were relegated to play for bronze the next day. We needed something to motivate us. At the restaurant that evening, some young ladies who had been at the game and who ran a hair salon were talking to us. They sensed that we were feeling low. One offered to open her shop and dye our hair blond to shock our team the next day, just for fun, you know. We went for it. It lifted our team and we won bronze. Again, it demonstrated the huge buy-in from the community.

Regarding the effect that the Viking Cup had on hockey, Thibodeau had this to say:

> The Viking Cup set a new tone in hockey. Now the AJHL and others in Canada and beyond hold a showcase weekend, with all teams involved, to show their players to the scouts and the public… No surprise that the AJHL has come to Camrose for their showcase five years in a row now. The Viking Cup was good for hockey and good for the AJHL. It was perfect for the NHL.

The Birth of the Camrose Kodiaks Junior Hockey Team

There were mutual advantages to both the Viking Cup and the AJHL emanating from Alberta Junior League All-Star participation in Viking Cup '96, and it led to another important beginning — a Junior A hockey franchise for Camrose.

Marty Knack saw Camrose as an ideal centre for an AJHL franchise, and talked at some length with me about how such a venture could be of benefit to Augustana's hockey program, especially the Viking Cup tournament. This was not exactly a new topic, as there had been sniffing in previous years from potential investors.

There was an opportunity at hand as the Sherwood Park Crusaders franchise was in financial difficulty and rumoured to be for sale.

After considering the alternatives with various stakeholders, including the City of Camrose, Augustana University College, and members of the Viking Cup steering committee, we decided to pursue the issue and offered to purchase the Crusaders franchise on April 1, 1996. After local consultation, the owners of the Crusaders decided that the team would not be for sale.

By this time, stakeholders had formed the Camrose Sport Development Society to own and manage the team. Many new members were Viking Cup committee members who were adamant that the team be operated in cooperation with the Augustana hockey program, including the Viking Cup. Like-minded new members were recruited to give a total of twenty-three directors when the society was formed. Two of the members were adamant that Augustana have direct representation, and thus paid for their membership. I had assumed the responsibility for raising the start-up funds through memberships to that point, when Verlyn Olson was elected first president of the society. The society was to be an umbrella organization that would support (and possibly own) any sport group needing assistance in the community. A junior hockey team would be their first project.

What were some of the reasons for the decision to proceed with a Camrose Junior A franchise?

1) In considering the attractiveness of Camrose as a centre for a franchise, it was felt that it would be best to have local control versus that of an outside group.

2) College hockey was not drawing well in the community at that time and had been struggling through the '90s to place well in ACAC league play. A local junior team could be a new source of good players for the Vikings and students for Augustana.

3) Improved facilities were necessary to accommodate a growing Viking Cup. A junior team, being an additional arena tenant to the Viking Cup and the Vikings, would lend much more credence to a push for new and better facilities.

4) A junior franchise would offer economic advantages for the community and offer young hockey players in the community an opportunity to develop skills at an advanced level.

With prospects of purchasing a franchise now faded beyond view, the Camrose Sport Development Society, with encouragement from the city, the college and the AJHL president, Marty Knack, decided to apply to the league for a new franchise. The letter of application was presented to President Knack by the new president of the Camrose Sport Development Society, Verlyn Olson, on May 27, 1996. The name Camrose Kodiaks was chosen for the new team, which began league play in September 1997 under its inaugural general manager/coach, Jeff Truitt.

It was initially intended that there would be joint initiatives of the Vikings, Viking Cup, and Kodiaks regarding sponsorships, advertising, scheduling, and Viking Cup participation. However, after one year of joint marketing (1998), the operations of college and junior hockey programs in Camrose were separated. The Kodiaks continue to be operated by the Camrose Sport Development Society.

Pullback of Canadian Junior Hockey from the Viking Cup

Canadian Junior Hockey continued to be strongly represented in Viking Cup 2000 and Viking Cup 2002, with all-star teams from all four Western Canada provinces. The Alberta Junior All-Stars won the silver medal in Viking Cup 2000. The BC Junior All-Stars won silver in Viking Cup 2002, and the Alberta Junior All-Stars won bronze.

With the additional Canadian junior teams, the Viking Cup expanded to ten-team tournaments in 2000 and 2002. However, the dominance of Canadian junior hockey representation may have been an Achilles' heel, as the following year all four teams, as a group, decided to withdraw from the Viking Cup to pursue a Junior A-Hockey Canada-sponsored international tournament now known as the World Junior A Challenge. The objective given was to showcase their best players to scouts of major hockey leagues while exposing them to international hockey at a high level.

Boris Rybalka, coordinator of Viking Cup 2000 and 2002, and now coach/general manager of the Camrose Junior A Kodiaks, saw the objectives of the Viking Cup as being much different than for the World Junior A Challenge: "The Viking Cup was an *event* and that was the main reason for its success. Billeting and cultural exchange was a great contributor to its success. It had a vision that should be continued. The purpose of the Junior A Challenge is narrower in scope."

The discontinuance of the Canadian junior All-Star teams from the Viking Cup upset the healthy balance of European to North American competition that had been an attractive feature, especially for the top European hockey nations.

Pipeline

Today, college hockey teams of the ACAC are made up almost entirely of graduates of Canadian Junior A hockey. The Viking Cup helped to build that pipeline that has given many junior players the opportunity to advance their education in combination with the sport they love.

CANADA

VIKING CUP PARTICIPANTS WHO PLAYED IN THE WINTER OLYMPICS (AS OF THE CONCLUSION OF 2018 GAMES)

Name	Viking Cup Team	Year(s)	Olympic Team	Year(s)
Robin Bartel	Prince Albert	1981, 1982	Canada	1984
Chris Kunitz	SJHL	1998	Canada	2014
Ken Lovsin	Camrose Luth. College	1986	Canada	1994
Greg Parks	St. Albert	1984	Canada	1994
James Patrick	Prince Albert	1981	Canada	1984
Ben Scrivens	AJHL North	2006	Canada	2018
Dave Tippett	Prince Albert	1981	Canada	1984, 1992

VIKING CUP PARTICIPANTS SELECTED IN NHL ENTRY OR SUPPLEMENTAL DRAFTS

Player	Viking Cup Team	Year(s)	Selected By	Draft	Round	Overall Selection
Joel Andresen	AJHL	2002	Los Angeles	2002 Entry	5	157
Gavin Armstrong	Notre Dame	1986	Edmonton	1987 Entry	9	189
Eric Aubertin	McGill	1990	Montreal	1986 Entry	5	94
Todd Bergen	Prince Albert	1982	Philadelphia	1982 Entry	5	98
Brent Bobyck	Notre Dame	1986	Montreal	1986 Entry	4	78
Paul Cabana	AJHL	1998	Vancouver	1996 Entry	6	149
Dean Clark	NAIT	1986	Edmonton	1982 Entry	8	167
Matt Cockell	MJHL	2000	Vancouver	1997 Entry	5	117
Mike Comrie	AJHL	1998	Edmonton	1999 Entry	3	91
Jesse Cook	AJHL	1998	Calgary	1999 Entry	5	153
Grant Couture	U of Alberta	1988	Pittsburgh	1982 Entry	7	136
Daryn Fersovich	St. Albert	1984	Philadelphia	1984 Entry	10	204
Glenn Fisher	AJHL	2002	Edmonton	2002 Entry	5	148
T.J. Galiardi	AJHL South	2006	Colorado	2007 Entry	2	55
Greg Geldart	NAIT	1992	Vancouver	1988 Entry	8	149
Rob Glasgow	U of Alberta	1988	Hartford	1986 Entry	9	179
Matthew Glasser	AJHL North	2006	Edmonton	2005 Entry	7	220
Warren Harper	Prince Albert	1981	Buffalo	1981 Entry	10	206
Gil Hudon	Prince Albert	1981, 1982	Philadelphia	1981 Entry	7	142
Ivan Huml	BCHL	2000	Boston	2000 Entry	2	59
Shane Hynes	BCHL	2002	Anaheim	2003 Entry	3	86
Connor James	AJHL	2000	Los Angeles	2002 Entry	9	279
Regan Kelly	SJHL	2000	Philadelphia	2000 Entry	8	259
Ken Lovsin	Camrose Luth. College	1986	Hartford	1987 Supplemental	1	6
Ken MacArthur	Notre Dame	1986	Minnesota	1988 Entry	8	148
Ryan MacMurchy	SJHL	2002	St. Louis	2002 Entry	9	284
Ken Magowan	BCHL	2000	New Jersey	2000 Entry	7	198
Jesse Martin	AJHL North	2006	Atlanta	2006 Entry	7	195
Nathan Martz	BCHL	2000	New York Rangers	2000 Entry	5	140
Scott McCallum	MJHL	2000	Phoenix	1997 Entry	4	96

Andrew Murray	MJHL	2000	Columbus	2001 Entry	8	242
Shaun Norrie	U of Lethbridge	2006	Edmonton	2000 Entry	6	184
Colin O'Hara	SJHL	1998	New Jersey	1995 Entry	9	226
Darryl Olsen	St. Albert	1984	Calgary	1985 Entry	9	185
Nathan Oystrick	BCHL	2002	Atlanta	2002 Entry	7	198
James Patrick	Prince Albert	1981	New York Rangers	1981 Entry	1	9
Fernando Pisani	AJHL	1996	Edmonton	1996 Entry	8	195
Parie Proft	University of Alberta	1988	Vancouver	1982 Entry	7	137
Gennady Razin	AJHL	1996	Montreal	1997 Entry	5	122
Jamie Reeve	McGill	1990	Washington	1982 Entry	9	173
Brent Regan	St. Albert	1984	Hartford	1984 Entry	10	193
Dave Reierson	Prince Albert	1981, 1982	Calgary	1982 Entry	2	29
Brent Severyn	University of Alberta	1988	Winnipeg	1984 Entry	5	99
Russell Spence	MJHL	2002	Phoenix	2002 Entry	9	280
Alan Stewart	Prince Albert	1982	New Jersey	1983 Entry	11	205
Jeff Tambellini	BCHL	2002	Los Angeles	2003 Entry	1	27
Billy Thompson	SJHL	2000	Florida	2001 Entry	5	136
Tim Tisdale	Notre Dame	1986	Edmonton	1988 Entry	12	250
David van der Gulik	BCHL	2002	Calgary	2002 Entry	7	206
Stephen Wagner						
John Walker	AJHL	1996	St. Louis	1996 Entry	7	159
	Camrose Luth.College	1984	New Jersey	1987 Supplemental	1	10
Blake Ward	NAIT	1986				
Bill Watson	U of Lethbridge	2006	Colorado	2000 Entry	9	285
Geoff Waugh	Prince Albert	1981, 1982	Chicago	1982 Entry	4	70
Dan Wiebe	SJHL	2002	Dallas	2002 Entry	3	78
Matthew Yeats	University of Alberta	1988	Quebec	1988 Entry	9	171
	AJHL	1998	Los Angeles	1998 Entry	9	248

VIKING CUP PARTICIPANTS WHO PLAYED IN NHL AND WERE NOT SELECTED IN NHL ENTRY OR SUPPLEMENTAL DRAFTS

Name	Viking Cup Team	Year(s)
Robin Bartel	Prince Albert	1981, 1982
Sheldon Brookbank	SJHL	2000
Greg Classen	SJHL	1998
Gary Emmons	Prince Albert	1982
Taylor Fedun	AJHL North	2006
Justin Fontaine	AJHL North	2006
Gabe Gauthier	BCHL	2002
Curtis Glencross	AJHL	2002
Mark Hartigan	SJHL	1998
Chris Kunitz	SJHL	1998
Junior Lessard	MJHL	2000
Mark Letestu	AJHL North	2006
Chris Levesque	MJHL	2000
Kael Mouillierat	AJHL North	2006

Greg Paslawski	Prince Albert	1981
Ben Scrivens	AJHL North	2006
Dave Tippett	Prince Albert	1981

Victorious Vikings

- photo by Elaine Pennington

Captain Chris Topp with Viking Cup (2002)

CHAPTER 11

Canadian College & University Connections

"The Viking Cup was a forerunner and a catalyst to better coaching in Alberta."

—Scott Robinson, executive director of Hockey Alberta Foundation/ executive director of the Canada Winter Games 2019

The ultimate success of the Viking Cup was evaluated on the basis of its educational value to the participants and the public in general. It was an exchange program established and operated by a college (which became a university) and therefore subject to its mandate. Augustana's goal is to educate the "whole person," and the more general mandate of the university is to serve the public good.

In keeping with these goals, the Viking Cup became much more than a hockey tournament. The Viking Cup was a laboratory of learning in all its facets—on and off the ice. It was a means through which Augustana, and other participating schools, could carry out the mission of leadership and learning, albeit in an unusual and stimulating setting.

Leadership in Coaching

During the Viking Cup era, many great coaches were coming out of the college and university systems, especially in Western Canada, where college hockey in Alberta was uniquely strong. Likewise, many great coaches performed in the Viking Cup, creating an excellent atmosphere of learning for all teams. Several of them instructed at Hockey Alberta coaching seminars in connection with the Viking Cup. For example, the *Viking Cup '81* souvenir magazine states the following:

> Dave King, coach of the University of Saskatchewan hockey team, is at the blackboard teaching. The scene is a level-four coaches' clinic during the Viking Cup. Dale Henwood, technical director of the AAHA (Hockey Alberta), says, "We try to hold the clinic in connection with a major hockey event. Last year it was the Olympic trials in Calgary; this year it's the Viking

Cup. Thanks to the Viking Cup, this year's list of 'professors' was long and impressive . . . including Scotty Bowman of the Buffalo Sabres, former NHL great Glenn Hall, the coaches of the Finnish and Swedish teams, a psychologist, a specialist in athletic injuries, an Olympic referee, a public relations director, and numerous university and college coaches. . . The students come from all over Alberta and Saskatchewan. . . The European flavour added so much.

"Everyone was very positive and instructive," said student Bob LeDrew as he lined up to get into the Viking Cup final between Prince Albert and Finland. Years later, when King was coaching Canada's national team, one of his players was Dave Tippett, who had played in Viking Cup '81 with Prince Albert.

Looking back, King comments: "It's no surprise that he became a coach. He had such a complete game. He understood the game so well and he had this poise and presence. Tippett's unflappable. That's just the way he is. It makes him a very impressive coach."

About his former coach, Tippett said King was a mad hockey scientist. He recalled a time during an intermission when King suggested playing two forwards and three defensemen for the next period. "He'd look at me with a smile and laugh. He would say things that were off the cuff that made you think."

Coach Terry Simpson of the 1981 Viking Cup Raiders couldn't resist a comment as well, "When I started coaching, I used to criticize the referees quite a bit. It didn't take long to realize that didn't help. You might as well just shut up and stand there. I can certainly see it in Tippett."

It seems to be a common trait amongst many great coaches. Augustana Vikings Coach Voytechek was known to be silent on referees . . . and respectful.

Mike Johnston, also a coach of the Vikings, was known as an effective recruiter of talented players, an important role for college coaches.

It wasn't only our team who benefited on the recruiting trail, it was the whole league.... Our players were highly motivated. Shortly after my first tournament, I asked the legendary coach Clare Drake if we could play his powerhouse University of Alberta Golden Bears in an exhibition game the next year. He said, No problem, and if there is ever a chance to get in the Viking Cup, let me know.

"Sport can be a real test to the inner emotions of players and coach, especially when the competition is intense," said Gary Snydmiller, a coach with the Augustana Vikings in the '90s until 2007. "The Viking Cup provided an unusual opportunity for coaches to develop skill, when under pressure."

Coach Blaine Gusdal set high standards for his teams on the ice but especially in their studies where they always excelled. Gus would often state that it was not the wins or accolades, but rather knowing the impact he made on the lives of the young men who came to Augustana.

"I played for Camrose in Viking Cup '88 and on their European tour in 1986–87." said Bill Peters, now a former coach of the Carolina Hurricanes and Calgary Flames and presently coaching in Russia. "We saw a great contrast in some of the best players from both sides of the Iron Curtain. The Viking Cup was a leader in bringing different styles and coaching strategies together. It was a great opportunity to learn from one another. The hockey was unbelievably good. It was a paradise for hockey scouts."

Former Augustana student Dave Hakstol, the first head coach of the expansion Seattle Kraken, former head coach of the Philadelphia Flyers, former assistant coach of the Toronto Maple Leafs and former coach at the University of North Dakota recalls his days in Camrose and his scouting visits to the Viking Cup.

> I see the Viking Cup from three levels. First, it gave players and coaches exposure at a very high level, and therefore great opportunity to achieve dreams and goals. The scouts were there in droves. Second, it may have been the one opportunity for players to play at the elite level—against the best in the world. And third, are the take-aways, the things that we remember twenty, thirty, forty, or fifty years later: understanding quality of play, friendships, cultural appreciation, and human values from rubbing shoulders with kids and hockey leaders from around the world.

"The Viking Cup was a step forward in coaching strategies for me," said Perry Pearn, coach of the two-time Viking Cup champion NAIT Ookpiks and long-time NHL assistant coach. "Cerebral challenges, for sure. It was a real-life laboratory setting to adjust to different styles and strategies from other countries, as well as to test my own ideas. . . . We faced quick mental challenges in coaching during games as well as preparation for each game in a tournament setting. It was a test in measuring up for us coaches." Off the ice, Perry recalled an interesting coaching session with Glenn Hall on "mindset and head fakes of goalies."

Ric Carriere, coach at NAIT and later assistant coach of the Edmonton Oilers, explains that they'd used the Viking Cup in the NAIT recruiting program. "Players were attracted to our program knowing that they would get to play in the Viking Cup. It got the Edmonton media more interested in our team at NAIT."

Al Ferchuk, coach of Red Deer College, three-time participants in the Viking Cup, commented: "From my coaching perspective, the Viking Cup was a key part of our seasonal plan—an improved Christmas break training focus and it made us a better hockey team in the second half of the season."

Mike Babcock, coach of the Red Deer College Kings at Viking Cup '90, said, "The Viking Cup was our benchmark for the whole year, and we had a real good team there."

"The Viking Cup was ahead of its time," said coach Ken Babey from the SAIT Trojans. "It became a premier event and it set a new standard for international hockey events in Canada. It opened up new opportunities for other hockey teams to compete at a high level with different systems from around the world and it made coaching more interesting. Hockey Canada and European hockey people talked about it a lot. SAIT was honoured to be a part of it."

Al Bohonus, director of athletics at Mount Royal College in Calgary, understood that his Cougars had achieved a high standard of excellence the day they were accepted into the Viking Cup. In 1993, he told the *Camrose Canadian,* "I know that winning is not the only aspect that is important for getting into this prestigious tournament. It is the type of team you have. It's the type of leadership from your coaching that you have and how you carry yourself off the ice. So, for me the fact that our team has been invited, tells me that we have achieved a goal in our program to have set that kind of standard for our team."

Augustana president Glenn Johnson and Dennis Cranston, U of A Golden Bears

"I am disappointed that I never got the opportunity to participate in the tournament as an athlete or coach because it was such a prestigious event," says Rob Daum, U of A Golden Bears coach from 1995 to 2005, and a professional, international, and junior coach and former player with the Augustana Vikings. "Whoever came up with the concept was a genius and for the college and the city of Camrose to make it happen year after year was incredible, a testament to small-town work ethic and hospitality. It is even more amazing that the tournament thrived because of all the obstacles that needed to be overcome at that time. It was groundbreaking in the sport and anyone who was involved with its success should be proud."

"To play in the Viking Cup was a special experience," remembers Bill Moores, coach of the U of A Golden Bears and assistant coach with the New York Rangers and Edmonton Oilers. "The competition was challenging and we had two particularly difficult games where we won against a tough Russian national team. Then, in the final, we won against a high-powered Czechoslovakian national squad. The attention to detail at the Viking Cup was second to none! This tournament made a special contribution to the growth of international hockey and we were fortunate to have been a part of it."

Clare Drake, who coached the U of A Golden Bears for twenty-eight seasons, calls the Viking Cup "quite an amazing story." The tournament has always been high calibre, he's said, and the recognition has improved because of that. "You have all the scouts watching. They recognize the fact that there are very talented players who are ready to go onto the next step in their career, whether it's in the university, college, or professional ranks. . . One of the hallmarks of the Viking Cup is the warmth between the community and the participants resulting from the billeting process."

And there were trivia riddles in the history of the Viking Cup to test the memory.

Riddle #1

What did the Russian Bear and the Golden Bear have in common?

Both Bears entered the Viking Cup in the same year, 1988. Viking Cup '88 is therefore remembered as the year of the Bears.

Legendary coach of the U of A Golden Bears, Clare Drake, had long been a student of Russian hockey, so when the opportunity to play the Russians in his own backyard in Camrose occurred, Coach Drake jumped at the thought with his team that had returned from the World University Games just days before the Viking Cup (see the full story of Drake's Russian connections in Chapter 8).

The Viking Cup was also a test to see if top national U18 teams from Europe could compete with Canadian university hockey. The test was especially stiff, as the U of A Bears were generally considered the best of university hockey in Canada and a step up from college hockey. The Alberta Bears won the gold medal with a perfect record, but it was a rare opportunity for the young Europeans to play some of the best amateur hockey possible in Canada. While 1988 was the only year that the U of A Bears participated in the Viking Cup, Clare Drake maintained an interest attending when he could. He was a guest presenter at Viking Cup seminars on coaching.

Riddle #2

Which famous coach played for McGill University, coached Red Deer College in Viking Cup '90, and coached Canada's Olympic gold team in the Vancouver 2010 Olympics?

The answer is Mike Babcock.

Mike coached in Viking Cup '90 against his former team, McGill University where he had been team captain. Although McGill took home gold in Viking Cup '90, the Babcock-coached Red Deer Kings managed to defeat the Montreal team, 3–2, in the first game of the tournament.

Mike recently commented, "It is only a community of Western Canada like Camrose that can pull off an event like that. It seemed that everybody got involved and the atmosphere was splendid."

From the Viking Cup, Mike went on to an impressive coaching career in university, major junior, professional, and international hockey. He is the only coach to have won six distinct national and international titles: a CIS title with the University of Lethbridge, the World Junior Championship in 1997, the Stanley Cup with the Detroit Red Wings (ten seasons with the Wings), IIHF World Championship with Team Canada in 2004, and the Olympics with Team Canada in 2010 (Vancouver) and 2014 (Sochi).

Riddle #3

Which Viking Cup team is generally considered to be the birthplace of the sport of ice hockey and when did that occur?

A press release in advance of McGill University's entry in Viking Cup '90 states:

When the McGill University hockey team makes its first appearance in the Viking Cup it will bring with it a tradition in hockey dating to the 1870s, and the beginning of organized hockey in this country. Among Canadian cities, Montreal, Halifax, and Kingston all claim to be hockey's birthplace. Yet Montreal's claim would appear to be the superior one insofar as the modern version of the game is concerned. It was there that hockey was first organized and played according to a clearly defined set of rules. McGill's role in this process seems to have been paramount. Indeed, one historian of the sport has claimed that:

"There is dependable evidence that three McGill University undergraduates drafted the rules that converted shinny to hockey; also, that McGill students captained the two teams that played the first indoor hockey match and organized the world's first hockey league. Amongst other firsts attributed to McGill students or teams are the introduction of the flat puck, the wearing of uniforms, restricting the number of players, and naming their positions; also, the possession of the world's oldest hockey trophy."

The McGill University hockey club can, moreover, claim to be the first team ever organized. At the very least, it was the first collegiate hockey team in the world. With the adoption of "McGill rules," hockey spread throughout Quebec and Ontario in the 1880s, and to Manitoba in the 1890s. In 1883, during Montreal's ice carnival week, a competition was held for the "World Championship." Six teams entered and McGill won.

Hockey underwent deep and significant change in the late nineteenth and early twentieth centuries under the impact of organizational growth and professionalism. In so doing, later organizers and innovators were building on the foundation already laid.

In Viking Cup '90, Al Grazys and former Montreal Canadiens great Jean Pronovost coached the Redmen (now the Redbirds). Pronovost asked for a large Viking Cup flag, which he placed in the McGill arena as a memento of their Viking Cup experience. Later, Augustana graduate Terry Bangen (1971) was head coach at McGill before joining the Vancouver Canucks coaching staff.

Riddle #4

Who was the coach of two different teams of the Viking Cup?

The answer is Mike Johnston.

Mike coached the hometown Vikings in Viking Cup '84 and '86, and the University of New Brunswick Red Devils in Viking Cup '92. He recalls his Viking Cup experiences:

> Personally, from a coaching perspective the chance for a young guy like me to be exposed to European tactics, strategies, style of practice, and off-ice training techniques had a major impact on my career. Later I would have an opportunity to coach in two World Junior Tournaments, U17 and U18 World Championships, seven Men's World Championships, and the Nagano Olympics. I attribute these experiences and the ability to move through the coaching ranks to what I learned in my time at Camrose.

Mike coached with the Vancouver Canucks, LA Kings, and Pittsburgh Penguins for a total of twelve years. He is currently general manager/head coach of the Portland Winterhawks of the WHL.

Riddle #5

What visiting ACAC teams played in the Viking Cup?

The NAIT Ookpiks (now Ooks) played in Viking Cups '84, '86, and '92, winning gold in both '84 and '86. Red Deer College's Kings played in Viking Cup '81, '88, and '90. SAIT Trojans played in Viking Cup '82. Mount Royal College Cougars played in Viking Cup '94.

In keeping with the high standard of the tournament and the goal of diversity, the intent was to invite the champion ACAC team from the previous year to each Viking Cup while also looking at rotational factors. The tournament champion was invited to return, but not more than two times in succession to give more teams the opportunity to participate.

ACAC teams were very competitive in the tournament, but as more European national junior and North American junior teams applied to participate, the Viking Cup took on more of a junior flavour. Other than the host Vikings, the last ACAC team to participate in the Viking Cup was in Viking Cup '94. The Cup gave more recognition and status to ACAC hockey through tournament marketing and a good showing by the ACAC teams.

Some ACAC coaches sum up the effect of the Viking Cup on ACAC hockey as follows.

NAIT Coach Perry Pearn: "It was a shot in the arm for ACAC recognition. ACAC hockey was able to take its place in the hierarchy levels of hockey, especially when considering NAIT's two gold championships. Many more eyes saw the product of the ACAC and media coverage was greatly enhanced. The Viking Cup provided the ACAC a great opportunity to better market its product . . . unfortunately, they could have done a better job of seizing upon the occasion. It had positive effects in recruiting talent to the ACAC."

RDC Coach Al Ferchuk: "I personally was proud to be a conference partner and all members shared in the prestige that this event brought to our conference and provided tremendous recognition of the quality of hockey in the ACAC. The profile of the ACAC benefited provincially, nationally, and internationally."

Augustana Vikings Coach Mike Johnston: "The Viking Cup put the ACAC on the map. Teams who were accepted to the Viking Cup tournament and the ones who were able to play in the European teams' exhibition games prior to the tournament all gained a recruiting advantage and valuable program exposure."

Riddle #6

Which ACAC team participated in all fourteen Viking Cup Tournaments in Camrose?

Of course, the answer is the host team, Augustana Vikings, known as the Camrose Lutheran College (CLC) Vikings prior to 1989. The Vikings' best achievement was in 2002, when the team won gold medals. As part of the Viking Cup exchange program, the Vikings played games in Europe on twelve different tours, from 1974 to 2001.

Important Milestones for Augustana Vikings Hockey in Fifty Years of ACAC League Play

- 1967– : Camrose Lutheran College director of athletics Garry Gibson appoints LeRoy Johnson, high school department principal, as coach/general manager of the Vikings hockey team to prepare for competitive hockey in the ACAC
- 1967– : Vikings play in a new Central Alberta Juvenile League
- 1969– : Vikings play in new Central Alberta Junior B League, of which Camrose Lutheran College was a founding member
- 1970– : Len Frankson appointed coach; LeRoy Johnson continues as general manager
- 1970– : Vikings hockey promotion committee (city businessmen) established. First scholarship established
- 1972– : Vikings enter ACAC college hockey (other teams: NAIT of Edmonton, Red Deer College, Mount Royal College, and SAIT of Calgary)
- 1973– : Joe Voytechek appointed head coach
- 1974–75: General manager LeRoy Johnson spearheads first trip to Europe and the Voytechek-coached team wins the ACAC and Canadian College Championship
- 1976–77: Vikings holiday hockey tour to Minnesota
- 1979–80: Vikings embark on second trip to Europe
- 1980– : Vikings promotion committee becomes Viking Cup steering committee
- 1980–81: First Viking Cup tournament in Camrose
- 1982–83: Mike Johnston appointed as coach/general manager; LeRoy Johnson continues as coordinator of the Viking Cup exchange program until 1998

- 1982–83: Vikings begin twenty-year exchange with Czechoslovakia Ice Hockey
- 1987–88: Dave Clement appointed interim coach/general manager while Mike Johnston attends the University of Calgary
- 1988–89: Bill Luke appointed coach/general manager (Mike Johnston continues at U of C and works with the national program)
- 1991–92: Gary Snydmiller appointed interim coach/general manager
- 1992–93: Bill Luke returns as coach/general manager
- 1993–94: Gary Snydmiller appointed coach/general manager
- 1994–97: Jeff Johnson appointed coordinator of Summer English Language and Conditioning camp
- 1998– : Jeff Johnson appointed Viking Cup Program Director
- 1999– : Boris Rybalka appointed Viking Cup coordinator
- 2002– : Augustana Vikings win gold – Viking Cup 2002
- 2003– : Verlyn Olson appointed Viking Cup steering committee chair
- 2005– : Len Frankson appointed Viking Cup steering committee chair
- 2008–2021: Blaine Gusdal Vikings coach/general manager
- 2009– : Augustana Vikings 1974–75 inducted into Alberta Hockey Hall of Fame
- 2011–12: Augustana Vikings win ACAC gold
- 2014– : LeRoy Johnson inducted into Alberta Hockey Hall of Fame (builder category)
- 2017– : Joe Voytechek inducted into ACAC Hall of Fame
- 2021– : Tim Green appointed Vikings coach/general manager

Induction into Alberta Hockey Hall of Fame 2009

When the 1974–75 Augustana Vikings were inducted into the Alberta Hockey Hall of Fame, all but two members of the team were present at the Hockey Alberta Awards Gala in Red Deer for the special occasion. The inscription in the Hall of Fame reads as follows:

> The first Alberta college team to win a national championship at the Canadian College Athletic Conference level, the Vikings of Camrose, were pioneers and leaders. Under Coach Joe Voytechek, a small college of only 390 students became a national champion by beating significantly larger schools such as NAIT and Red Deer College for the Alberta colleges' crown. The Vikings defeated Selkirk College in the Four West Championship and then St. Clair College of Quebec for the CCAA National Championship which was held in Sydney, NS. The Vikings were also one of the first colleges to take a team over to Europe and tour, which through establishing international contacts became the birth of the Viking Cup in Camrose, AB, one of the most significant international tournaments in our history.

Canadian Champions—'74 –75 Vikings

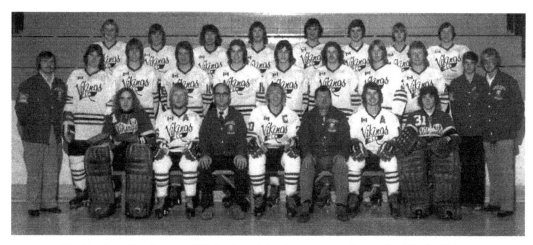

The first Canadian Colleges Athletic Association hockey champions -- the 1974-75 Vikings.

L to R back row: Dennis Dunn, Elston Solberg, Larry Stewart, Don Boyce,
John Danko, Morley Dunlop, Ken Alackson, Russ Shandro
Middle row: Dennis Becker, Kirk Davies, Tom Gould, Peter Hanson, Darryl Runka,
Joe Miller, Bob Large, Harley Johnson, Lynn Getz, Jim Voytechek, Karl Faltin
Front row: Svend Green, Lee Cumberland, LeRoy Johnson (GM), Bill Andreassen,
Joe Voytechek (Coach), Phil Irwin, Gary Fortier

Following that famous championship game, the local Sydney, Nova Scotia newspaper reported:

> Fundamental and disciplined positional play will more often than not lead to championships and this theory prevailed here Saturday night when Alberta's Camrose Lutheran College Vikings were crowned as the first Canadian Colleges Athletic Association's national hockey champions following a 6–2 victory over Ontario's St. Clair College Saints in the CCAA's national tournament.

"We have no excuses to make," said St. Clair coach, Father John Sullivan. "They played excellent hockey, played their positions well, and forechecked strongly. I guess we underestimated the Vikings."

"We definitely played a most fundamental style," said winning coach Joe Voytechek. "We forechecked, backchecked, played a good clean game, and didn't take any unnecessary penalties. I'm very proud of the way my players disciplined themselves on and off the ice and that's really what made us the winners because they want to play hockey."

Team reporter Rodney Lee phoned the game results to the Augustana Cafeteria where the annual "Boys party for the Gals" was in progress. "Sarge [Vi Furman] answered and I gave the game results I can still hear the eruption at the other end of the line. When it died down, I got a chance to also announce that Dennis Dunn had been chosen MVP! The whole college was so involved. Everyone in Camrose celebrated!"

A Tribute to Coach Joe Voytechek, 1923-2020

When Camrose Lutheran College jumped into the rapids of Alberta college hockey, Joe Voytechek was chosen to steer the boat.

Joe had grown up in the Coal Branch on the eastern slopes of the Rocky Mountains, but moved to Camrose in the late '40s to play defense for the Camrose Maroons Hockey Club. Joe married a local nurse, Phyllis, whom he met at the Camrose hospital following a hockey injury. Together, they raised six children (Charlotte, Marlene, Mike, Wes, Jim, and Pat), all of whom were heavily involved in sports, from swimming to archery to hockey. And Joe and Phyllis coached them all.

Joe was a local plumber, and since his regular customers in town included the doctors from the local medical clinic, he became known as the Drain Surgeon

Joe Voytechek

of Camrose—and beyond. One of his regular customers was his hunting buddy, Chicago Blackhawk goaltender Glenn Hall, living at Stony Plain.

In his rookie campaign at the helm of the Vikings in 1973–74, the team placed first in the ACAC, but lost to Mount Royal College in the playoffs. Joe commented, "There was a good base left for me. The kids were hungry. It was a new league. Things kind of fell together."

The following season, Voytechek coached the Vikings to their first and only Canadian College Championship. At that time, Joe had told his team, "Winning this championship will mean more to you in twenty-five years than it does today." Thirty-five years later (2009), that team was inducted into the Alberta Hockey Hall of Fame.

Joe coached the Viking for nine seasons, which included two hockey tours of northern Europe, a tour of Minnesota, and the first two years of the Viking Cup in Camrose (VC '81 and VC '82). He was the first coach to reach the 200-ACAC game milestone (217 upon retirement). Voytechek was inducted into the ACAC Hall of Fame in 2017, and the Camrose City Sports Hall of Fame much earlier, for outstanding leadership and achievement in sport and recreation.

Joe ran a tight ship and no one entered the dressing room but the members of his team . . . except for one time!

"Nobody ever got into our dressing room—never, never, never. Except for one of those crucial games," Joe remembers. "One of the girls said, 'Look, can we sneak into that dressing room and sew the pant legs and shirt sleeves of these players?' I said, 'OK. You can during the last period, but make it snappy!' They did. . . The guys came running out of the shower and wanted to go out in a hurry! They went to put on their trousers and the pant legs were sewn up. After 'de-stitching,' they grabbed their shirts! Oh, no! It was all in good fun!"

The international aspect of the Vikings program was the highlight for Joe. "We made some good friends," he's said. "I still hear from some of the people over there. Some of them even come over to visit. It was wonderful! The atmosphere in the Viking Cup was incredible. The college had a band there, and they were thumping it up with all the hoopla imaginable!"

Colleagues in the coaching realm had high praise for Joe. As an inexperienced coach coming into the ACAC, NAIT coach Perry Pearn was looking for coaching role models. "In Joe, I saw someone whose teams played with speed, skill, intensity, and structure but were always disciplined. I knew Joe was a coach I would learn from, and I did. He had integrity and class, traits I knew I should try to acquire."

Player John Danko (1974–76) summarizes the comments of many Voytechek-coached players: "Joe simplified things. He got us in good shape and did the basic things, then turned us loose to be creative."

Gold-Medal Champions, Viking Cup 2002

Front Row (L-R): Heath Klein, Tylor Keller, Kris Topp, Chad Rycroft, Jamie Wilson, Lonnie Letawsky, Travis Harrington
Second Row (L-R): Doug Fleck, Chris Gonzalez, Lonnie Granley, Darren Cameron, Jared Jowett, Karl Gartly, Rob McCracken, Ryan Trottier, Mike Young, Gary Snydmiller
Third Row (L-R): Terry Ofrim, Sean Byrne, Marty Chief, Spencer Vanhereweghe, Shane Christiansen, Matt Suchodolski, Greg Lamson, Mike Klug, Marty Palechuk
Fourth Row (L-R): Marcus Ryan, Blake Parker, David St. Cyr, Neil Spiller, John Heinen, Blake Vanhereweghe

As reported in the *Viking Cup 2004* magazine:

> After doubling the Augustana Vikings 10–5 during the round-robin portion of the tournament, the BCHL All-Star Selects set their sights on a similar outcome

in front of a sellout crowd at the championship game. Early on, the representatives from the BCHL executed their game plan to perfection. A pair of goals from Myles Kuharski gave the Selects a 2–0 advantage, with just over eight minutes gone in the contest. Jeff Tambellini's powerplay marker late in the first period and Michel Leveille's short-handed tally early in the middle stanza increased BCHL's lead to 4–0. Viking goaltender Chad Rycroft then kept his team in the game, making big saves time and time again. Augustana's Karl Gartly and Spencer VanHereweghe cut the margin to two later in the second period as they bent the twine at 12:21 and 15:25 respectively. With less than four minutes left in regulation, the Vikings received markers from Lonnie Letawsky, Tyler Keller, and Lonnie Granly in a span of 124 seconds to complete one of the greatest comebacks in Viking Cup history and give the host team a 5–4 victory.

On their way to the championship game, the Vikings had defeated the Manitoba Junior Hockey League All-Stars 5–4 in OT, the Saskatchewan Junior Hockey League All-Stars 5–0 and the Alberta Junior League All-Stars 3–1. This was, indeed, the greatest accomplishment for the Vikings in Viking Cup history.

Augustana Vikings Tylor Keller, who was MVP of the gold-medal game, had this to say as he reminisced in later years: "Before the final game I was interviewed by a radio announcer. I said, 'We are going to win.' WE WON! [It was the] top highlight of my hockey life! The perception was that BC would win. My favourite memory was watching the game on TV the next day, over and over and . . . with my teammates, Rycroft, and the rest, in our living room."

"We had a good team and we were really a close-knit group of guys," team captain Chris Topp reflects.

> We bonded well with our coaches, Gary Snydmiller and Doug Fleck. The players themselves did a lot of recruiting that year—friends, you know. The Viking Cup was a big draw for our players. We wanted to prove that we were there for more than just hosting the event. We really wanted to win, and we believed we could. I remember the full house for the championship game. The crowd loved it—and so did we! I have absolutely great memories of my time at Augustana.

Defenseman David St. Cyr was one of five players who had come from Notre Dame College in Saskatchewan to play with this Viking team. After graduating from Augustana, he went on to play in Britain and Germany. David enthusiastically recalls that gold feeling in 2002:

> The leader of the team was Topp, and he set the standard. You were either working for the greater good of the team or you were not going to be a part of it. He let everyone know at the beginning that the goal was Viking Cup. . . Everyone brought their strengths and the coaches blended them together. They put trust in us. When we won, our captain received the trophy and took it right to Gary Snydmiller, first! That is a great memory and a great

statement from team to coach! I think Gary learned a lot as a coach from this team. Assistant coach Doug Fleck was the best I have had. He taught me how to penalty kill. I was almost hoping for a call against us so that I could try and excel for the team in my role. . . I remember playing against Sweden's Robert Nilsson, Kent's son. He had lightning-quick hands, but I just stayed with him and he didn't get around me. I felt good about that. . .The crowds were fantastic—final game sold out and wild! The place erupted for the winning goal with just two minutes remaining, and we did, too!

Gary Snydmiller, Coach:

"I have to give the players on that team a lot of credit. In the 2002 tournament, they played some very good games against some very good teams and just seemed determined to put themselves in the gold-medal game. As the tournament wore on, they just played solid hockey with very few mistakes. Sport is sometimes a real test to your inner emotions.

"In the third period, it was getting late in the game. We were down, 4-2, but pressing. I think we got three goals in just over two minutes to take a 5-4 lead with a little over a minute to go in the game. It was a storybook ending. The tension was unbearable in that last minute and to get the win was a great achievement for the group, one that I will remember forever."

ACAC (Alberta) Champions 2012

Joel Danyluk, Shawn Jacklin, Brendan Stephen, Jorden MacSwain, Harrison Trible, Scott Aucoin, Torrie Dyck, Quinn Amiel, Kenny Bradley, Casey Rempel, Matthew Foster, Daniel Hope, Devan Hobbs, Tanner Korchinski, Richard Dupre, Darryl Gagnon, Dean Prpick, Dane Bonish, Brendan Lamb, Paul Kolida, Brad Bourke, David Ritz, Ryan Cornforth, Ian Grant, Jeremy Belmes, Adam Johnson, Blaine Gusdal (coach), Paul King (assistant coach), Tyler Bellamy (assistant coach), Dr. Greg Ninian, Dr. Dave Hewko, Adam Tresoor (video coach), Chance Reinhart (trainer)

Torrie Dyck, team captain, Augustana Athlete of the Year:

We had an awesome group of guys. The school and community were really supportive and involved that year, including Dean Dr. Allen Berger. It was so amazing. It was so enjoyable. I played Junior hockey before my three years at Augustana, and then I played for the U of A Golden Bears for two years, followed by several years of Senior hockey. I never saw a team bond like the Vikings of 2012 in Camrose.

Dean Prpick scored the winning goal in the second overtime period, "It was my biggest memory. It was my highest point in hockey—such a cool thing!"

Tanner Korchinski commented, "We are always talking about it. We had the right combination of guys. All got along well—we peaked."

Kenny Bradley remembers, "We were heroes at the school for weeks . . . even showed a video in some of the classes." Kenny had played for the Camrose Kodiaks in the Canadian Championships (RBC Cup) in Camrose the previous year—a double thrill for sure.

Joel Danyluk, ACAC Playoffs MVP and all-star goaltender recalls with enthusiasm:

> Community is the biggest take-away during my time at Augustana, and it was never so prevalent as during the championship run. My best memory will be coming out to the roar of close to 2,000 fans! . . . I was one of the few hockey players who lived on campus and I remember the cafeteria workers made me a special homemade lasagna during the playoffs and had a signed card by all the staff wishing for a championship win. . . No number of awards and accolades lives up to that feeling of taking our championship picture in front of our crowd hanging over the boards. The win was so much more rewarding knowing that we had done it for each other, but the school and community, as well.

Coach Blaine Gusdal:

"I was blessed with a group of young men who truly cared about each other and understood the opportunity to accomplish something very special. Man-for-man, this group bought into 'Vikings hockey', and they'll forever have that bond with each other."

So, too, will all the Vikings who played for Camrose Lutheran College and Augustana of the University of Alberta.

For a list of NHL drafts/Olympians from Viking Cup Canadian college and university teams, see the end of Chapter 10: Canadian Junior Connections.

Battle River Valley by Jim Brager (The Battle River to the Arctic Ocean)

CHAPTER 12

Legacy

Paul Henderson scored the most famous goal in international hockey history.

In the top 100 hockey stories of all time, the IIHF places the Henderson goal in the Summit Series of September 28, 1972, as the number-two story, just behind the Miracle on Ice Olympic game of 1980. It was a goal like all goals—across the line…in the net. But the impact it had at a particular time in sport and political history is what made the difference. It is the most defining play in the development of international hockey—just one goal with a whopping impact.

Other sporting plays, events, and movements have also had their impacts, especially those that have occurred at opportune times in history. Think of the impact of the Spengler Cup following WWI, or the lift that the Czech nation experienced in their only Olympic victory in hockey in 1998, or Sidney Crosby's "golden goal" for Canada in the more recent Vancouver Olympics of 2010.

The Viking Cup occurred over a period when international sport broke away from political control in the Cold War and into an environment of open competition. A new era in hockey was set to begin, and the Viking Cup helped to usher in many changes at a grassroots level that have left a lasting impact on the game and everyone involved. Just one sport exchange program, leaving a significant impression on a broad scale.

For Paul Henderson, his famous goal was not the real prize. There is something more important, he says. "I'm a very, very proud Canadian, and having the privilege to represent my country on the international level was the highlight of my eighteen-year career."

The Flag

To any participant of the Viking Cup, the Canadian flag holds a special meaning. It symbolizes the many great lessons and experiences that each Viking Cup brought to each player, leader, worker, and fan. It flew high and stately at each game in Canada, and it flew wherever the Vikings travelled in Europe. In international hockey, players play for the flag. They play for their country with passion and pride regardless of the political picture of the time.

Captain Dale Pilon of the first Vikings team to travel behind the Iron Curtain in Czechoslovakia (1982–83) knows that. "When I saw the large poster advertising our first game, it read KANADA (with a maple leaf) vs CZECHOSLOVAKIA," he has remembered. "The real meaning hit me hard. And then at the game, our flag was raised and we heard our national anthem for the first time in the Communist world. It was a serious and slightly tearful moment of reflection. We really were representing our country."

It was in those moments that the Augustana Vikings truly understood what was behind the tradition of the Joe Voytechek-coached teams to face the flag at attention and never move until the last note of the national anthem was complete—the expression of respect.

No one in that curious Czechoslovakian crowd knew that we were from Camrose Lutheran College. To them, we were the Canadians—and that was the simple but powerful message of our flag. Wrapped up in that flag were many reminders of our freedoms and privileged way of life back home. It was the first of many impacts behind the Iron Curtain.

To know the message of a flag is one thing; to experience it is another, even in a far-off land—a far-off land like Canada to the Czechoslovakians, Swedes, Finns, Russians, and whoever played in the Viking Cup.

It is no surprise then that large, colourful flags of each country graced the most prominent area of the Camrose Arena, surrounded by an array of Viking Cup and provincial flags. To enhance their meaning, the national anthem of each country was always sung in special harmony by the famed Viking Cup Trio in the first language of each country, a lasting feature that enhanced the memory and meaning of the flag at the Viking Cup.

The national flags carried meaning outside the arena, as well.

The Camrose Rotary Club purchased four tall silver flagpoles topped with gold balls as a gift to the Viking Cup to centrally fly the flag of each game's participating countries with the Canadian and Alberta flag on either side. Today, these same flagpoles with prominent flags welcome visitors as they enter the new Camrose Sport Development Centre, a permanent footprint of the Viking Cup era on a new age of sport in Camrose, and a reminder of the importance of the flag in international sport events.

Community "Connectedness" and Safety

In a ceremony on March 19, 2019, RCMP Deputy Commissioner Curtis Zablocki, Augustana graduate and former Viking Cup '86 player, stated: "I am extremely honoured and humbled to be selected as the twenty-fifth commanding officer of the Alberta RCMP."

Just months before, Zablocki, as commanding officer of the Saskatchewan RCMP, had led the investigation into the April 6, 2018 Humboldt Broncos tragic bus crash.

> Many may not consider or realize the positive impact that the Viking Cup has had on the city of Camrose and area when it comes to community safety. This tournament hosted hundreds of young hockey players, relied on its residents to billet many of these players, relied on the community as a whole to welcome and host thousands of visitors from across Canada, USA, and Europe, and in

the end met the challenge in ensuring that all who came to this central Alberta community were able to enjoy the high calibre of competition.

It is not just any community that can successfully host an international tournament such as the Viking Cup, particularly during a time when relationships between countries and international travel were quite different from what we see today. The community was able to come together to give confidence to the visiting countries that their hockey players would be safe and looked after. These efforts in hosting the Viking Cup tournaments have resulted in a legacy of community connectedness that to this day continues to make the city of Camrose and area a safe place to live, work, and raise a family.

Zablocki was well aware of the strong confidence that Communist countries placed in the Viking Cup to look after their U18 national teams during Cold War times.

Relative to his days as an Augustana student Zablocki commented:

I had heard of the Vikings through the Prince Albert Raiders of my area, playing in the Viking Cup. I knew it was good hockey and a credible program. The Viking Cup was the highlight of my hockey time at Augustana. There was a bonus, too. I met my wife Debbie Traptow of Bashaw, who was also a student of Augustana!

Camrose Sport Development Centre

Ironically, the impressive Camrose Recreation Centre was built in the same year of the demise of the Viking Cup. The role of the Viking Cup in the development of the arena project is nevertheless indelibly implanted in its history.

As a member of Camrose City Council from 1986 to 1992, it was no problem for me to keep council abreast of Viking Cup developments and achievements. Prior to Viking Cup '94, a meeting occurred regarding updated facilities. In June 1995, a formal brief was presented to council on plans for Viking Cup '96, with a request for new or improved facilities. The Viking Cup was expanding. For the first time, all the visiting "hockey power" countries would be represented by their national U18 teams.

By this time, the provincial government was taking special notice of the Camrose event. Former Premier Don Getty had described it as "a prestigious amateur hockey event, known worldwide, incredibly successful."

The brief acknowledged the need for additional tenants should a new arena be built, and broached the subject of a Junior A team for Camrose, which we thought would support the Viking Cup's expanding facility needs.

Camrose Junior A Kodiaks

At this time, Marty Knack, president of the Alberta Junior Hockey League, was pushing for AJHL involvement in the Viking Cup (see full story in Chapter 10). The end result occurred rather quickly when the Viking Cup spawned the Camrose Sport Development Society, bringing a Junior A franchise to Camrose in 1997—the Camrose Kodiaks. This additional tenant fortified the Viking Cup's drive for a new arena, even though the Camrose Sport Development Society was devoting its full time and energies into the development of their new team at the time.

Alignment and Timing to Act – A New Recreation Centre

In 1997, I was elected to the Alberta Legislature and was now in a position to pursue provincial support for the constituency.

By the early part of the new century, the economy of the province was improving and Premier Ralph Klein announced a new $4-billion infrastructure capital grants program for Alberta municipalities. The City of Camrose channelled a good portion of its grant into the regional recreation centre project. Additionally, the province celebrated its centennial in 2005 by introducing a centennial grants program for community development projects.

Later, a sum of money was made available to encourage the completion of joint community and college/university cooperative capital projects. The program was timely for Camrose as by now Augustana had merged with the University of Alberta, creating new needs for facility expansion. Most of the grant funds from this program were channelled to the new performing arts centre, which was another joint project of the University of Alberta (Augustana) and the city and county of Camrose at the time.

This was a time in our history when the stars lined up and many communities that noticed were the benefactors. The economy was strong, the Alberta Centennial era had arrived, rural development was strong on the government agenda, the University of Alberta expanded into Camrose, and the Viking Cup was bringing international attention to Alberta and had spawned a new junior hockey franchise in the Camrose Kodiaks.

Camrose and Camrose County, through their government and university leaders, responded and today the community enjoys a state-of-the-art sport development centre, a new performing arts centre, the Kodiak junior hockey team and a vastly expanded university campus.

Unfortunately, the Viking Cup never used the new recreation centre. Augustana closed the door on the tournament following Viking Cup 2006, bringing to an end this remarkable exchange program. The city lost its long-time tenant that had ironically spearheaded the drive for the new spectator-friendly recreation centre.

Camrose recreation superintendent of the time, Paul Nielsen, reflects on the new Camrose recreation project, for which he played an important role.

> The legacy of the Viking Cup is still being written. Another chapter is written each time the facility brings a new attraction to Camrose . . . national curling Championships, Oiler/Flames/Canucks rookie tournament, Royal Bank

Canadian Junior Hockey Championships and so on. It brings a focus and it brings people to our city. It stimulates our economy. Camrose is a beacon for others to emulate—and it wouldn't be what it is without the Viking Cup. It is a tragedy that the Viking Cup was dropped, but its legacy is not finished.

The recreation centre is a reminder of an era when Camrose and its college opened its doors and windows to the world through the Viking Cup.

A Stronger Augustana Vikings Hockey Team

Captain Bill Andreassen, now an Alberta Judge, receives the ACAC trophy on way to the first ever Canadian College Athletic Championship in 1975. Player Tom Gould, now a lawyer, looks on.

The Augustana Vikings' entry into the ACAC hockey league in the 1972–73 season was a bold step for the small school it was at the time. By 1974–75, the Vikings discovered the right stone in their armour and victoriously claimed the Canadian College Championship. That rock was their first encounter with European hockey.

The introduction of international hockey was as much magnet as it was artillery. The international exchange drew the interest of many talented players to the program, and the glitter of gold at each succeeding Viking Cup established a new level of credibility and attraction that became part of its tradition.

Alumnus Larry Espe (1977–78) comments, "The Viking Cup amplified my pride in being an alumnus of the program. It makes me feel good—especially when talking to others about it. Actually, I brag about it."

The Viking Cup even rescued the team that bore it.

When college finances were in desperate straits and consideration was being given to discontinuing the hockey program, the Viking Cup was that valuable possession to the institution that likely saved its hockey team. After all, it would not make sense to run a tournament without a home team. Later, in 2020, the legacy of the Viking Cup was once more an important factor in keeping the program alive in the face of severe budget cutbacks for the university.

Raising the Bar

Every Viking Cup had its unique memories, and each succeeding tournament was generally described as the best. For me, Viking Cup '88 warrants special recognition. It marked the introduction of the Russian and University of Alberta Golden Bears (major university) participation. Amid the build-up of community interest in Viking Cup '88, a pre-tournament exhibition game between the Czechoslovakian national Selects and the Augustana Vikings was scheduled in Camrose before the Christmas break.

Bill Peters, former head coach of the Carolina Hurricanes and the Calgary Flames, was attending Camrose Lutheran College and playing for the hometown Vikings at the time. Bill recently reflected upon the experience and commented to me:

> Before the tournament we played an exhibition game with the Czechs in Camrose – packed house, noisy crowd. This was a new level of hockey for me, for sure. I will never forget the experience.
>
> The score was 8–7 for the Czechs who had players like Bobby Holik [a first-round draft] and Roman Turek [later to play goal for the Calgary Flames]. We played beyond our level because they forced us, and the crowd did, too. I tasted it and wanted more. I traded sticks with a Czech after the game—I still have it in my most prized collection of souvenirs. A jubilant fan came to our dressing room right after the game and gave each of our players twenty bucks. It never happened before, nor has it happened since. My first payment for playing—one of my most memorable moments in hockey.

The river flowed high for guest teams as well, and that is what brought them back.

The organization and operation of the Viking Cup was likewise a blend of the best practices from Canadian and European hockey nations, and many of its practices were copies of ideas garnered from tours or World Championships. Alternatively, European hockey leaders visited the Viking Cup to observe successful practices as well.

David St Cyr played on the Augustana Vikings gold team of Viking Cup 2002 and upon his graduation played in Britain and France. He sums up his Viking Cup experience.

> Looking back, this must be one of the best examples of over-the-top com-mitment and achievement for the talent assembled of any team. The Viking Cup was a great motivator in itself and so were the competing teams. It was our 'World Juniors—one time.' There was just something about the tourna-ment—people speak of it with respect and enthusiasm. I hope my kids can experience something like it.

Opportunities for Youth

In the end, the greatest legacy of the Viking Cup may lie in the young minds and hearts of those who were touched by it. Seeds were sown that influenced the goals and direction of our growing youth in intrinsic ways that may never be known. Yet, end points may have had their beginnings in the Viking Cup, as illustrated by the following two families of the Camrose community.

The Green Family
"It started my fire burning"

Josh Green had a twenty-year career in professional hockey, including stints with the Edmonton Oilers, Calgary Flames and Vancouver Canucks. He completed his career playing three seasons in the Finnish Elite Liiga, and is now coaching with the Winnipeg Ice in the WHL.

Brother Tim Green played in the WHL for four seasons and added six years of semi-pro hockey in the US before beginning his university program at Augustana while playing with the Vikings. He played in Viking Cup 2000. Today, he is teaching hockey skills at a hockey academy and coaching the Vikings.

Any player who succeeds in the upper levels of sport must have more than the necessary skills. They must be motivated and dedicated at a very high level.

Recently, Josh and Tim spoke of their young days in sport in Camrose. Josh commented:

> The Viking Cup started my fire burning. I was with the Camrose Elks Pee Wee team in '86, when they were assigned to be the cheerleaders for Team Finland (Kärpät) in the Viking Cup. That was so much fun, to sit right behind the team. They seemed like the best players in the world to me, like they were as good as the NHL. We had Finnish flags and we all were waving

them for Finland. My dream then was to play for the Vikings so that I could play in the Viking Cup.

The memories seemed dear and clear as Josh continued.

Two of the Finnish players were billeted at our place—three times, in fact. One of those players was Ari Hilli, a goaltender. I couldn't see how they could understand each other with such strange noises [the Finnish language]. Of course, I didn't know then that I would be playing in Finland and trying to learn a few of those long words myself.

Thirty years later when I was playing for Tampere in Finland, we played a game at Kärpät. Sure enough, Ari was the goalie coach for their team. My parents were visiting and caring for our son, so we all had a great time reminiscing with Ari about Viking Cup days.

Tim lit up when talking Viking Cup as well.

I grew up with the Viking Cup. It was my inspiration to move on in hockey. Christmas and Viking Cup went hand in hand for many years. I remember that we felt it was really cool billeting Finns. We played hand hockey downstairs. It felt like they were part of our family. The games were so exciting. My favourite player was Olli Jokinen.

Getting to play in the Viking Cup was therefore a great experience for me. I knew the tradition and it was everything I thought it to be. It was special for me because I got Player of the Game in our first game with Norway and Josh was there to make the presentation. That was REAL special.

But the Green family story was burning much earlier.

Father Svend chose to attend and play goal for Camrose Lutheran College Vikings on their first trip to Europe to start the Viking Cup exchange program in the 1974–75 season. He was the all-star goaltender in the Canadian Championships, won by Augustana. Since then, he, his wife Carol Ofrim, and their family have been avid supporters in the Camrose community sport programs…and Tim was recently appointed as head coach of the Augustana Vikings!

The Stollery Family
"My dream started with the Viking Cup"

International hockey seemed so far away for Karl Stollery, and then it was right there in his hometown.

The Viking Cup was the beginning of my hockey career, which took me to the Seoul Olympics with Team Canada, where we earned a bronze medal for our country. My best memories of the Viking Cup were in billeting the players and in going with them to the games. That was fun. One year, we billeted Marek Svatoš and Peter Gajdoš of team Slovakia. I was only nine then and still learning how to play hockey. We had so much fun playing shinny on the rink that my dad (Keith & mom Connie) made on our garden on the farm. Oh, how I wanted to be skillful like them; and so, I was motivated to work hard to make the Camrose Kodiaks, begin my education at Augustana, and receive a scholarship to Merrimack College in the US. After college, I signed with the Colorado Avalanche and, in a preseason conditioning camp, I caught the eye of Marek Svatoš, about the same time as he caught mine in the dressing room. My friend Marek of the Viking Cup, fifteen years earlier, had been playing for the Avalanche and now we were back together. What a joyful reunion and a mammoth coincidence.

Karl played for Riga, Latvia in the Russian League in 2018, and was invited to try out for Canada's Olympic team. Coincidentally (again), Hockey Canada chose Riga as its pre-Olympic training centre. Karl said:

> I could have slept in my own bed, but I chose to live with my teammates at the hotel. . . And then it was on to Seoul, my dream come true. . . The following year I played for Jari Kurri's team, Jokerit, in Helsinki. I think he managed the team as smoothly as my dad said he played for the Oilers – Great guy. I am now playing for Frölunda in the Swedish Elite League in Göteborg. The Frölunda Junior team played in the Viking Cup in 1982, about the same time my Uncle Randy played for the Vikings.

Karl is but one of hundreds of youth who were motivated to achieve excellence in sport throughout the Viking Cup era in Camrose, whether through shinny games, billeting, watching the best junior international hockey, or simply being a part of the spirit of the Viking Cup.

"No matter which team I play for," Karl has said, "when I say I am from Camrose, there is always someone that says, 'Oh, I played in the Viking Cup there.'"

Another Dimension for Education

The question was asked, "Is the university in the business of running hockey tournaments?" All programs and projects of the university should be evaluated on the basis of educational value, and the Viking Cup was no exception.

Dr. Henry Marshall Tory, first president of the University of Alberta, once said the university exists to be of service and to "uplift the whole people . . . people with ideas, talent, and purpose. Then, we act. . . We ask the big questions. We push the limits of human understanding and knowledge. We engage with partners and communities close to home and around the world to lead positive change. We empower creative people to take risks and make imaginative leaps toward yet undetermined futures."

In consideration of the university's mission, the greatest legacy of the Viking Cup is described in the educational accomplishments of all who participated. The classroom of the Viking Cup was different. It was on an ice surface, in the stands, in family homes, on European tours, and in the intercultural connections and dialogue where learning flowed, even through barriers of language and political ideology.

In the end, the Viking Cup was a lab for the engagement, understanding, and goodwill of all people. It led to a better game and a better tournament through international exposure. It was our recipe for positive change and growth. And it was a window of new career opportunity and service for its many students, local and global, of the experience.

Scott Robinson of Red Deer relates his story. "I was an assistant coach for Red Deer College when the Viking Cup brought the Russian team to Red Deer to play us in an exhibition game just prior to Viking Cup '88. It was a rare high-level game for us—our first opportunity to play international hockey. It fired me up and got me going on my career in sport. I started with Hockey Alberta in 1992, and spent many years in leadership positions there."

Dr. Yvonne Becker, former physical education instructor and Augustana athletics director (1986–2007), speaks of the value of the Viking Cup to Augustana:

> It was the perfect experience that could be created for a group of student athletes on campus. The education piece was so important. The reciprocity of cultural difference and similarities was experienced by so many in such an effective way. It was the perfect fit for Augustana and the whole Camrose community. And it was the forerunner to other international exchange programs, making Augustana a leader in the field. It led to opportunities for ACAC teams and players to travel and play overseas and it brought respect to the league.

Dennis Dunn, CLC Vikings (1973–75) and MVP at the Canadian College Championships (1975), remembers the lessons learned. "Coach Joe always said, 'Gentlemen, you have the world by the tail on a downhill pull.' I know that the values and principles that were forged inside me during those days have been instrumental in whatever success I have enjoyed in life, whether raising our children, coaching sport, or serving on a board. Wherever I go, I can honestly say this was much more than the game of hockey. There were lessons in the game of life."

Ken Lovsin, CLC Vikings (1984–86), ACAC Hall of Famer and Lillehammer Olympian in 1994 recalls, "This was the era of taking on the best qualities of the European game, an important step forward, and I was privileged to be a part of it. Our game developed in quality and style. It changed much for the better. What a privilege to see it all happen, and to be a part of it. I played for Canada in the Olympics and I got my degree."

Joel Danyluk, Augustana Vikings (2011–15), ACAC hockey gold medalist and MVP, knew of the Viking Cup. "As players, we were all aware of the nostalgia and glory days of the Viking Cup. I really wanted to be a part of the story, even though I was not on one of the teams of that era. The heart of the Viking Cup was still there. We felt it in the crowds and community and it was inspiring for us. It was a valuable part of my education. It will always be with me."

Bobby Holík, a star player from Czechoslovakia in Viking Cup '88, and with two Stanley Cups in New Jersey, now speaks of the educational value of the Viking Cup from personal experience.

The Viking Cup was my first time in North America. Here I was at the impressionable age of seventeen, on the opposite side of the planet. It was an important step for me in hockey, but more so in life. I didn't just learn to play on North American rinks. I learned about the people of Canada. Living with the Johnsons was part of my learning experience. For example, I improved my communication skills and saw what North American food was like—I had never eaten peas before. I found out Canadians were normal, just like us. Absolutely, the Viking Cup experience was an important step for me. My Camrose experience was extraordinary. . . I am living in America now, but I don't regret growing up and living in the Communist system. Now I realize it gives me a different perspective because here too, I experienced an alternative. It was an education that many others don't get. You are always building your identity from your experiences in life. Hockey is not only to be a sport but to make better human beings—you still have to be a person.

Bobby Holík with the Stanley Cup. (Read more about Robert in Chapter 6.)
Photo by Jonathan Selkowitz

Community Dynamics

Each person who was touched by the Viking Cup will describe the impact in his or her own unique way. The collective impact on Camrose and the wider community is somewhat more complicated to assess. Nevertheless, there was a significant impact and its measurement is described through the observations, feelings, hearts, and eyes of those involved. Some quotes relating to community relations and dividends from the Viking Cup era follow.

Verlyn Olson (twenty-five-year Viking Cup committee chair and former MLA/Minister, Alberta government):

> The Viking Cup experience exposed us to the world and made us more aware. While we all like to share memories of our high-profile Viking Cup visitors, I have a feeling that there was also a more subtle, but no less important, benefit of being one of the 400 Viking Cup volunteers for each tournament and the thousands of fans in the stands. That benefit was getting to meet and work with many other community members who one may not have otherwise gotten to know. It's always worthwhile to roll up one's sleeves with neighbours and friends for a cause that will benefit the community. And many of these "strangers in our backyard" became friends, associates, clients, or customers for life. So, all these years after this successful hockey tournament left us, it is, through these relationships, that we are still being paid a dividend as individuals and as a community. No matter the initiative, the lesson to be learned is "a community in which citizens mobilize to boldly tackle new initiatives will be a strong, growing, and successful community." That is what happened in the Viking Cup; and it made Camrose the envy of many other communities.

> Camrose is blessed to be a university town. I'd like to think that this very significant partnership between Augustana, community volunteers, and businesses, and of course the city and county of Camrose paved the way for many great initiatives that followed the Viking Cup. We got far more than just a new arena. The Camrose Sport Development Centre has become a hub that also houses a primary care network as well as health- and sports-medicine-related facilities used by Augustana students and the community.

> The history of successful collaboration of various levels of government and the community in expanding the sport and public health infrastructure in Camrose also pointed the way for further initiatives, most notably the stunning Jean and Peter Lougheed Performing Arts Centre on the Augustana campus. From a cultural and sport perspective, Camrose now has the capacity to host many more events than it did before the Viking Cup era began.

Jeff Johnson (player, project coordinator, former MLA/Minister with the Alberta government): "Everybody pitched in and nobody seemed to care about who should have the credit. It was a good example to youth growing up in this environment."

Dr. John Stuart (billet): "The Viking Cup took tribalism out of the picture. It transcended politics . . . people were dealing directly with people on a human level."

Joan Petruk (billet): "The Viking Cup brought the community together more than any event I am aware of. It was amazing how connections were made and maintained. We became a more open-minded and tolerant people."

Don Hutchinson (billet): "Real community spirit was the result of so many from the community working collaboratively. The Camrose community became well known internationally."

Yvon de Champlain (player): "It opened our eyes to the world. We experienced a different life. It helped us to communicate with people who did not speak our language and to be more accepting of other people for who they are. It made us more appreciative of what we have at home after experiencing a different way of life in a Communist country."

Bill Keech (player and Viking Cup worker): "The Viking Cup changed hockey in Camrose. Now young, promising players wanted to stay and play in Camrose. The bar was moved up."

Rob and Liz Rolf (billets): "It felt like we were visiting with the world. . . You can't replicate that feeling, and we still have it."

Rick Jarrett (player and committee member): "It stands alone. No other event in Camrose can parallel the Viking Cup in mobilizing and endearing the citizens to this community. I don't know of anything like it—anywhere. It has left a lasting impression. The spirit was lifted. Camrose embraced it."

Footprints That Remain

When I enter the bright new Camrose Recreation Centre, I find myself making a little diversion through the Max McLean Arena to reflect, one more time, on the banners that permanently mark the year and place where a great hockey team was crowned with gold in the Viking Cup. Sometimes, I visit the Wall of Fame to consider the hockey careers of the many who called Camrose home for just a short while. Somehow, I feel there are others who do the same. Viking Cup paintings from the brush of commissioned artists hang in offices and homes around our town and far beyond, and a Viking Cup Endowment helps to keep the Augustana Vikings hockey program alive. Let this all be a proud reminder that Camrose and its esteemed college welcomed the world to one of the finest events in international sport exchange where the stars shone bright.

"The Viking Cup is a lasting mark on Camrose and we all need to retouch it and relive it" says Paul St. Cyr, Edmonton educator, former assistant coach of NAIT in the Viking Cup, and father of former Augustana Viking player, David St. Cyr. "It gave Camrose a special identity. There should be a monument to the Viking Cup in the new arena for all to see. . . . I am happy a book is being written on the Viking Cup. It will awaken the feeling of the people to this exceptional event. People need to reflect on their history—especially on great achievements like the Viking Cup."

In the Big Picture of Sport

A look at history will reveal an amazing array of stories on the role of sport in serving the best interests of the people. Sport can activate, enlighten, and unite; give leadership and security; develop pride and tolerance; and provide opportunity where none may have existed.

The Viking Cup was there in its own supporting humble way to ignite and inspire a small community (and province) to dwell on the qualities that can tear down walls of division in our world, and build a wider window of promise and freedom for all. The river of Camrose is but a small creek, but its waters have reached the oceans.

EPILOGUE

It is 2021 and the Alberta economy has been struck by the COVID pandemic and the serious downfall of its important energy industry. Post-secondary education has been forced by the Alberta Government to accept massive budget cuts and the University of Alberta - Augustana Campus has not been spared. Amongst the cuts is the decision by Augustana to discontinue their Vikings hockey program.

Fortunately, the team has been rescued by the Augustana Hockey Alumni Association which was formed only a few years earlier. Hockey at Augustana will continue as an ACAC sport financed and managed by its Alumni Association. Its membership has grown significantly during a long history of ACAC and Viking Cup participation.

As the Alumni Association examines past successes in planning a future direction, the Viking Cup program immediately becomes part of the discussion. Many have asked, "Can the Viking Cup be revived or reestablished in some form?" I believe it can and there are helpful lessons to be learned from our history.

The Viking Cup found a niche and built on it. That niche was centered around International hockey. The niche today might be related or something completely different. Creative minds, strong wills, and dedicated leadership must find and develop that special area of opportunity and need in this post pandemic era.

The legacy of the Viking Cup leaves strengths that a Viking Cup in a new generation can build on. Hopefully, this book in describing where the Viking Cup has been can be helpful in setting a new course. Facilities awaiting a new venture are vastly superior to former times and a new agenda of activity can create a new interest and enthusiasm reminiscent of how the people of the community gravitated to the Viking Cup in former times. After all, Camrose is a college town and the support of college sport is well engrained.

Viking Cup Endowment*: A Viking Cup Endowment Fund was established from the proceeds of the Viking Cup, with the annual Interest generated from the fund applied to the Augustana hockey budget. Donations to the Endowment are gratefully accepted and will assist the Hockey Alumni Association and the team in achieving goals.*

I look forward to hearing your thoughts on this endeavor. Please visit my website to continue the conversation: **thevikingcup.com**

REFERENCES

Allen, Kevin. *Mr. and Mrs. Hockey: A Tribute to Sport's Greatest Couple.* Detroit, MI: Immortal Investments Publishing, 2004.

Athletic Daily, various issues.

Babcock, Mike. *Leave No Doubt: A Credo for Chasing Your Dreams.* Montreal, QC: McGill-Queen's University Press, 2012.

Brown, Daniel James. *The Boys in the Boat: Nine Americans and Their Epic Quest for Cold at the 1936 Berlin Olympics.* New York, NY: Penguin Books, 2013.

Čornej, Petr. *Fundamentals of Czech History.* Prague, Czech Republic: Nakladatelství Práh/Práh Publishers, 1992.

Drager, Derek. *Clare Drake, The Coaches' Choice: Hockey's Quiet Revolutionary.* Winnipeg, MB: Friesen Press, 2007.

Dryden, Ken. *Scotty: A Hockey Life Like No Other,* Penguin Random House (McCLelland & Stewart): Canada, 2019.

Furlong, John. *Patriot Hearts: Inside the Olympics that Changed a Country.* Vancouver, BC: Douglas & McIntyre, 2011.

Gave, Keith. *The Russian Five: A Story of Espionage, Defection, Bribery and Courage.* Cleveland, OH: Gold Star Publishing, 2018.

Hock, Jonathan, dir. *Of Miracles and Men.* Bristol, CN: ESPN, 2015.

Howe, Gordie. *Mr. Hockey: The Autobiography of Gordie Howe.* Toronto: ON: Penguin Canada Books, 2014.

Jones, Terry. *Wayne Gretzky, An Oiler Forever.* Edmonton, AB: Quebecor Jasper Printing, 1999.

Merron, Jeff. "Russians regroup on other side of the red line." *ESPN*, February 14, 2002. https://www.espn.com/olympics/winter02/hockey/story?id=1326249

Morreale, Mike G. "Sweden's new-look hockey model paying dividends." *NHL.com*, October 31, 2011. https://www.nhl.com/news/swedens-new-look-hockey-model-paying-dividends/c-598251

Ossipov, Vassili. "'Russian Five' changed hockey's fabric forever." *NHL.com*, October 27, 2015. https://www.nhl.com/news/russian-five-changed-hockeys-fabric-forever/c-784942

Riehl, Joshua, dir. *The Russian Five*. Ferndale, MI: Parliament Studios, 2018.

Robinson, Peter & Locke, Kim. "The Building of a Canadian Dream." Hockey Canada – The First 25 Years (1969-1994).

Shoalts, Adam. *A History of Canada in Ten Maps: Epic Stories of Charting a Mysterious Land*. Toronto, ON: Penguin Canada, 2017.

Spector, Mark. *The Battle of Alberta: The Historic Rivalry Between the Edmonton Oilers and the Calgary Flames*. Toronto, ON: Penguin Random House, 2015.

Stern, Steven, dir. *Miracle on Ice*. Bryan, OH/Sonoma County, CA: Moonlight Productions / Filmways Television, 1981.

Tuma, Oldrich, Prozumenschikov, Mikhail, Soares, John, and Kramer, Mark. "The (Inter-Communist) Cold War on Ice: Soviet-Czechoslovak Ice Hockey Politics, 1967–69." Working Paper #69, Cold War International History Project, Wilson Center, February 2014. https://www.wilsoncenter.org/publication/the-inter-communist-cold-war-ice-soviet-czechoslovak-ice-hockey-politics-1967-1969

Viking Cup Magazine (various issues).

Wikipedia, s.v. "Velvet Revolution," last modified February 7, 2021, 11:25. https://en.wikipedia.org/wiki/Velvet Revolution

Willes, Ed (1998), "Dominik Hasek: Hockey's Improving Golden Glove." *New York Times*, March 2, 1998. https://archive.nytimes.com/www.nytimes.com/library/sports/hockey/030298hkn-hasek.html

Zeman, Gary W. *Alberta On Ice*. Edmonton, AB: Westweb Press, 1985.

Zeman, Gary W. *The Real Hansen Brothers*, Article 2020. Living Heritage.weebly.com (Camrose County)

CPSIA information can be obtained
at www.ICGtesting.com
Printed in the USA
BVHW060940291021
619982BV00002B/7